DEVELOPING MANAGEMENT SKILLS

* * *

The Suffolk University MBA Program

David A. Whetten

Kim S. Cameron

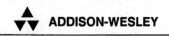
ADDISON-WESLEY

An Imprint of Addison Wesley Longman, Inc.

Reading, Massachusetts • Menlo Park, California • New York • Harlow, England
Don Mills, Ontario • Sydney • Mexico City • Madrid • Amsterdam

Manager of Addison Wesley Longman Custom Publishing: Lynn Colgin
Production Administrator: Cynthia Cody

Developing Management Skills for the Suffolk University MBA Program consists of materials from *Developing Management Skills* by David A. Whetten and Kim S. Cameron (0-321-01308-5).

Copyright © 1999 Addison Wesley Longman, Inc.

ISBN: 0-201-68023-8

99 00 01 9 8 7 6 5 4 3 2 1

Brief Contents

Developing Self-Awareness

skill development

Skill Assessment

Diagnostic Surveys for Self-Awareness

Self-Awareness

Step 1: Before you read the material in this chapter, please respond to the following statements by writing a number from the rating scale below in the left-hand column (Preassessment). Your answers should reflect your attitudes and behavior as they are now, not as you would like them to be. Be honest. This instrument is designed to help you discover how self-aware you are so you can tailor your learning to your specific needs. When you have completed the survey, use the scoring key in Appendix I to identify the skill areas discussed in this chapter that are most important for you to master.

Step 2: After you have completed the reading and the exercises in this chapter and, ideally, as many of the Skill Application assignments at the end of this chapter as you can, cover up your first set of answers. Then respond to the same statements again, this time in the right-hand column (Postassessment). When you have completed the survey, use the scoring key in Appendix I to measure your progress. If your score remains low in specific skill areas, use the behavioral guidelines at the end of the Skill Learning section to guide further practice.

Rating Scale

1	Strongly disagree	4	Slightly agree
2	Disagree	5	Agree
3	Slightly disagree	6	Strongly agree

Assessment

Pre-   Post-

Pre-	Post-	
1	1	1. I seek information about my strengths and weaknesses from others as a basis for self-improvement.
5	5	2. When I receive negative feedback about myself from others, I do not get angry or defensive.
6	4	3. In order to improve, I am willing to be self-disclosing to others (that is, to share my beliefs and feelings).
6	6	4. I am very much aware of my personal style of gathering information and making decisions.
4	4	5. I am very much aware of my own interpersonal needs when it comes to forming relationships with other people.
5	5	6. I have a good sense of how I cope with situations that are ambiguous and uncertain.
6	6	7. I have a well-developed set of personal standards and principles that guide my behavior.

6   6   8. I feel very much in charge of what happens to me, good and bad.

2   7   9. I seldom, if ever, feel angry, depressed, or anxious without knowing why.

4   4   10. I am conscious of the areas in which conflict and friction most frequently arise in my interactions with others.

6   6   11. I have a close personal relationship with at least one other person with whom I can share personal information and personal feelings.

The Defining Issues Test

This instrument assesses your opinions about controversial social issues. Different people make decisions about these issues in different ways. You should answer the questions for yourself without discussing them with others. You are presented with three stories. Following each story are 12 statements or questions. Your task after reading the story is to rate each statement in terms of its importance in making a decision. After rating each statement, select the four most important statements and rank them from one to four in the spaces provided. Each statement should be ranked in terms of its relative importance in making a decision.

Some statements will raise important issues, but you should ask yourself whether the decision should rest on that issue. Some statements sound high and lofty but are largely gibberish. If you cannot make sense of a statement, or if you don't understand its meaning, mark it 5—"Of no importance."

For information about interpreting and scoring the Defining Issues Test, refer to Appendix I. Use the following rating scale for your response.

Rating Scale

1	Of great importance	This statement or question makes a crucial difference in making a decision about the problem.
2	Of much importance	This statement or question is something that would be a major factor (though not always a crucial one) in making a decision.
3	Of some importance	This statement or question involves something you care about, but it is not of great importance in reaching a decision.
4	Of little importance	This statement or question is not very important to consider in this case.
5	Of no importance	This statement or question is completely unimportant in making a decision. You would waste your time thinking about it.

The Escaped Prisoner

A man had been sentenced to prison for 10 years. After one year, however, he escaped from prison, moved to a new area of the country, and took on the name of Thompson. For eight years he worked hard, and gradually he saved enough money to buy his own business. He was fair to his customers, gave his employees top wages, and gave most of his own profits to charity. Then one day, Ms. Jones, an old neighbor, recognized him as the man who had escaped from prison eight years before and for whom the police had been looking.

Should Ms. Jones report Mr. Thompson to the police and have him sent back to prison? Write a number from the rating scale on the previous page in the blank beside each statement.

____ Should report him

____ Can't decide

____ Should not report him

Importance

__5__ 1. Hasn't Mr. Thompson been good enough for such a long time to prove he isn't a bad person?

__2__ 2. Every time someone escapes punishment for a crime, doesn't that just encourage more crime?

__5__ 3. Wouldn't we be better off without prisons and the oppression of our legal systems?

__1__ 4. Has Mr. Thompson really paid his debt to society?

__5__ 5. Would society be failing what Mr. Thompson should fairly expect?

__5__ 6. What benefit would prison be apart from society, especially for a charitable man?

__5__ 7. How could anyone be so cruel and heartless as to send Mr. Thompson to prison?

__5__ 8. Would it be fair to prisoners who have to serve out their full sentences if Mr. Thompson is let off?

__5__ 9. Was Ms. Jones a good friend of Mr. Thompson?

__1__ 10. Wouldn't it be a citizen's duty to report an escaped criminal, regardless of the circumstances?

__5__ 11. How would the will of the people and the public good best be served?

__5__ 12. Would going to prison do any good for Mr. Thompson or protect anybody?

From the list of questions above, select the four most important:

__10__ Most important

__4__ Second most important

__2__ Third most important

__11__ Fourth most important

The Doctor's Dilemma

A woman was dying of incurable cancer and had only about six months to live. She was in terrible pain, but was so weak that a large dose of a pain killer such as morphine would probably kill her. She was delirious with pain, and in her calm periods, she would ask her doctor to give her enough morphine to kill her. She said she couldn't stand the pain and that she was going to die in a few months anyway.

What should the doctor do? (Check one.)

___✗___He should give the woman an overdose that will make her die

_____Can't decide

_____Should not give the overdose

Importance

_4_	1.	Is the woman's family in favor of giving her the overdose?
_1_	2.	Is the doctor obligated by the same laws as everybody else?
_5_	3.	Would people be better off without society regimenting their lives and even their deaths?
_5_	4.	Should the doctor make the woman's death from a drug overdose appear to be an accident?
_5_	5.	Does the state have the right to force continued existence on those who don't want to live?
_5_	6.	What is the value of death prior to society's perspective on personal values?
_4_	7.	Should the doctor have sympathy for the woman's suffering, or should he care more about what society might think?
_2_	8.	Is helping to end another's life ever a responsible act of cooperation?
_5_	9.	Can only God decide when a person's life should end?
_1_	10.	What values has the doctor set for himself in his own personal code of behavior?
_1_	11.	Can society afford to let anybody end his or her life whenever he or she desires?
_1_	12.	Can society allow suicide or mercy killing and still protect the lives of individuals who want to live?

From the list of questions above, select the four most important:

_2_	Most important
_12_	Second most important
_11_	Third most important
_10_	Fourth most important

The Newspaper

Fred, a senior in high school, wanted to publish a mimeographed newspaper for students so that he could express his opinions. He wanted to speak out against military build-up and some of the school's rules, such as the rule forbidding boys to wear long hair.

When Fred started his newspaper, he asked his principal for permission. The principal said it would be all right if before every publication Fred would turn in all his articles for the principal's approval. Fred agreed and turned in several articles for approval. The principal approved all of them and Fred published two issues of the paper in the next two weeks.

But the principal had not expected that Fred's newspaper would receive so much attention. Students were so excited by the paper that they began to organize protests against the hair regulation and other school rules. Angry parents objected to Fred's opinions. They phoned the principal telling him that the newspaper was unpatriotic and should not be published. As a result of the rising excitement, the principal wondered if he should order Fred to stop publishing on the grounds that the controversial newspaper articles were disrupting the operation of the school.

What should the principal do? (Check one.)

_____ Should stop it

_____ Can't decide

___X___ Should not stop it

Importance

_1_	1.	Is the principal more responsible to the students or to the parents?
_5_	2.	Did the principal give his word that the newspaper could be published for a long time, or did he just promise to approve the newspaper one issue at a time?
_5_	3.	Would the students start protesting even more if the principal stopped the newspaper?
_3_	4.	When the welfare of the school is threatened, does the principal have the right to give orders to students?
_1_	5.	Does the principal have the freedom of speech to say no in this case?
_1_	6.	If the principal stopped the newspaper, would he be preventing full discussion of important problems?
_4_	7.	Would the principal's stop order make Fred lose faith in him?
_5_	8.	Is Fred really loyal to his school and patriotic to his country?
_2_	9.	What effect would stopping the paper have on the students' education in critical thinking and judgment?
_1_	10.	Is Fred in any way violating the rights of others in publishing his own opinions?
_3_	11.	Should the principal be influenced by some angry parents when it is the principal who knows best what is going on in the school?
_2_	12.	Is Fred using the newspaper to stir up hatred and discontent?

From the list of questions above, select the four most important:

___5___ Most important

___10___ Second most important

___6___ Third most important

___1___ Fourth most important

Source: Rest, 1979.

The Cognitive Style Instrument

In this instrument, you should put yourself in the position of someone who must gather and evaluate information. The purpose is to investigate the ways you think about information you encounter. There are no right or wrong answers, and one alternative is just as good as another. Try to indicate the ways you do or would respond, not the ways you think you should respond.

For each scenario, there are three pairs of alternatives. For each pair, select the alternative that comes closest to the way you would respond. Answer each item. If you are not sure, make your best guess. When you have finished answering all the questions, compare the scoring key in Appendix I as a basis for comparing your score with others.

Suppose you are a scientist in NASA whose job it is to gather information about the moons of Saturn. Which of the following would you be more interested in investigating?

_B_ 1. a. *How the moons are similar to one another*

b. How the moons differ from one another

_B_ 2. a. *How the whole system of moons operates*

b. The characteristics of each moon

_A_ 3. a. *How Saturn and its moons differ from Earth and its moon*

b. How Saturn and its moons are similar to Earth and its moon

Suppose you are the chief executive of a company and have asked division heads to make presentations at the end of the year. Which of the following would be more appealing to you?

_A_ 4. a. *A presentation analyzing the details of the data*

b. A presentation focused on the overall perspective

_A_ 5. a. *A presentation showing how the division contributed to the company as a whole*

b. A presentation showing the unique contributions of the division

_A_ 6. a. *Details of how the division performed*

b. General summaries of performance data

Suppose you are visiting an Asian country, and you are writing home to tell about your trip. Which of the following would be most typical of the letter you would write?

_A_ 7. a. *A detailed description of people and events*

b. General impressions and feelings

_A_ 8. a. *A focus on similarities of our culture and theirs*

b. A focus on the uniqueness of their culture

_B_ 9. a. *Overall, general impressions of the experience*

b. Separate, unique impressions of parts of the experience

Suppose you are attending a concert featuring a famous symphony orchestra. Which of the following would you be most likely to do?

_A_ 10. a. *Listen for the parts of individual instruments*

b. Listen for the harmony of all the instruments together

_B_ 11. a. *Pay attention to the overall mood associated with the music*

b. Pay attention to the separate feelings associated with different parts of the music

_B_ 12. a. *Focus on the overall style of the conductor*

b. Focus on how the conductor interprets different parts of the score

Suppose you are considering taking a job with a certain organization. Which of the following would you be more likely to do in deciding whether or not to take the job?

_A_ 13. a. *Systematically collect information on the organization*

b. Rely on personal intuition or inspiration

_A_ 14. a. *Consider primarily the fit between you and the job*

b. Consider primarily the politics needed to succeed in the organization

_A_ 15. a. *Be methodical in collecting data and making a choice*

b. Mainly consider personal instincts and gut feelings

Suppose you inherit some money and decide to invest it. You learn of a new high-technology firm that has just issued stock. Which of the following is most likely to be true of your decision to purchase the firm's stock?

_B_ 16. a. *You would invest on a hunch*

b. You would invest only after a systematic investigation of the firm

_B_ 17. a. *You would be somewhat impulsive in deciding to invest*

b. You would follow a pre-set pattern in making your decision

_A_ 18. a. *You could rationally justify your decision to invest in this firm and not in another*

b. It would be difficult to rationally justify your decision to invest in this firm and not another

Suppose you are being interviewed on TV, and you are asked the following questions. Which alternative would you be most likely to select?

_B_ 19. *How are you more likely to cook?*

a. With a recipe

b. Without a recipe

_A_ 20. *How would you predict the Super Bowl winner next year?*

a. After systematically researching the personnel and records of the teams

b. On a hunch or by intuition

_B_

21. *Which games do you prefer?*

    a. Games of chance (like Bingo)

    b. Chess, checkers, or Scrabble

Suppose you are a manager and need to hire an executive assistant. Which of the following would you be most likely to do in the process?

_A_

22. a. *Interview each applicant using a set outline of questions*

    b. Concentrate on your personal feelings and instincts about each applicant

_A_

23. a. *Consider primarily the personality fit between yourself and the candidates*

    b. Consider the match between the precise job requirements and the candidates' capabilities

_A_

24. a. *Rely on factual and historical data on each candidate in making a choice*

    b. Rely on feelings and impressions in making a choice

Locus of Control Scale

This questionnaire assesses your opinions about certain issues. Each item consists of a pair of alternatives marked with *a* or *b*. Select the alternative with which you most agree. If you believe both alternatives to some extent, select the one with which you most strongly agree. If you do not believe either alternative, mark the one with which you least strongly disagree. Since this is an assessment of opinions, there are obviously no right or wrong answers. When you have finished each item, turn to the Scoring Key in Appendix I for instructions on how to tabulate the results and for comparison data.

This questionnaire is similar, but not identical, to the original locus of control scale developed by Julian Rotter. The comparison data provided in Appendix I comes from research using Rotter's scale instead of this one. However, the two instruments assess the same concept, are the same length, and their mean scores are similar.

_A_

1. a. *Leaders are born, not made.*

   b. Leaders are made, not born.

_A_

2. a. *People often succeed because they are in the right place at the right time.*

   b. Success is mostly dependent on hard work and ability.

_B_

3. a. *When things go wrong in my life, it's generally because I have made mistakes.*

   b. Misfortunes occur in my life regardless of what I do.

_B_

4. a. *Whether there is war or not depends on the actions of certain world leaders.*

   b. It is inevitable that the world will continue to experience wars.

_A_

5. a. *Good children are mainly products of good parents.*

   b. Some children turn out bad no matter how their parents behave.

_B_

6. a. *My future success depends mainly on circumstances I can't control.*

   b. I am the master of my fate.

_B_   7.   a. History judges certain people to have been effective leaders mainly because circumstances made them visible and successful.

           b. Effective leaders are those who have made decisions or taken actions that resulted in significant contributions.

_A_   8.   a. To avoid punishing children guarantees that they will grow up irresponsible.

           b. Spanking children is never appropriate.

_A_   9.   a. I often feel that I have little influence over the direction my life is taking.

           b. It is unreasonable to believe that fate or luck plays a crucial part in how my life turns out.

_A_   10.   a. Some customers will never be satisfied no matter what you do.

           b. You can satisfy customers by giving them what they want when they want it.

_B_   11.   a. Anyone can get good grades in school if he or she works hard enough.

           b. Some people are never going to excel in school no matter how hard they try.

_B_   12.   a. Good marriages result when both partners continually work on the relationship.

           b. Some marriages are going to fail because the partners are just incompatible.

_B_   13.   a. I am confident that I can improve my basic management skills through learning and practice.

           b. It is a waste of time to try to improve management skills in a classroom.

_A_   14.   a. More management skills courses should be taught in business schools.

           b. Less emphasis should be put on skills in business schools.

_B_   15.   a. When I think back on the good things that happened to me, I believe they happened mainly because of something I did.

           b. The bad things that have happened in my life have mainly resulted from circumstances outside my control.

_A_   16.   a. Many exams I took in school were unconnected to the material I had studied, so studying hard didn't help at all.

           b. When I prepared well for exams in school, I generally did quite well.

_B_   17.   a. I am sometimes influenced by what my astrological chart says.

           b. No matter how the stars are lined up, I can determine my own destiny.

_B_   18.   a. Government is so big and bureaucratic that it is very difficult for any one person to have any impact on what happens.

           b. Single individuals can have a real influence on politics if they will speak up and let their wishes be known.

_A_   19.   a. People seek responsibility in work.

           b. People try to get away with doing as little as they can.

_A_   20.   a. The most popular people seem to have a special, inherent charisma that attracts people to them.

           b. People become popular because of how they behave.

21. a. *Things over which I have little control just seem to occur in my life.*

    b. Most of the time I feel responsible for the outcomes I produce.

22. a. *Managers who improve their personal competence will succeed more than those who do not improve.*

    b. Management success has very little to do with the competence possessed by the individual manager.

23. a. *Teams that win championships in most sports are usually the teams that, in the end, have the most luck.*

    b. More often than not, teams that win championships are those with the most talented players and the best preparation.

24. a. *Teamwork in business is a prerequisite to success.*

    b. Individual effort is the best hope for success.

25. a. *Some workers are just lazy and can't be motivated to work hard no matter what you do.*

    b. If you are a skillful manager, you can motivate almost any worker to put forth more effort.

26. a. *In the long run, people can improve this country's economic strength through responsible action.*

    b. The economic health of this country is largely beyond the control of individuals.

27. a. *I am persuasive when I know I'm right.*

    b. I can persuade most people even when I'm not sure I'm right.

28. a. *I tend to plan ahead and generate steps to accomplish the goals that I have set.*

    b. I seldom plan ahead because things generally turn out OK anyway.

29. a. *Some things are just meant to be.*

    b. We can change anything in our lives by hard work, persistence, and ability.

Tolerance of Ambiguity Scale

Please respond to the following statements by indicating the extent to which you agree or disagree with them. Fill in the blanks with the number from the rating scale that best represents your evaluation of the item. The scoring key is in Appendix I.

Rating Scale

1	Strongly disagree	5	Slightly agree
2	Moderately disagree	6	Moderately agree
3	Slightly disagree	7	Strongly agree
4	Neither agree nor disagree		

1. An expert who doesn't come up with a definite answer probably doesn't know too much.

2. I would like to live in a foreign country for a while.

3. There is really no such thing as a problem that can't be solved.

4. People who fit their lives to a schedule probably miss most of the joy of living.

5.	A good job is one where what is to be done and how it is to be done are always clear.
6.	It is more fun to tackle a complicated problem than to solve a simple one.
7.	In the long run it is possible to get more done by tackling small, simple problems rather than large and complicated ones.
8.	Often the most interesting and stimulating people are those who don't mind being different and original.
9.	What we are used to is always preferable to what is unfamiliar.
10.	People who insist upon a yes or no answer just don't know how complicated things really are.
11.	A person who leads an even, regular life in which few surprises or unexpected happenings arise really has a lot to be grateful for.
12.	Many of our most important decisions are based upon insufficient information.
13.	I like parties where I know most of the people more than ones where all or most of the people are complete strangers.
14.	Teachers or supervisors who hand out vague assignments give one a chance to show initiative and originality.
15.	The sooner we all acquire similar values and ideals the better.
16.	A good teacher is one who makes you wonder about your way of looking at things.

Source: Budner, 1962.

Fundamental Interpersonal Relations Orientation-Behavior (FIRO-B)

For each statement below, decide which of the following answers best applies to you. Place the number of the answer at the left of the statement. When you have finished, turn to the scoring key in Appendix I.

Rating Scale

1	Usually	4	Occasionally
2	Often	5	Rarely
3	Sometimes	6	Never

1.	I try to be with people.
2.	I let other people decide what to do.
3.	I join social groups.
4.	I try to have close relationships with people.
5.	I tend to join social organizations when I have an opportunity.
6.	I let other people strongly influence my actions.
7.	I try to be included in informal social activities.
8.	I try to have close, personal relationships with people.

9.   I try to include other people in my plans.

10.   I let other people control my actions.

11.   I try to have people around me.

12.   I try to get close and personal with people.

13.   When people are doing things together, I tend to join them.

14.   I am easily led by people.

15.   I try to avoid being alone.

16.   I try to participate in group activities.

For each of the next group of statements, choose one of the following answers:

Rating Scale

1	Most people	4	A few people
2	Many people	5	One or two people
3	Some people	6	Nobody

17.   I try to be friendly to people.

18.   I let other people decide what to do.

19.   My personal relations with people are cool and distant.

20.   I let other people take charge of things.

21.   I try to have close relationships with people.

22.   I let other people strongly influence my actions.

23.   I try to get close and personal with people.

24.   I let other people control my actions.

25.   I act cool and distant with people.

26.   I am easily led by people.

27.   I try to have close, personal relationships with people.

28.   I like people to invite me to things.

29.   I like people to act close and personal with me.

30.   I try to influence strongly other people's actions.

31.   I like people to invite me to join in their activities.

32.   I like people to act close toward me.

33.   I try to take charge of things when I am with people.

34.   I like people to include me in their activities.

35.   I like people to act cool and distant toward me.

36.   I try to have other people do things the way I want them done.

37.   I like people to ask me to participate in their discussions.

38.   I like people to act friendly toward me.

_____ 39.   I like people to invite me to participate in their activities.

_____ 40.   I like people to act distant toward me.

For each of the next group of statements, choose one of the following answers:

Rating Scale

1	Usually	4	Occasionally
2	Often	5	Rarely
3	Sometimes	6	Never

_____ 41.   I try to be the dominant person when I am with people.

_____ 42.   I like people to invite me to things.

_____ 43.   I like people to act close toward me.

_____ 44.   I try to have other people do things I want done.

_____ 45.   I like people to invite me to join their activities.

_____ 46.   I like people to act cool and distant toward me.

_____ 47.   I try to influence strongly other people's actions.

_____ 48.   I like people to include me in their activities.

_____ 49.   I like people to act close and personal with me.

_____ 50.   I try to take charge of things when I'm with people.

_____ 51.   I like people to invite me to participate in their activities.

_____ 52.   I like people to act distant toward me.

_____ 53.   I try to have other people do things the way I want them done.

_____ 54.   I take charge of things when I'm with people.

Source: Schutz, 1958.

■ Skill Learning

Key Dimensions of Self-Awareness

For more than 300 years, knowledge of the self has been considered to be at the very core of human behavior. The ancient dictum "Know thyself" has been variously attributed to Plato, Pythagoras, Thales, and Socrates. Plutarch noted that this inscription was carved on the Delphic Oracle, that mystical sanctuary where kings and generals sought advice on matters of greatest importance to them. As early as 42 B.C., Publilius Syrus proposed: "It matters not what you are thought to be, but what you are." Alfred Lord Tennyson said: "Self-reverence, self-knowledge, self-control, these three alone lead to sovereign power." Probably the most oft-quoted passage on the self is Polonius' advice in Hamlet: "To thine own self be true, and it must follow as the night the day, thou canst not then be false to any man."

This chapter on self-awareness, along with the material on time and stress management in the next chapter, allows us to construct a hierarchy of self-management skills. As Messinger reminded us, "He that would govern others must first master himself." Self-management depends first and foremost on self-awareness, but as illustrated in Figure 1, other skills are also closely linked to, and build upon, self-awareness. Setting personal priorities and goals, for example, helps individuals direct their own lives, and time and stress management helps individuals adapt to and organize their environments. This chapter centers around the core aspects of self-management and serves as the foundation for the following chapter on stress and time management. Moreover, as Figure 1 illustrates, when problems arise in personal management, the easily recognized symptoms are often time pressures or experienced stress. However, those symptoms are often linked to more fundamental problems with self-awareness and out-of-balance priorities. Enhancing these aspects of self-awareness leads to long-term strategic improvement.

Students of human behavior have long known that knowledge of oneself—self-awareness, self-insight, self-understanding—is essential to one's productive personal and interpersonal functioning and in understanding and empathizing with other people. A host of techniques and methods for achieving self-knowledge have therefore been devised. Various therapies, group methods, meditation techniques, and exercise programs have been touted as enhancing insight into the self and bringing inner peace. This chapter does not aim to summarize those procedures, nor does it espouse any one procedure in particular. Rather, we discuss here the importance of self-awareness in managerial behavior and introduce several

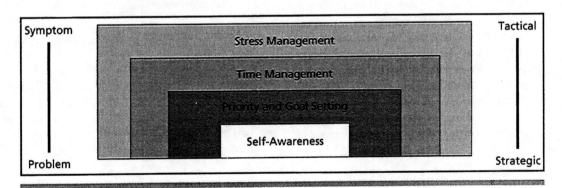

Figure 1 A Hierarchy of Personal Life-Management Skills

self-assessment instruments that research has shown to relate to managerial success. Our emphasis is on scientifically validated information linking self-awareness to the behavior of managers, and we try to avoid generalizations that have not been tested in research.

The Enigma of Self-Awareness

Erich Fromm (1939) was one of the first behavioral scientists to observe the close connection between one's self-concept and one's feelings about others: "Hatred against oneself is inseparable from hatred against others." Carl Rogers (1961) later proposed that self-awareness and self-acceptance are prerequisites for psychological health, personal growth, and the ability to know and accept others. In fact, Rogers suggested that the basic human need is for self-regard, which he found to be more powerful in his clinical cases than physiological needs. Hayakawa (1962) has asserted that the first law of life is not self-preservation, but self-image preservation. "The self-concept," he states, "is the fundamental determinant of all our behavior. Indeed, since it is an organization of our past experiences and perceptions as well as our values and goals, it determines the character of the reality we see" (p. 229). There is considerable empirical evidence that self-awareness and self-acceptance are strongly related to personal adjustment, interpersonal relationships, and life success. Brouwer (1964, p. 156) asserted:

> The function of self-examination is to lay the groundwork for insight, without which no growth can occur. Insight is the "Oh, I see now" feeling which must consciously or unconsciously precede change in behavior. Insights—real, genuine glimpses of ourselves as we really are—are reached only with difficulty and sometimes with real psychic pain. But they are the building blocks of growth. Thus, self-examination is a preparation for insight, a groundbreaking for the seeds of self-understanding which gradually bloom into changed behavior.

There is little question that the knowledge we possess about ourselves, which makes up our self-concept, is central to improving our management skills. We cannot improve ourselves or develop new capa-bilities unless and until we know what level of capability we currently possess. On the other hand, self-knowledge may inhibit personal improvement rather than facilitate it. The reason is that individuals frequently evade personal growth and new self-knowledge. They resist acquiring additional information in order to protect their self-esteem or self-respect. If they acquire new knowledge about themselves, there is always the possibility that it will be negative or that it will lead to feelings of inferiority, weakness, evilness, or shame. So they avoid new self-knowledge. As Maslow (1962, p. 57) notes:

> We tend to be afraid of any knowledge that would cause us to despise ourselves or to make us feel inferior, weak, worthless, evil, shameful. We protect ourselves and our ideal image of ourselves by repression and similar defenses, which are essentially techniques by which we avoid becoming conscious of unpleasantness or dangerous truths.

We avoid personal growth, then, because we fear finding out that we are not all that we would like to be. If there is a better way to be, our current state must therefore be inadequate or inferior. The realization that one is not totally adequate or knowledgeable is difficult for many people to accept. This resistance is the "denying of our best side, of our talents, of our finest impulses, of our highest potentialities, of our creativeness. In brief, this is the struggle against our own greatness" (Maslow, 1962, p. 58). Freud (1956) asserted that to be completely honest with oneself is the best effort an individual can make, because complete honesty requires a continual search for more information about the self and a desire for self-improvement.

Seeking knowledge of the self, therefore, seems to be an enigma. It is a prerequisite for and motivator of growth and improvement, but it may also inhibit growth and improvement. It may lead to stagnation because of fear of knowing more. How, then, can improvement be accomplished? How can management skills be developed if the self-knowledge necessary for the development of those skills is resisted?

The Sensitive Line

One answer relies on the concept of the **sensitive line.** This concept refers to the point at which individuals become defensive or protective when encountering information about themselves that is inconsistent with their self-concept or when encountering pressure to alter their behavior. Most people regularly experience information about themselves that doesn't quite fit or that is marginally inconsistent. For example, a friend might say, "You look tired today. Are you feeling okay?" If you are feeling fine, the information is inconsistent with your self-awareness. But because the discrepancy is relatively minor, it would not be likely to offend you or evoke a strong defensive reaction. That is, it would probably not require that you reexamine and change your self-concept. On the other hand, the more discrepant the information or the more serious its implications for your self-concept, the closer it would approach your sensitive line, and you would feel a need to defend yourself against it. For example, having a coworker judge you incompetent as a manager may cross your sensitive line if you think you have done a good job as a manager. This would be especially true if the coworker was an influential person. Your response would probably be to defend yourself against the information to protect the image you hold of yourself.

Hayakawa (1962, p. 230) stated the point differently. He asserted that the self-concept "tends to rigidify under threat," so that if an individual encounters discrepant information that is threatening, the current self-concept is reasserted with redoubled force. Haney (1979) refers to a "comfort zone" similar to a thermostat. When the situation becomes too uncomfortable, protective measures are brought into play that bring the situation back to normal. When marked discrepancies in the self-image are experienced, in other words, the validity of the information or its source is denied, or other defensive mechanisms are used to ensure that the self-concept remains stable.

In light of this defensiveness, then, how can increased self-knowledge and personal change ever occur? There are at least two answers. One is that information that is verifiable, predictable, and controllable is less likely to cross the sensitive line than information without those characteristics. That is, if an individual can test the validity of the discrepant information (for example, if some objective standard exists), if the information is not unexpected or "out-of-the-blue" (for example, if it is received at regular intervals), and if there is some control over what, when, and how much information is received (for ex-

ample, if it is requested), it is more likely to be heard and accepted. The information you receive about yourself in this chapter possesses those three characteristics. You have already completed several self-assessment instruments that have been used extensively in research. Their reliability and validity have been established. Moreover, they have been found to be associated with managerial success. Therefore, in your analysis of your scores, you can gain important insight that can prove helpful to you.

A second answer to the problem of overcoming resistance to self-examination lies in the role other people can play in helping insight to occur. It is almost impossible to increase skill in self-awareness unless we interact with and disclose ourselves to others. Unless one is willing to open up to others, to discuss aspects of the self that seem ambiguous or unknown, little growth can ever occur. Self-disclosure, therefore, is a key to improvement in self-awareness. Harris (1981) points out:

> In order to know oneself, no amount of introspection or self-examination will suffice. You can analyze yourself for weeks, or meditate for months, and you will not get an inch further—any more than you can smell your own breath or laugh when you tickle yourself.
>
> You must first be open to the other person before you catch a glimmering of yourself. Our self-reflection in a mirror does not tell us what we are like; only our reflection in other people. We are essentially social creatures, and our personality resides in association, not in isolation.

As you engage in the practice exercises in this chapter, therefore, you are encouraged to discuss your insights with someone else. A lack of self-disclosure not only inhibits self-awareness but also may affect adversely other aspects of managerial skill development. For example, several studies have shown that low self-disclosers are less healthy and more self-alienated than high self-disclosers. College students give the highest ratings for interpersonal competence to high self-disclosers. Individuals are liked best who are high self-disclosers, and excessive or insufficient self-disclosure results in less liking and acceptance by others (see, for example, Jourard, 1964; Covey, 1989). Some of the exercises in this chapter will require you to discuss your experiences with others. This is done because involving others in your acquisition of self-understanding will be a critical aspect of your personal growth.

The enigma of self-awareness can be managed, then, by exercising some control over when and what kind of information you receive about yourself, and by involving others in your pursuit of self-understanding. The social support individuals receive from others during the process of self-disclosure, besides helping to increase feedback and self-awareness, helps information contribute to greater self-awareness without crossing the sensitive line.

Important Areas of Self-Awareness

We focus on four major areas of self-awareness that have been found to be key in developing successful management: personal values, cognitive style, orientation toward change, and interpersonal orientation. These areas of self-awareness have been found to be important predictors of various aspects of effective management such as successful team membership and team leadership, life success, personal learning and development, creativity, communication competency, and effective empowerment (Schutz, 1989; Lawrence & Kleiner, 1987; Marshall, 1986; Parker & Kram, 1993; Atwater & Yammarino, 1992). **Personal values** are discussed first because they are "the core of the dynamics of behavior, and play so large a part in unifying personality" (Allport, Gordon, & Vernon, 1931, p. 2). That is, all other attitudes, orientations, and behaviors arise out of individuals' values. Two major types of values are considered: instrumental and terminal (Rokeach, 1973). We present research findings that relate personal development in these two types of values to successful managerial performance. The assessment instrument designed to assess your values development is discussed, along with information concerning the scores of other groups of people so that you can compare your scores with those of more and less successful managers. Because this discussion of values development is connected to ethical decision making, the implications of managerial ethics are also discussed.

The second area of self-awareness is **cognitive style,** which refers to the manner in which individuals gather and process information. A discussion of the critical dimensions of cognitive style is presented, based on the assessment instrument that you used to assess your own style. Empirical research linking cognitive style to managerial behavior is discussed, and your scores are compared to other successful managers in a variety of organizations.

Third, a discussion of **orientation toward change** focuses on the methods people use to cope with change in their environment. Everyone, but especially a manager, is faced with increasingly fragmented, rapidly changing, tumultuous conditions. It is important that you become aware of your orientation toward adapting to these conditions. Two important dimensions—locus of control and intolerance of ambiguity—have been measured by two assessment instruments. Research connecting these two dimensions to effective management is discussed in the sections that follow.

Finally, **interpersonal orientation,** or the tendency to interact in certain ways with other people, is explained. We provided an assessment instrument for measuring certain aspects of interpersonal orientation, and in this section we discuss its relevance to managerial behavior. By analyzing your scores, you can obtain useful insights not only into yourself but also into the quality of your relationships with others.

These four areas of self-awareness—personal values, cognitive style, orientation toward change, and interpersonal orientation—constitute the very core of the self-concept. Values define an individual's basic *standards* about what is good and bad, worthwhile and worthless, desirable and undesirable, true and false, moral and immoral. Cognitive style determines individual *thought processes* and perceptions. It determines not only what kind of information is received by an individual, but how that information is interpreted, judged, and responded to. Orientation toward change identifies the *adaptability* of individuals. It includes the extent to which individuals are tolerant of ambiguous, uncertain conditions, and the extent to which they are inclined to accept personal responsibility for their actions under changing conditions. Interpersonal orientation determines the *behavior patterns* that are most likely to emerge in interactions with others. The extent to which an individual is open or closed, assertive or retiring, controlling or dependent, affectionate or aloof depends to a large degree on interpersonal orientation. Figure 2 summarizes these four aspects of self-awareness, along with their functions in defining the self-concept.

Of course, there are many other aspects of self-awareness that could be considered in this chapter, for

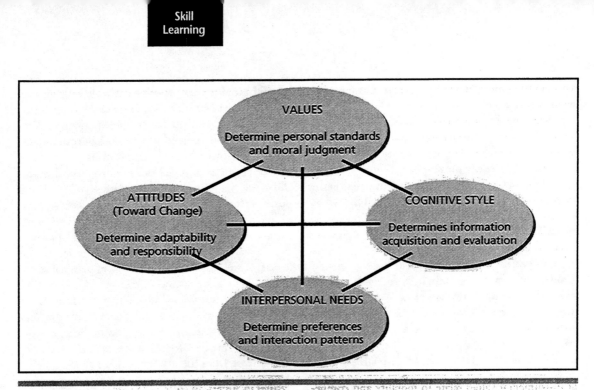

Figure 2 Four Core Aspects of the Self-Concept

example, emotions, attitudes, temperament, personality, and interests. But all these aspects of the self are related fundamentally to the four core concepts. What we value, how we feel about things, how we behave toward others, what we want to achieve, and what we are attracted to all are strongly influenced by our values, cognitive style, orientation toward change, and interpersonal orientation. These are among the most important building blocks upon which other aspects of the self emerge. On the other hand, if you want to do a more in-depth analysis of multiple aspects of self-awareness, instruments such as the Strong-Campbell Vocational Inventory, the Minnesota Multiphasic Personality Inventory, the Myers-Briggs Type Indicator, the Sanford-Binet Intelligence Test, and a host of other instruments are available in most college counseling centers or testing centers. No one, it should be emphasized, can get too much self-knowledge.

Values

Values are among the most stable and enduring characteristics of individuals. They are the foundation upon which attitudes and personal preferences are formed. They are the basis for crucial decisions, life directions, and personal tastes. Much of what we are is a product of the basic values we have developed throughout our lives. An organization, too, has a value system, usually referred to as its organizational culture. Research has found that employees who hold values that are congruent with their organization's values are more productive and satisfied (Posner & Kouzes, 1993). Holding values that are inconsistent with company values, on the other hand, is a major source of frustration, conflict, and nonproductivity. Being aware of one's own priorities and values, therefore, is important if one expects to achieve compatibility at work and in a long-term career (Lobel, 1992).

However, as Simon (1974) and others have suggested, people sometimes lose touch with their own values, behaving in ways that are inconsistent with those values. That is, they pursue lower priorities at the expense of higher priorities, substituting goals with immediate payoffs for those with more long-term, central value. They may pursue an immediate reward or a temporary satisfaction, for example, in place of longer-term happiness and inner peace. Not being cognizant of one's own value priorities can lead to misdirected decisions and frustration in the long term.

As in many areas of self-awareness, however, many people feel that they have a clear understanding of their values. Because their values are seldom challenged, they don't think much about the extent to which they hold certain values more highly than others. On the other hand, it is precisely because they are seldom challenged that people tend to forget value priorities and behave in incongruous ways. Until people encounter a contradiction or threat to their values, they seldom assert them or seek to clarify them.

Rokeach (1973) argued that the total number of values people possess is relatively small and that all individuals possess the same values, but in different degrees. For example, everyone values peace, but some make it a higher priority than others. Two general types of values were identified by Rokeach, and independent priority ratings have been found to exist for each type (that is, the two sets of values are largely unrelated). One general type of values is labeled instrumental, or means-oriented; the other type is terminal, or ends-oriented.

Instrumental values prescribe desirable standards of conduct or methods for attaining an end. Two types of instrumental values relate to morality and competence. Violating moral values (for example, behaving wrongly) causes feelings of guilt, while violating competence values (for example, behaving incapably) brings about feelings of shame.

Terminal values prescribe desirable ends or goals for the individual. There are fewer of them, according to Rokeach, than there are instrumental values, so the sum total for all individuals in all societies can be identified. Terminal values are either personal (for example, peace of mind) or social (for example, world peace). Rokeach has found that an increase in the priority of one personal value tends to increase the priority of other personal values and decrease the priority of social values. Conversely, an increase in the priority of one social value tends to increase the priority of other social values and decrease the value of personal values. Individuals who increase their priority for "a world at peace," for example, would also increase their priority for "equality" while decreasing their priority for "pleasure" or "self-respect." People tend to differ, in other words, in the extent to which they are self- versus others-orientated in their values. Table 1 lists the 18 terminal values "judged to represent the most important values in American society" (Rokeach, 1973, p. 29).

In a national study of 1,460 American managers, Schmidt and Posner (1982) assessed which of these values were most important in the workplace. Using Rokeach's instrumental values list, they asked managers

TERMINAL VALUES	INSTRUMENTAL VALUES
A comfortable life (a prosperous life)	Ambitious (hard-working, aspiring)
An exciting life (a stimulating, active life)	Broadminded (open-minded)
A sense of accomplishment (lasting contribution)	Capable (competent, effective)
A world at peace (free of war and conflict)	Cheerful (lighthearted, joyful)
A world of beauty (beauty of nature and the arts)	Clean (neat, tidy)
Equality (brotherhood, equal opportunity for all)	Courageous (standing up for your beliefs)
Family security (taking care of loved ones)	Forgiving (willing to pardon others)
Freedom (independence, free choice)	Helpful (working for the welfare of others)
Happiness (contentedness)	Honest (sincere, truthful)
Inner harmony (freedom from inner conflict)	Imaginative (daring, creative)
Mature love (sexual and spiritual intimacy)	Independent (self-reliant, self-sufficient)
National security (protection from attack)	Intellectual (intelligent, reflective)
Pleasure (an enjoyable, leisurely life)	Logical (consistent, rational)
Salvation (saved, eternal life)	Loving (affectionate, tender)
Self-respect (self-esteem)	Obedient (dutiful, respectful)
Social recognition (respect, admiration)	Polite (courteous, well-mannered)
True friendship (close companionship)	Responsible (dependable, reliable)
Wisdom (a mature understanding of life)	Self-controlled (restrained, self-disciplined)

Table 1 Terminal and Instrumental Values
Source: Rokeach, 1973.

to identify those that were most desired in the workplace. "Responsible" and "honest" were by far the most desired values in employees (over 85 percent of the managers selected them), followed by "capable" (65 percent), "imaginative" (55 percent), and "logical" (49 percent). "Obedient," "clean," "polite," and "forgiving" were the least important, being selected by fewer than 10 percent of the managers.

Different groups of people tend to differ in the values they hold. For example, business school students and professors tend to rate "ambition," "capability," "responsibility," and "freedom" higher than people in general. They tend to place lower importance than people in general on concern and helpfulness to others, aesthetics and cultural values, and overcoming social injustice (Cavanaugh, 1980). In a study that compared highly successful, moderately successful, and unsuccessful managers, highly successful managers gave significantly higher scores to values relating to economic (for example, a comfortable life) and political values (for example, social recognition) than less successful managers (Rokeach, 1973).

Compared to the population in general, managers place substantially more value on "sense of accomplishment," "self-respect," "a comfortable life," and "independence" (Clare & Sanford, 1979). The instrumental value managers held highest for themselves, in fact, was "ambition"; their highest held terminal value was "sense of accomplishment." In other words, personal values (rather than social values) and those oriented toward achievement predominate among managers.

These value preferences may explain why business students and even managers themselves have been criticized for being too self-centered and impatient for personal achievement and promotion (see Introduction). A balance of personal values and social values, such as justice and helpfulness, may characterize a more adaptable manager in the future.

Simply esteeming certain personal and achievement-oriented values does not mean, of course, that one will be a successful manager. On the other hand, it is clear that values do affect individual behavior. For example, Kohlberg (1969), Graves (1970), and Flower, Hughes, Myers, and Myer (1975) all argue that the behavior displayed by individuals (that is, the means used to achieve their valued ends) is a product of their level of values maturity. Individuals differ in their level of values development, according to these authors, so different sets of instrumental values are held by individuals at different stages of development. People progress from one level of maturity to another, and as they do, their value priorities change. Individuals who have progressed to more mature levels of values development possess a qualitatively different set of instrumental values than individuals who are at less mature levels.

This theory of values or moral development has received a great deal of attention from researchers, and research findings have some important implications for self-awareness and managerial effectiveness. Therefore, we shall discuss in some detail this notion of values maturity.

Kohlberg's model is the best known and most widely researched approach to values maturity. It focuses on the kind of reasoning used to reach a decision about an issue that has value or moral connotations. The model consists of three major levels, each of which contains two stages. Table 2 summarizes the characteristics of each stage. In brief, the stages are sequential (for example, a person can't progress to stage 3 before passing through stage 2), and each stage represents a higher level of maturity. Kohlberg uses the terms *preconventional, conventional,* and *postconventional* to describe these three levels. In the following discussion, we have chosen to use different terms that capture the dominant characteristics of each stage.

The first level of maturity, the **self-centered level,** includes the first two stages of values development. Moral reasoning and instrumental values are based on personal needs or wants and on the consequences of an act. For example, something could be judged as right or good if it helped an individual obtain a reward or avoid punishment and if the consequences were not negative for someone else. Stealing $50,000 is worse than stealing $500 in the self-centered level because the consequences (that is, the losses) are more negative for someone else.

The second level, or **conformity level,** includes stages 3 and 4. Moral reasoning is based on conforming to and upholding the conventions and expectations of society. This level is sometimes referred to as the "law and order" level because the emphasis is on conformity to laws and norms. Right and wrong are judged on the basis of whether or not behaviors conform to the rules of those in authority. Respect from others based on obedience is a prized outcome. Stealing $50,000 and stealing $500 are equally wrong in this level because both violate the law. Most American adults function at this level of values maturity.

LEVEL	BASIS OF MORAL JUDGMENT	STAGE OF DEVELOPMENT
I	Moral value resides in external, quasiphysical happenings, in bad acts, or in quasiphysical needs, rather than in persons and standards.	1. *Obedience and punishment orientation.* Egocentric deference to superior power or prestige, or a trouble-avoiding set. Objective responsibility. 2. *Naively egotistic orientation.* Right action is that instrumentally satisfying the self's needs and occasionally others'. Awareness of relativism of value to each actor's needs and perspectives. Naive egalitarianism and orientation to exchange and reciprocity.
II	Moral value resides in performing good or right roles, in maintaining the conventional order and the expectancies of others.	3. *Good-person orientation.* Orientation to approval and to pleasing and helping others. Conformity to stereotypical images of majority or natural role behavior, and judgment by intentions. 4. *Orientation to "doing duty,"* showing respect for authority, and maintaining the social order for its own sake. Regard for earned expectations of others.
III	Moral value resides in conformity by the self to shared or sharable standards, rights, or duties.	5. *Contractual legalistic orientation.* Recognition of an arbitrary element or starting point in rules or expectations for the sake of agreement. Duty defined in terms of contract, general avoidance of violation of the will or rights of others, and majority will and welfare. 6. *Conscience of principle orientation.* Orientation not only to actually ordained social rules, but to principles of choice involving appeal to logical universality and consistency. Orientation to conscience as a directing agent and to mutual respect and trust.

Table 2 Classification of Moral Judgment into Levels and Stages of Development
Source: Kohlberg, 1969.

Third is the **principled level.** It includes the final two stages of maturity and represents the most mature level of moral reasoning and the most mature set of instrumental values. Right and wrong are judged on the basis of the internalized principles of the individual. That is, judgments are made on the basis of a set of principles or core values that have been developed from individual experience. In the highest stage of maturity, this set of principles is comprehensive (it covers all contingencies), consistent (it is never violated), and universal (it does not change with the situation or circumstance). Thus, stealing $50,000 and stealing $500 are still judged to be wrong, but the basis for the judgment is not the violation of laws or rules; rather, it is the violation of a set of comprehensive, consistent, universal prin-

ciples developed by the individual. Few individuals, according to Kohlberg, reach this highest level of maturity on a consistent basis.

In short, self-centered individuals view rules and laws as outside themselves, but they obey because, by doing so, they may obtain rewards or avoid punishment. Conformist individuals view rules and laws as outside themselves, but they obey because they have learned and accepted those rules and laws, and they seek the respect of others. Principled individuals examine the rules and laws and develop a set of internal principles that they believe are morally right. If there is a choice to be made between obeying a law or obeying a principle, they choose the principle. Internalized principles supersede rules and laws in principled individuals.

To understand the different levels of values maturity, consider the following story used by Kohlberg (1969):

In Europe a woman was near death from a special kind of cancer. There was one drug that the doctors thought might save her. It was a form of radium that a druggist in the same town had recently discovered. The drug was expensive to make, but the druggist was charging ten times what the drug cost to make. He paid $200 for radium and charged $2000 for a small dose of the drug. The sick woman's husband, Heinz, went to everyone he knew to borrow the money, but he could get together only about $1000, which was half of what it cost. He told the druggist that his wife was dying and begged him to sell the drug at a lower price or let him pay later. But the druggist said, "No, I discovered the drug and I'm going to make money from it." So Heinz grew desperate and began to think about breaking into the store to steal the drug for his wife.

Now answer the following questions in reaction to the story:

YES   NO

_____ _____ 1. Would it be wrong for Heinz to break into the store?

_____ _____ 2. Did the druggist have the right to charge that much for the product?

_____ _____ 3. Did Heinz have an obligation to steal the drug for his wife?

_____ _____ 4. What if Heinz and his wife did not get along? Should Heinz steal the drug for her?

_____ _____ 5. Suppose Heinz's best friend were dying of cancer, rather than Heinz's wife. Should Heinz steal the drug for his friend?

_____ _____ 6. Suppose the person dying was not personally close to Heinz. Should Heinz steal the drug?

_____ _____ 7. Suppose Heinz read in the paper about a woman dying of cancer. Should he steal the drug for her?

_____ _____ 8. Would you steal the drug to save your own life?

_____ _____ 9. Suppose Heinz was caught breaking in and brought before a judge. Should he be sentenced to jail?

For individuals in the self-centered level of maturity, stealing the drug might be justified because Heinz's wife had instrumental value: she could provide companionship, help rear the children, and so on. A stranger, however, would not have the same instrumental value for Heinz, so it would be wrong to steal the drug for a stranger. Individuals in the conformity level would base their judgments on the closeness of the relationship and on law and authority. Heinz has an obligation to steal for family members, according to this reasoning, but not for nonfamily members. A governing principle is whether or not an action is against the law (or society's expectations). Principled individuals base their judgments on a set of universal, comprehensive, and consistent principles. They may answer any question yes or no, but their reasoning will be based on their own internal principles, not on externally imposed standards or expectations. (For example, they might feel an obligation to steal the drug for anyone because they value human life more than property.)

Research on Kohlberg's model of values development reveals some interesting findings that have relevance to managerial behavior. For example, moral judgment stories were administered to college students who had earlier participated in Milgram's (1963) obedience study. Under the guise of a reinforcement-learning experiment, Milgram's subjects had been directed to give increasingly intense electric shocks to a person who was observed to be in great pain. Of the respondents at the principled level (stages 5 and 6), 75 percent refused to administer the shocks (i.e., to hurt someone), while only 12.5 percent of the respondents at the conformity level refused. Higher levels of values development were associated with more humane behavior toward other people. Haan, Smith, and Block (1968) found that although both principled and self-centered individuals are inclined to join in mass social protests, the self-centered individuals are motivated by the desire to better themselves individually, while principled individuals are motivated by a sense of justice and by a desire to uphold the rights of the larger community.

It should also be noted that Kohlberg's model has been criticized by Carol Gilligan (1979, 1980, 1982, 1988) as containing a male bias. In her investigations of moral dilemmas among women, Gilligan indicated that women tend to value care, relationships, and commitment more highly than do males. The Kohlberg model, which tends to emphasize justice as the highest moral value, is more typical of males than females, she claimed. Whereas Gilligan's criticisms are somewhat controversial among researchers, they are less relevant to our discussion here because of our emphasis on the development of internalized principles for guiding behavior, whatever their basis. For our purposes in this chapter, the debate about whether justice is a male value and caring is a female value is largely beside the point.

Becoming more mature in values development requires that individuals develop a set of internalized principles by which they can govern their behavior. The development of those principles is enhanced and values maturity is increased as value-based issues are confronted, discussed, and thought about. Lickona (1976, p. 25) notes, "Simply increasing the amount of reciprocal communication that occurs among people is likely to enhance moral development."

To help you determine your own level of values maturity, an instrument developed by James Rest at the University of Minnesota's Moral Research Center was included in the Assessment section. It has been used extensively in research because it is easier to administer than Kohlberg's method for assessing maturity. According to Kohlberg (1976, p. 47), "Rest's approach does give a rough estimate of an individual's moral maturity level." Rather than placing a person on one single level of values maturity, it identifies the stage that the person relies on most. That is, it assumes that individuals use more than one level of maturity (or set of instrumental values), but that one level generally predominates. By completing this instrument, therefore, you will identify your predominant level of values maturity. To determine your maturity level, refer to the self-scoring instructions in the Appendix at the end of this chapter. An exercise in the Skill Practice section will help you develop or refine principles at the stage 5 and stage 6 level of maturity.

Ethical Decision Making and Values

In addition to its benefits for self-understanding, awareness of your own level of values maturity also has important practical implications for ethical decision making. By and large, the American public rates the honesty, integrity, and concern for moral values of American business executives as abysmal. A large majority of the public indicate that they think executives are dishonest, overly profit-oriented, and willing to step on other people to get what they want (Andrews, 1989). Although nine out of 10 companies have a written code of ethics, evidence exists to support public perceptions that these documents are not influential in assuring high moral conduct. For example, Ford Motor Company refused to alter the dangerous gas tank on the Pinto in order to save $11 per car. It cost Ford millions of dollars in lawsuits and cost many people their lives. Equity Funding tried to hide 64,000 phony insurance claims, but went bankrupt when the truth came out. Firestone denied that its 500-series tire was defective, but eventually took losses in the millions when the accident reports were publicized. A. H. Robins knew of problems with its Dalcon Shield for years before informing the public. The billion dollars set aside for lawsuits against the company was dwarfed by the actual claims, and the company filed Chapter 11. E. F. Hutton, General Dynamics, General Electric, Rockwell, Martin Marietta, Lockheed, Bank of Boston, Dow Corning, and a host of other firms have also been in the news for violating ethical principles. One cartoon that seems to summarize these goings-on shows a group of executives sitting at a conference table. The leader remarks, "Of course, honesty is one of the better policies."

Corporate behavior that exemplifies unethical decision making is not our principal concern here. More to the point is a study by the American Management Association that included 3,000 managers in the United States. It reported that most individual managers felt they were under pressure to compromise personal standards to meet company goals (Cavanaugh, 1980). As an illustration, consider the following true incident (names have been changed). How would you respond? Why?

> Dale Monson, a top manufacturing manager at Satellite Telecommunications, walked into the office of Al Lake, the head of quality control.

Dale was carrying an assembled part that was to be shipped to a customer on the West Coast. Dale handed Al the part and said, "Look Al, this part is in perfect shape electronically, but the case has a gouge in it. I've seen engineering and they say that the mark doesn't affect form, fit, or function. Marketing says the customer won't mind because they are just going to bury the unit anyway. We can't rework it, and it would cost $75,000 to make new cases. We will only do 23 units, and they're already made. The parts are due to be shipped at the end of the week." Al responded, "Well, what do you want from me?" "Just sign off so we can move forward," said Dale. "Since you're the one who needs to certify acceptable quality, I thought I'd better get this straightened out now rather than waiting until the last minute before shipping."

Would you ship the part or not? Discuss this with class members. Generate a recommendation for Al.

This case exemplifies the major values conflict faced over and over again by managers. It is a conflict between maximizing the economic performance of the organization (as indicated by revenues, costs, profits, and so forth) or the social performance of the organization (as indicated by obligations to customers, employees, suppliers, and so forth). Most ethical tradeoffs are conflicts between these two desirable ends: economic versus social performance (Hosmer, 1987). Making these kinds of decisions effectively is not merely a matter of selecting between right and wrong alternatives or between good and bad choices. Most of these choices are between right and right or between one good and another. Individuals who effectively manage these kinds of ethical tradeoffs are those who have a clear sense of their own values and who have developed a principled level of moral maturity. They have articulated and clarified their own internal set of universal, comprehensive, and consistent principles upon which to base their decisions. It is seldom the case, of course, that a manager could choose economic performance goals every time or that he or she could choose social performance goals every time. Tradeoffs are inevitable.

It is not a simple matter, on the other hand, to generate a personal set of universal, comprehensive, and consistent principles that can guide decision making. According to Kohlberg's research, most adults have nei-

ther constructed, nor do they follow, a well-developed set of principles in making decisions. One reason is that they have no model or example of what such principles might be. We offer some standards against which to test your own principles for making moral or ethical choices. These standards are neither comprehensive nor absolute, nor are they independent of one another. They simply serve as reference against which to test the principles that you include in your personal values statement.

Front page test: Would I be embarrassed if my decision became a headline in the local newspaper? Would I feel comfortable describing my actions or decision to a customer or stockholder?

Golden rule test: Would I be willing to be treated in the same manner?

Dignity and liberty test: Are the dignity and liberty of others preserved by this decision? Is the basic humanity of the affected parties enhanced? Are their opportunities expanded or curtailed?

Equal treatment test: Are the rights, welfare, and betterment of minorities and lower status people given full consideration? Does this decision benefit those with privilege but without merit?

Personal gain test: Is an opportunity for personal gain clouding my judgment? Would I make the same decision if the outcome did not benefit me in any way?

Congruence test: Is this decision or action consistent with my espoused personal principles? Does it violate the spirit of any organizational policies or laws?

Procedural justice test: Can the procedures used to make this decision stand up to scrutiny by those affected?

Cost-benefit test: Does a benefit for some cause unacceptable harm to others? How critical is the benefit? Can the harmful effects be mitigated?

Good night's sleep test: Whether or not anyone else knows about my action, will it produce a good night's sleep?

In the Skill Application section of this chapter, you may want to consider these alternatives when constructing your own set of comprehensive, consistent, and universalistic principles. You also should be aware, however, that your set of personal principles will also be influenced by your orientation for acquiring and responding to the information you receive. This orientation is called cognitive style.

Cognitive Style

Cognitive style consists of a large number of factors that relate to the way individuals perceive, interpret, and respond to information. There are literally scores of dimensions used in the research literature to define cognitive style (for examples, see Eckstrom, French, & Harmon, 1979). In this chapter, however, we consider the two major dimensions of cognitive style discussed in research literature that have been shown to have particular relevance to managerial behavior: (1) the manner in which individuals gather information; and (2) the manner in which they evaluate information they receive.

The basic premise underlying cognitive style is that every individual is faced with an overwhelming amount of information, and only part of it can be given attention and acted upon at any one time. Individuals, therefore, develop strategies for assimilating and interpreting the information they receive. No strategy is inherently good or inherently bad, and not everyone adopts an identifiable, consistent set of strategies that become part of his or her cognitive style. However, about 80 percent of individuals do eventually develop (mostly unconsciously) a preferred set of information-processing strategies, and these make up their particular cognitive styles. The Cognitive Style instrument in the Assessment section assesses the two core dimensions of your information-processing preferences.

In order for your scores on the Cognitive Style instrument to be meaningful to you, you must understand the theory on which the model is based. It is grounded in the work of Jung (1923). Figure 3 illustrates the two cognitive dimensions. The information-gathering dimension distinguishes an intuitive strategy from a sensing strategy, and the information evaluation dimension distinguishes a thinking strategy from a feeling strategy.

Different strategies for taking in, coding, and storing information (information gathering) develop as a result of certain cognitive filters used by individuals to select the information to which they pay attention. An **intuitive strategy** takes a holistic view and emphasizes commonalities and generalizations, that is, the relationships among the various elements of data. Intuitive

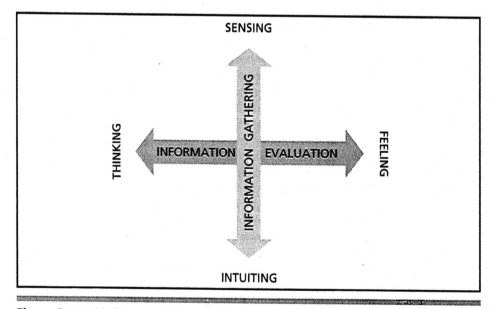

Figure 3   Model of Cognitive Style Based on Two Dimensions

thinkers often have preconceived notions about what sort of information may be relevant, and they look at the information to find what is consistent with their preconceptions. They tend to be convergent thinkers.

The **sensing strategy** focuses on detail, or on the specific attributes of each element of data, rather than on relationships among the elements. Sensing thinkers are rational and have few preconceptions about what may be relevant, so they insist on a close and thorough examination of the information. They are sensitive to the unique attributes of various parts of the information they encounter and tend to be divergent thinkers.

In simple terms, an intuitive strategy focuses on the whole whereas a sensing strategy looks at the parts of the whole. An intuitive strategy seeks commonalities and overall categories, while a sensing strategy looks for uniqueness, detail, and exceptions to general rules.

The second dimension of Jung's model refers to strategies for interpreting and judging information (information evaluation). These strategies develop from reliance on a particular problem-solving pattern. A **thinking strategy** evaluates information using a systematic plan with specific sequential steps. There is a focus on appropriate methods and logical progressions. Individuals who use a thinking style generally rely on objective data. Attempts are made to fit problems into a known model or framework. When such people defend their solutions, they emphasize the methods and procedures used to solve the problems. Vertinsky (1976) refers to these individuals as members of a "continuous culture," meaning that they operate consistently with existing patterns of thought.

A **feeling strategy,** on the other hand, approaches a problem on the basis of "gut feel," or an internal sense of how to respond. Problems are often defined and redefined, and approaches are based on trial and error rather than logical procedures. Feeling individuals have a penchant for subjective or impressionistic rather than objective data, and frequently cannot describe their own problem-solving processes. Problem solutions are often found through using analogies or seeing unusual relationships between the problem and a past experience. Vertinsky (1976) refers to these individuals as members of a "discontinuous culture."

These different strategies have important implications for managerial behavior. Each has advantages and disadvantages. For example, when faced with a large amount of data, sensing managers, because they focus on detail, experience information overload and personal stress more readily than intuitive managers do. When they encounter too much detail, or too much heterogeneity, sensing managers become overloaded because each detail receives attention.

Intuitive managers, on the other hand, focus on the relationships among elements and the whole and handle additions of detail relatively easily. However, when diversity or ambiguity is encountered in the information, when aberrations from expected relationships occur, or when preformed categories don't fit, intuitive managers are likely to have more difficulty processing the information than sensing managers are. Encountering exceptions or the absence of a clear set of relationships among elements is particularly problematic for intuitive managers. Sensing managers are likely to handle these situations more easily because of their tendency to do "fine-grained analyses" of problems.

Thinking managers are less likely to be effective when encountering problems requiring creativity and discontinuous thinking or when encountering highly ambiguous problems that have only partial information available. When no apparent system exists for solving a problem, these individuals are likely to have more difficulty than feeling managers are.

On the other hand, when one program or system will solve a variety of problems, that is, when the information suggests a straightforward, computational solution, feeling managers are less effective because of their tendency to try new approaches, to redefine problems, and to reinvent the solution over and over without following past programs. This generally leads to inefficient problem solving or even solving the wrong problem. Thinking managers have less difficulty in such situations.

Research on these cognitive dimensions has found that no matter what type of problem they face, most individuals use their preferred cognitive style to approach it. They prefer, and even seek, decision situations and problem types that are consistent with their own cognitive style (for example, individuals scoring high on thinking prefer problems with a step-by-step method of solution). In one study, for example, managers who were more thinking-oriented than feeling-oriented implemented more computer-based systems and rational procedures for decision making. Managers in another study defined identical problems differently depending on their different cognitive styles. Another study found that differences in cognitive style led to significantly different decision-making processes in managers (see Henderson & Nutt, 1980; Chenhall & Morris, 1991; Ruble & Cosier, 1990).

Students with different cognitive styles also have been found to approach learning differently, and different kinds of educational experiences hold meaning for different types of people. For example, individuals who emphasize intuitive strategies tend to do better in conceptual courses; they learn more easily through reading and through discussing general relationships. Exam questions with only one right answer may be easier for them than for those who emphasize sensing. Individuals who emphasize sensing strategies tend to do better in factual courses or courses in which attention to detail and dissimilarity is important. Critical and analytical learning activities (for example, debates) facilitate their learning, and exams emphasizing implications and applications may be easiest for these individuals.

Individuals who emphasize a thinking strategy do best in courses (such as mathematics) that take an orderly, step-by-step approach to the subject and where what is learned builds on, and follows directly from, what was learned earlier. On the other hand, feeling individuals do best in courses requiring creativity and idea generation. Learning activities in which the student must rely on a personal sense of what is appropriate (for example, sculpting) are likely to be preferred by these individuals.

Knowing one's own cognitive style can prove advantageous to managers in numerous ways, such as identifying career options, choosing appropriate business environments and managerial assignments, and selecting teams of complementary members to solve problems. It also is useful in helping students to capitalize on their academic strengths and enhance their study skills. Table 3 summarizes some personal characteristics associated with each of these major cognitive orientations.

Attitude Toward Change

In order to capitalize fully on the strengths of your own cognitive style, you also should be aware of your orientation toward change. This is important because, as the environment in which managers operate continues to become more chaotic, more temporary, more complex, and more overloaded with information, your ability to process information is at least partly constrained by your fundamental attitude about change.

Almost no one disagrees with the prediction that change will increase. Toffler (1980) stated it this way:

A powerful tide is surging across much of the world today, creating a new, often bizarre, environment in which to work, play, marry, raise children, or retire. In this bewildering context, businessmen swim against highly erratic economic currents; politicians see their ratings bob wildly up and down; universities, hospitals, and other institutions battle desperately against inflation. Value systems splinter and crash, while lifeboats of family, church, and state are hurled madly about.

Many observers have suggested that we have now entered a "post-industrial environment," characterized by more and increasing information, more and increasing turbulence, and more and increasing complexity (Huber, 1984; Grayson & O'Dell, 1988). For example, the number of academic journals currently is increasing at the rate of 11 percent per year from a base of approximately 100,000. Laser disc technology makes possible the storage of the equivalent of a law library on a 10.5-inch disc, and visual scanners can rapidly transfer the contents of printed material to a disc. The information explosion, including instantaneous mail and voice communication, immediate document retrieval, and desktop libraries, has changed the environment of modern management dramatically. Access to more information in increasing amounts almost instantaneously leads to increased turbulence and complexity for managers. They must make decisions ever faster as both the amount and the rapidity of the information encountered increase (Cameron & Ulrich, 1986; Peters, 1987). On the other hand, the human mind is capable of processing only a certain amount of information at a time, so more and more decisions have to be made on the basis of incomplete and ambiguous information (Simon, 1973). Individuals must manage now more than ever in conditions of ambiguity and turbulence, and cognitive style is sometimes at the mercy of orientation toward change.

Being aware of your own orientation toward change, therefore, is an important prerequisite for successfully coping with it. Two dimensions of change orientation particularly relevant for managers are discussed on the following pages.

INFORMATION GATHERING

INTUITIVE TYPES	SENSING TYPES
Like solving new problems.	Dislike new problems unless there are standard ways to solve them.
Dislike doing the same thing over and over again.	Like an established routine.
Enjoy learning a new skill more than using it.	Enjoy using skills already learned more than learning new ones.
Work in bursts of energy powered by enthusiasm, with slack periods in between.	Work more steadily, with realistic idea of how long it will take.
Jump to conclusions frequently.	Must usually work all the way through to reach a conclusion.
Are patient with complicated situations.	Are impatient when the details are complicated.
Are impatient with routine details.	Are patient with routine details.
Follow inspirations, good or bad.	Rarely trust inspirations, and don't usually feel inspired.
Often tend to make errors of fact.	Seldom make errors of fact.
Dislike taking time for precision.	Tend to be good at precise work.

INFORMATION EVALUATION

FEELING TYPES	THINKING TYPES
Tend to be very aware of other people and their feelings.	Are relatively unemotional and uninterested in people's feelings.
Enjoy pleasing people, even in unimportant things.	May hurt people's feelings without knowing it.
Like harmony. Efficiency may be badly disturbed by office feuds.	Like analysis and putting things into logical order. Can get along without harmony.
Often let decision be influenced by their own or other people's personal likes and wishes.	Tend to decide impersonally, sometimes ignoring people's wishes.
Need occasional praise.	Need to be treated fairly.
Dislike telling people unpleasant things.	Are able to reprimand people or fire them when necessary.
Relate well to most people.	Tend to relate well only to other thinking types.
Tend to be sympathetic.	May seem hardhearted.

Table 3   Characteristics of Cognitive Styles

Tolerance of Ambiguity

The first important dimension is **tolerance of ambiguity,** which refers to the extent to which individuals are threatened by or have difficulty coping with situations that are ambiguous, where change occurs rapidly or unpredictably, where information is inadequate or unclear, or where complexity exists. Stimulus-rich and information-overloaded environments (for example, air traffic control towers) are examples. Regardless of their cognitive style, people vary in their aptitude for operating in such circumstances.

People differ in the extent to which they are "cognitively complex" or in the extent to which they can cope with ambiguous, incomplete, unstructured, dynamic situations. Individuals who have a high tolerance of ambiguity also tend to be more cognitively complex. They tend to pay attention to more information, interpret more cues, and possess more sense-making categories than less complex individuals do. Research has found that cognitively complex and tolerant individuals are better transmitters of information (Bieri et al., 1966), more sensitive to internal (non-superficial) characteristics of others when evaluating their performance at work (Schneier, 1979), and more behaviorally adaptive and flexible under ambiguous and overloaded conditions than less tolerant and less cognitively complex individuals (Haase, Lee, & Banks, 1979). Managers with higher tolerance-of-ambiguity scores are more likely to be entrepreneurial in their actions (Schere, 1982), to screen out less information in a complex environment (Haase et al., 1979), and to choose specialties in their occupations that possess less-structured tasks (Budner, 1962). It also should be pointed out, however, that individuals who are more tolerant of ambiguity have more difficulty focusing on a single important element of information—they are inclined to pay attention to a variety of items—and they may have somewhat less ability to concentrate without being distracted by interruptions. However, for the most part, in an information-rich environment, tolerance of ambiguity and cognitive complexity are more adaptive than the opposite characteristics.

In the Skill Assessment section of this chapter, a Tolerance of Ambiguity Scale (Budner, 1962) assesses the extent to which you have a tolerance for these kinds of complex situations. In scoring the Tolerance of Ambiguity Scale (see Appendix I) three different sub-scale scores are assessed. One is the **Novelty** score, which indicates the extent to which you are tolerant of new, unfamiliar information or situations. The second sub-scale is the **Complexity** score, which indicates the extent to which you are tolerant of multiple, distinctive, or unrelated information. The third sub-scale is the **Insolubility** score, which indicates the extent to which you are tolerant of problems that are very difficult to solve because, for example, alternative solutions are not evident, information is unavailable, or the problem's components seem unrelated to each other. In general, the more tolerant people are of novelty, complexity, and insolubility, the more likely they are

to succeed as managers in information-rich, ambiguous environments. They are less overwhelmed by ambiguous circumstances.

It is important to note that cognitive complexity and tolerance for ambiguity are not related to intelligence (Smith & Leach, 1972), and your score on the Tolerance of Ambiguity Scale is not an evaluation of how smart you are. Most important, individuals can learn to tolerate more complexity and more flexibility in their information-processing abilities. The first step toward increasing tolerance is becoming aware of where you are now by completing the Skill Assessment section. Then the Skill Analysis and Skill Practice sections of this chapter, along with discussions such as the one in the chapters on problem solving and creativity, provide ways to improve your tolerance for ambiguity and your cognitive complexity.

It is also interesting to note that a positive correlation exists between tolerance of ambiguity and the second dimension of orientation toward change discussed here, internal locus of control.

Locus of Control

The second dimension of orientation toward change is **locus of control.** It is one of the most studied and written-about aspects of orientation toward change. Locus of control refers to the attitude people develop regarding the extent to which they are in control of their own destinies. When individuals receive information about the success or failure of their own actions, or when something changes in the environment, they differ in how they interpret that information. People receive reinforcements, both positive or negative, as they attempt to make changes around them. If individuals interpret the reinforcement they receive to be contingent upon their own actions, it is called an **internal locus** of control (that is, "I was the cause of the success or failure of the change"). If they interpret the reinforcement as being a product of outside forces, it is called an **external locus** of control (that is, "Something or someone else caused the success or failure"). Over time, people develop a "generalized expectancy" about the dominant sources of the reinforcements they receive. Thus, they become largely internally focused or largely externally focused with regard to the source of control they perceive in a changing environment.

Over 1,000 studies have been done using the locus of control scale. In general, the research suggests that, in American culture, internal locus of control is associated with the most successful managers (for reviews of the literature, see Hendricks, 1985; Spector, 1982). For example, the author of the scale, Julian B. Rotter (1966), summarized several studies of locus of control and reported that people with an internal locus of control are more likely to (1) be attentive to aspects of the environment that provide useful information for the future, (2) engage in actions to improve their environment, (3) place greater emphasis on striving for achievement, (4) be more inclined to develop their own skills, (5) ask more questions, and (6) remember more information than people with an external locus of control (see also Seeman, 1982).

In the management literature, individuals who have an internal locus of control are less alienated from the work environment (Mitchell, 1975; Seeman, 1982; Wolf, 1972), more satisfied with their work (Organ & Green, 1974; Pryer & Distefano, 1971), and experience less job strain and more position mobility (promotions and job changes) than do individuals with an external locus of control (Gennill & Heisler, 1972; Newton & Keenan, 1990). A study of leadership and group performance found that internals were more likely to be leaders and that groups led by internals were more effective than those led by externals (Anderson & Schneider, 1978; Blau, 1993). Internals also were found to outperform externals in stressful situations (Anderson, Hellriegel, & Slocum, 1977), to engage in more entrepreneurial activity (Durand & Shea, 1974; Cromie, Callahan, & Jansen, 1992; Bonnett & Furnharn, 1991), to be more active in managing their own careers (Hammer & Vardi, 1981), and to have higher levels of job involvement than externals (Runyon, 1973; Kren, 1992). Differences have also been found regarding how power and authority are utilized by externals and internals (see the chapter on Gaining Power and Influence). External leaders tend to use coercive power and threat, whereas internal leaders rely more on persuasion and expertise as a source of power (Goodstadt & Hjelle, 1973; Mitchell, Smyser, & Weed, 1975; Sweeney, McFarlin, & Cotton, 1991). Moreover, internals both demonstrate and are more satisfied with a participative management style than externals are (Runyon, 1973; Colarelli & Bishop, 1990). A study of locus of control among top executives found that the firms led by internals engaged in more innovation, more risky projects, more leadership in the marketplace, longer planning horizons, more scanning of

the environment, and a more highly developed technology than external-led firms did (Miller, Kets de Vries, & Toulouse, 1982). In summarizing his conclusions about locus of control, McDonald (1970) stated, "all research points to the same conclusion: In the American culture, people are handicapped by external locus of control."

On the other hand, research also has found that an internal locus of control is not a panacea for all management problems. Internal locus of control is not always a positive attribute. For example, individuals with an external locus of control have been found to be more inclined to initiate structure as leaders (to help clarify roles) and to show consideration to people (Durand & Shea, 1974). Internals are less likely to comply with leader directions and are less accurate in processing feedback about successes and failures than are externals (Cravens & Worchel, 1977). Internals also have more difficulty arriving at decisions with serious consequences for someone else (Wheeler & Davis, 1979).

It is important to note that locus of control can shift over time, particularly as a function of the position held at work (Harvey, 1971), and that external locus of control does not inhibit individuals from attaining positions of power and influence at the top of organizations (Rothenberg, 1980). Therefore, no matter what your Internal-External score, you can be a successful manager in the right setting, or you can alter your locus of control. Research has shown that people who interpret information about change as if they are in control of it, and who perceive themselves to be in charge of their own performance (and hence able to control outcomes related to that performance), are more likely to be effective managers in most circumstances in our culture.

The Locus of Control Scale in the Skill Assessment section helps you generate a score showing the extent to which you have an internal or external locus of control. The scoring key and some comparison information are located in Appendix I.

In summary, two key attitudes toward change, tolerance of ambiguity and locus of control, have been found to be associated with success in management roles. Knowing your scores on these two factors can help you capitalize on your strengths and enhance your potential for management success. While substantial research exists associating some positive managerial behaviors with internal locus of control and tolerance of ambiguity, possessing these orientations is neither an assurance of success as a manager nor a solution to the problems that managers face. By knowing your scores, however, you will be able to choose situations in which you are more likely to feel comfortable, perform effectively, and understand the point of view of those whose perspectives differ from yours. Self-understanding is a prerequisite to self-improvement and change.

Interpersonal Orientation

The fourth critical area of self-awareness is interpersonal orientation. This aspect of self-awareness differs from the first three in that it relates to behavioral tendencies and to relationships with other people, not just to one's own personal inclinations and psychological attributes. Because the manager's job has been characterized as overwhelmingly interpersonal, interpersonal orientation, or the tendency to behave in certain ways around other people, is an especially important aspect of self-awareness. Sayles (1964, p. 38) suggests that management involves virtually constant contact with people, and managers whose personalities do not dispose them toward a high amount of interpersonal activity are likely to be frustrated and dissatisfied. The quality and type of this interpersonal activity can vary widely, however. Therefore, it is important for you to know your own interpersonal tendencies and inclinations to maximize the probabilities of successful interactions.

Interpersonal orientation does not reflect the actual behavior patterns displayed in interpersonal situations. Rather, it refers to the underlying tendencies to behave in certain ways, regardless of the other person involved or the circumstance. Interpersonal orientation generally arises from certain basic needs in the individual that relate to relationships with others.

A well-known and thoroughly researched theory of interpersonal orientation was proposed by Schutz (1958). The basic assumption of his model is that people need people and that all individuals seek to establish compatible relationships with other individuals in their social interactions. As people form relationships and begin striving for compatibility in interactions, three interpersonal needs develop that must be satisfied if the individual is to function effectively and avoid unsatisfactory relationships.

The first is the **need for inclusion.** Everyone needs to maintain a relationship with other people, to be included in their activities, and to include them in one's own activities. To some extent all individuals seek to belong to a group, but at the same time they want to be

left alone. They need to ensure that others are not left out while at the same time giving them independence. There is always a tradeoff between tendencies toward extroversion and introversion. Therefore, individuals differ in the strength of their relative needs: (1) the need to include others, or expressed inclusion, and (2) the need to be included by others, or wanted inclusion.

A second interpersonal need is the **need for control.** This is the need to maintain a satisfactory balance of power and influence in relationships. All individuals need to exert control, direction, or structure over other people while also remaining independent from them. All individuals also have a need to be controlled, directed, or structured by others but at the same time to maintain freedom and discretion. Essentially, this is a tradeoff between authoritarianism and dependency. Individual differences arise, therefore, in the need to control others, or expressed control, and the need to be controlled by others, or wanted control.

A third need is the **need for affection,** or the need to form close personal relationships with others. This need is not restricted to physical affection or romantic relationships but includes needs for warmth, intimacy, and love apart from overt behaviors. All individuals need to form close, personal relationships with other people, but at the same time they want to avoid becoming overcommitted or smothered. All individuals need to have others show warmth and affection to them but also need to maintain some distance. This is a tradeoff between high affiliative needs and high independence needs. Individuals therefore vary in their needs for expressing affection toward other people and for wanting affection to be expressed toward them.

Each of the three interpersonal needs has two aspects, a desire to express the need and a desire to receive the needed behavior from others. These three needs determine an individual's interpersonal orientation. Individuals differ uniquely in their need to give or receive certain behaviors when interacting with others. Table 4 summarizes these three needs and illustrates characteristics of each.

In the Skill Assessment section, we provided the instrument Schutz developed to assess inclusion, control, and affection needs. Using the scoring sheet and instructions in Appendix I, compute your score for each interpersonal need. The discussion of interpersonal orientation in this section will be more meaningful to you if you have completed the FIRO-B survey in the Assessment section. If you have not done so, please take

	INCLUSION	CONTROL	AFFECTION
Expressed Toward Others	I join other people, and I include others.	I take charge, and I influence people.	I get close and personal with people.
Wanted from Others	I want other people to include me.	I want others to lead me or give me directions.	I want people to get close and personal with me.

Table 4   Descriptors of Fundamental Interpersonal Relations Orientation-Behavior (FIRO-B) Needs

time to complete it now. It should take you no more than 10 minutes.

There are several ways your scores on this questionnaire can be analyzed and interpreted. For example, you can compare your *expressed* total with your *wanted* total to determine the extent to which you are willing to give as much behavior as you want to get. Individuals who have high expressed scores and low wanted scores are called "controllers" by Ryan (1970) because they want to express but are unwilling to accept in return. The reverse pattern, high wanted scores and low expressed scores, is called a "passive" pattern by Ryan because these individuals want to receive but are unwilling to initiate interaction.

By comparing each need score, you can determine which is your most important interpersonal need. Your highest score may indicate the need that is least satisfied.

Another way to interpret your scores is to compare them with the national norm data in Table 5. The numbers at the top of each box (for example, 4 to 7) refer to the average range of scores. At least 50 percent of adults fall within that range. The numbers at the

bottom (for example, 5.4) refer to the average scores in the cells. At least 50 percent of adults score within 1.5 of those scores. If you scored 6 in the expressed control cell, for example, you score higher than 75 percent of the people on that need; if you scored 2 in the expressed affection cell, you score lower than 75 percent.

The score in the lower-right-hand corner (the total of the expressed and wanted scores) is called the *social interaction index*. This score represents the overall interpersonal need level. The highest possible score is 54. Individuals with high scores have strong needs to interact with other people. They are likely to be gregarious, friendly, and involved with others. Low scores are more typical of shy, reserved people.

Hill (1974) found that business school students differ significantly on the social interaction index, depending on their majors. Accounting and systems analysis students in his study had means of 22.3 and 22.6, respectively (lower than average), while marketing and human resource majors had means of 31.0 and 31.9, respectively (higher than average). Finance, small business, and engineering students were in the middle.

	INCLUSION	CONTROL	AFFECTION	ROW TOTALS
Expressed Toward Others	4 to 7 5.4	2 to 5 3.9	3 to 6 4.1	9 to 18 13.4
Wanted from Others	5 to 8 6.5	3 to 6 4.6	3 to 6 4.6	11 to 20 15.9
Column Totals	9 to 15 11.9	5 to 11 8.5	6 to 12 8.9	20 to 38 29.3

Table 5   Average FIRO-B Scores and Ranges

This difference turned out to be statistically significant, which suggests that career selection may have something to do with interpersonal orientation.

Probably the greatest usefulness of the scores lies in analyzing **interpersonal compatibility**—that is, in matching one person's scores with those of another. Individuals can be interpersonally incompatible in three ways. To explain these three incompatibilities, two hypothetical scores are used in Table 6.

The first type of incompatibility is **reciprocal**. It refers to the match between one person's expressed behavior and another person's wanted behavior. For example, if one person has a high need to express control but the other person does not want to be controlled, there is a reciprocal incompatibility. The formula for computing reciprocal incompatibility is

$$| \text{Manager's } e - \text{Subordinate's } w | + | \text{Subordinate's } e - \text{Manager's } w |$$

The straight lines indicate absolute values (no minus numbers). The data in Table 6 show that in the inclusion area, for example, a reciprocal incompatibility exists between the manager and the subordinate. Using the formula above, we have

$$| 9 - 2 | + | 3 - 8 | = 12$$

Any score higher than 6 means that there is a strong possibility of incompatibility. In this case, the manager has a strong need to include others and to be included by them, but the subordinate has low needs in both aspects of inclusion. There is a potential for interpersonal conflict to arise in this area, particularly if inclu-

sion behavior (for example, teamwork) is required in the relationship.

Originator incompatibility is the second type. This refers to the match between the expressed scores of both individuals. Originator incompatibility occurs either when both people want to initiate in an area or when neither wants to initiate. The formula for computing originator incompatibility is

$$(\text{Manager's } e - \text{Manager's } w) + (\text{Subordinate's } e - \text{Subordinate's } w)$$

The parentheses in the formula indicate that minus numbers should be computed. The data from Table 6 in the control area make clear that an originator incompatibility exists. Both the manager and the subordinate want to control, but neither has a high need to be controlled. Their incompatibility score is computed as follows:

$$(9 - 4) + (8 - 2) = +11$$

Any score higher than +6 indicates high competitive originator incompatibility. A score of less than -6 indicates high apathetic originator incompatibility. Apathetic incompatibility occurs either when neither individual wants to initiate in the area or, in this case, when neither person wants to control or take charge; both want the other to do it.

The third type of incompatibility is **interchange**. This refers to the extent to which two individuals emphasize the same or different interpersonal needs. For example, interchange incompatibility exists if one person emphasizes control needs highly while the other

	MANAGER			
	INCLUSION	**CONTROL**	**AFFECTION**	
Expressed *(e)*	9	9	1	19
Wanted *(w)*	8	4	3	15
	17	13	4	34
	SUBORDINATE			
	INCLUSION	**CONTROL**	**AFFECTION**	
Expressed *(e)*	3	8	6	17
Wanted *(w)*	2	2	8	12
	5	10	14	29

Table 6 Examples of Two FIRO-B Scores

emphasizes affection needs highly. When interpersonal problems arise, one person would likely define the problem as one of control, direction, or influence, while the other person would likely define the problem as one of closeness, warmth, and affection. The difficulty would be in getting the two people to see the situation as the same problem. The formula for computing interchange incompatibility is

$$| \text{Manager's } e + \text{Manager's } w | - | \text{Subordinate's } e + \text{Subordinate's } w |$$

Again, the straight lines in the formula enclose absolute values. In the affection area in Table 6, an interchange incompatibility exists. Affection is a high need area for the subordinate but a low need area for the manager. (The reverse case exists in the inclusion area.) Computing the interchange incompatibility score gives us

$$| 1 + 3 | - | 6 + 8 | = 10$$

Scores above 6 indicate a strong possibility of incompatibility. The need of the subordinate in the affection area is likely to be ignored or rejected in the relationship.

Using these three incompatibility formulas allows us to compute a **total incompatibility** score, which combines the three types of incompatibilities in the three need areas. These are computed in Table 7 for the hypothetical manager and subordinate.

The incompatibility scores indicate that this manager and subordinate have a high probability of interpersonal difficulty in their relationship. Potential problems of not meeting one another's needs in any of the three interpersonal need categories (reciprocal incompatibility), of both wanting to control but not wanting to be controlled (originator incompatibility in

the control area), and of having different need emphases (interchange incompatibility in the inclusion and affection areas) would probably lead these two people to have a conflict-ridden relationship.

Research confirms this prediction. For example, DiMarco (1974) has found that low incompatibility scores result in more favorable attitudes of subordinates toward managers. Obradovic (1962) has found teacher attitudes are more favorable toward students when compatibility scores are high. Hutcherson (1963) has found that students achieve higher levels in classes when compatibility with the teacher is high. More often, friends are chosen from among those with compatible scores. Sapolsky (1965) and Mendelsohn and Rankin (1969) have even found that the success of therapist-patient treatment is affected by interpersonal incompatibility.

There is strong evidence that groups composed of compatible individuals are more satisfying to members and more effective than groups composed of incompatible individuals. The following are some characteristics that studies have found typical of interpersonally compatible groups (Hewett, O'Brien, & Hornik, 1974; Liddell & Slocum, 1976; Reddy & Byrnes, 1972; Shalinsky, 1969; Schutz, 1958; Smith & Haythorn, 1973):

1. More interpersonal attraction among members.

2. More positive group climate.

3. More cooperative behavior on tasks.

4. More productivity in accomplishing tasks.

5. Faster problem solving.

6. Fewer errors in solving problems.

7. Less hostility among members.

	INCLUSION	CONTROL	AFFECTION
Reciprocal incompatibility	12	11	10
Originator incompatibility	2	11	−4
Interchange incompatibility	12	3	10
Total incompatibility (Sum of absolute values)			75

Table 7 Incompatibility Scores for a Hypothetical Manager and a Subordinate

Knowing your interpersonal orientation, then, can be an important factor in your managerial success. Not only does it enhance good interpersonal relations by helping you diagnose potential areas of incompatibility, but it also helps you generate alternatives for behavior when you attempt to solve interpersonal difficulties. For example, some problems can be solved simply by increasing inclusion activities, by allowing someone else to express a little more control, or by redefining an issue as an affection problem instead of a control problem.

Summary

Corporate America increasingly has begun to discover the power of developing self-awareness among its managers. Each year, millions of executives complete instruments designed to increase self-awareness in companies such as Apple, AT&T, Citicorp, Exxon, General Electric, Honeywell, 3M, and the U.S. Army. An awareness of how individuals differ in their values priorities and values maturity, cognitive style, orientation toward change, and interpersonal orientation has helped many companies cope better with interpersonal conflicts, botched communications, breakdowns in trust, and misunderstandings. For example, after requiring his top 100 managers to undergo self-awareness training, the president of the computer reservations company of Hilton Hotels and Budget Rent-a-Car stated:

We had some real morale problems. I realized I had a mixed bag of people reporting to me and that this training could help us better understand each other and also understand how we make decisions. We wouldn't have made it through [a recent company crisis] without self-awareness training (Moore, 1987).

Not only does self-awareness training assist individuals in their ability to understand, and thereby manage, themselves, but it also is important in helping individuals develop understanding of the differences in others. Most people will regularly encounter individuals who possess different styles, different sets of values, and different perspectives than they do. Most work forces are becoming more, not less, diverse. Self-awareness training as discussed in this chapter, therefore, can be a valuable tool in helping individuals develop empathy and understanding for the expanding diversity they will face in work and school settings. The relationship between the four critical areas of self-awareness and these management outcomes is summarized in Figure 4.

Most of the following chapters relate to skills in interpersonal or group interaction, but successful skill development in those areas will occur only if individuals

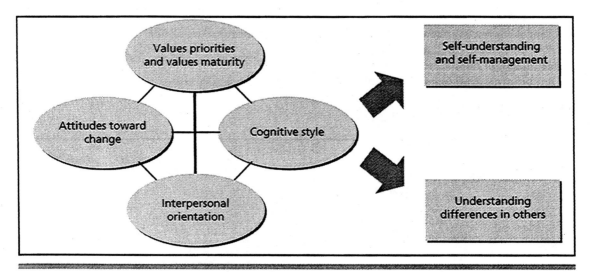

Figure 4   Core Aspects of Self-Awareness and the Managerial Implications

have a firm foundation in self-awareness. In fact, there is an interesting paradox in human behavior: *We can know others only by knowing ourselves, but we can know ourselves only by knowing others.* Our knowledge of others, and therefore our ability to manage or interact successfully with them, comes from relating what we see in them to our own experience. If we are not self-aware, we have no basis for knowing certain things about others. Self-recognition leads to recognition and understanding of others. As Harris (1981) puts it:

> Nothing is really personal that is not first interpersonal, beginning with the infant's shock of separation from the umbilical cord. What we know about ourselves comes only from the outside, and is interpreted by the kind of experiences we have had; and what we know about others comes only from analogy with our own network of feelings.

Behavioral Guidelines

Following are the behavioral guidelines relating to the improvement of self-awareness. These guidelines will be helpful to you as you engage in practice and application activities designed to improve your self-awareness.

1. Identify your sensitive line. Determine what information about yourself you are most likely to defend against.

2. Identify a comprehensive, consistent, and universal set of principles on which you will base your behavior. Identify the most important terminal and instrumental values that guide your decisions.

3. Expand your cognitive style, your tolerance of ambiguity, and your internal locus of control by increasing your exposure to new information and engaging in different kinds of activities than you are used to. Seek ways to expand and broaden yourself.

4. Compute incompatibility scores on those with whom you regularly interact and identify areas in which potential incompatibilities may arise. Apply principles of supportive communication (Chapter 4) and conflict management (Chapter 7) when disagreements do arise.

5. Engage in honest self-disclosure with someone who is close to you and accepting of you. Check out aspects of yourself that you are not sure of.

6. Keep a journal, and make time regularly to engage in self-analysis. Balance life's activities with some time for self-renewal.

Skill Analysis

Cases Involving Self-Awareness

Communist Prison Camp

To find examples of an intensive destruction of identification with family and reference groups and the destruction of social role and self-image, we turn to the experiences of civilian political prisoners interned in Chinese Communist prisons.

In such prisons the total regimen, consisting of physical privation, prolonged interrogation, total isolation from former relationships and sources of information, detailed regimentation of all daily activities, and deliberate humiliation and degradation, was geared to producing a confession of alleged crimes, the assumption of a penitent role, and the adoption of a Communist frame of reference. The prisoner was not informed what his crimes were, nor was he permitted to evade the issue by making up a false confession. Instead, what the prisoner learned he must do was reevaluate his past from the point of view of the Communists and recognize that most of his former attitudes and behavior were actually criminal from this point of view. For example, a priest who had dispensed food to needy peasants in his mission church had to "recognize" that he was actually a tool of imperialism and was using his missionary activities as cover for exploitation of the peasants. Even worse, he had used food as blackmail to accomplish his aims.

The key technique used by the Communists to produce social alienation to a degree sufficient to allow such redefinition and reevaluation to occur was to put the prisoner into a cell with four or more other prisoners who were somewhat more advanced in their "thought reform" than he. Such a cell usually had one leader who was responsible to the prison authorities, and the progress of the whole cell was made contingent upon the progress of the least "reformed" member. This condition meant in practice that four or more cell members devoted all their energies to getting their least "reformed" member to recognize "the truth" about himself and to confess. To accomplish this they typically swore at, harangued, beat, denounced, humiliated, reviled, and brutalized their victim twenty-four hours a day, sometimes for weeks or months on end. If the authorities felt that the prisoner was basically uncooperative, they manacled his hands behind his back and chained his ankles, which made him completely dependent on his cellmates for the fulfillment of his basic needs. It was this reduction to an animal-like existence in front of other humans which constituted the ultimate humiliation and led most reliably to the destruction of the prisoner's image of himself. Even in his own eyes he became something which was not worthy of the regard of his fellow man.

If, to avoid complete physical and personal destruction, the prisoner began to confess in the manner desired of him, he was usually forced to prove his sincerity by making irrevocable behavioral commitments, such as denouncing and implicating his friends and relatives in his own newly recognized crimes. Once he had done this he became further alienated from his former self, even in his own eyes, and could seek security only in a new identity and new social relationships. Aiding this process of confessing was the fact that the crimes gave the prisoner something concrete to which to attach the free-floating guilt which the accusing environment and his own humiliation usually stimulated.

. . . A good example was the plight of the sick and wounded prisoners of war who, because of their physical confinement, were unable to escape from continual conflict with their interrogator or instructor, and who therefore often ended up forming a close relationship with him. Chinese Communist instructors often encouraged prisoners to take long walks or have informal talks with them and offered as incentives cigarettes, tea, and other rewards. If the prisoner was willing to cooperate and become a "progressive," he could join with other "progressives" in an active group life.

Within the political prison, the group cell not only provided the forces toward alienation but also offered the road to a "new self." Not only were there available among the fellow prisoners individuals with whom the prisoner could identify because of their shared plight, but once he showed any tendency to seek a new identity by truly trying to reevaluate his past, he received again a whole range of rewards, of which perhaps the most important was the interpersonal information that he was again a person worthy of respect and regard.

Source: Schein, 1960.

Discussion Questions

1. To what extent is the self-concept a product of situational factors or inherited factors?

2. What is the relationship between self-knowledge and social pressure?

3. Is self-awareness constant, or do people become more and less self-aware over time?

4. What mechanisms could have been used by prisoners of war to resist the destruction of their self-concepts?

5. What could have been done to facilitate the reform of the self-concepts of prisoners? What can be done to enhance an already-positive self-concept?

Decision Dilemmas

For each of the five scenarios below, select the choice you would make if you were in the situation.

1. A young manager in a high technology firm was offered a position by the firm's chief competitor for almost double her salary. Her firm sought to prevent her from changing jobs, arguing that her knowledge of certain specialized manufacturing processes would give the competitor unfair advantage. Since she had acquired that knowledge through special training and unique opportunities in her current position, the firm argued that it was unethical for her to accept the competitor's offer. What should the young manager do?

   ____✓____ Accept the offer

   _____ Reject the offer

2. A consumer advocate organization conducted a survey to determine whether Wendy's hamburgers were really any more "hot and juicy" than any other hamburgers. After testing a Big Mac, a Whopper, a Teen Burger, and a Wendy's Hot and Juicy, each hamburger brand received approximately the same number of votes for being the juiciest. The consumer group advocated that Wendy's not advertise its hamburgers to be the juiciest. The

company indicated that its own tests showed different results and that the image of the burger was the important thing, not the test results. Should the advertisements cease or not?

_____ Cease to advertise

_____ Continue to advertise

3. After several profitable years, the Bob Cummings Organic Vitamin Company was made available for sale. Bob's movie and TV appearances precluded him from keeping track of a large company, and it became apparent that, if present trends continued, the company would either have to expand substantially or lose a large share of the market. Several firms were interested in purchasing the company for the asking price, but one firm was particularly aggressive. It sponsored several parties and receptions in Bob's honor; a 35-foot yacht was made available for his use during the summer; and several gifts for family members arrived during the holidays. Bob's wife questioned the propriety of these activities. Was it appropriate for Bob to accept the gifts? Should he sell to that firm?

_____ Proper to accept

_____ Not proper

_____ Should not sell

_____ Should sell

4. John Waller was hired to coach football. After two seasons, he was so successful that he was named coach of the year by UPI, *Sporting News,* and ESPN. He was also very vocal about the need to clean up cheating in college athletics, especially among competitor schools in his own conference. He heard rumors about inappropriate alumni gifts to some of his own athletes, but after confronting those involved, he received assurances that the rumors weren't true. At the beginning of the next season, however, he received conclusive evidence that seven of the starters on his team, including an All-American, had received financial benefits from a wealthy booster. What should Waller do?

_____ Kick them off the team

_____ Suspend them for several games

_____ Warn them but do nothing

5. Roger's company had been battered by competition from Asian firms. Not only were Asian products selling for less money, but their quality was substantially higher. By investing in some high technology equipment and fostering better union-management relations, Roger was relatively certain that the quality gap could be overcome. But his overhead rate was more than 40 percent above that of the competitor firms. He reasoned that the most efficient way to lower costs would be to close one of his older plants, lay off the employees, and increase production in the newer plants. He knew just which plant would be the one to close. The trouble was, the community was dependent on that plant as its major employer and had recently invested a great deal of money for highway repair and streetlight construction around the plant. Most of the work force were older people who had lived in the area most of their lives. It was improbable that they could obtain alternative employment in the same area. Should Roger close the plant or not?

_____ Close the plant

_____ Do not close

Discussion Questions

Form a small group and discuss the following questions regarding these five scenarios:

1. Why did you make the choices you did in each case? Justify each answer.

2. What principles or basic values for decision making did you use in each case?

3. What additional information would you need in order to be certain about your choices?

4. What circumstances might arise to make you change your mind about your decision? Could there be a different answer to each case in a different circumstance?

5. What do your answers tell you about your own values, cognitive style, attitude toward change, and interpersonal orientation?

Skill Practice

Exercises for Improving Self-Awareness Through Self-Disclosure

Through the Looking Glass

In the 19th century, the concept of "looking-glass self" was developed to describe the process used by people to develop self-awareness. It means simply that other people serve as a "looking-glass" for each of us. They mirror back our actions and behaviors. In turn, we form our opinions of ourselves as a result of observing and interpreting this mirroring. The best way to form accurate self-perceptions, therefore, is to share your thoughts, attitudes, feelings, actions, and plans with others. This exercise helps you do that by asking you to analyze your own styles and inclinations and then share and discuss them with others. They may provide insights that you haven't recognized before.

Assignment

In a group of two or three, share your scores on the Skill Assessment instruments. Determine what similarities and differences exist among you. Do systematic ethnic or gender differences exist? Now read aloud the 11 statements listed below. Each person should complete each statement, but take turns going first. The purpose of your completing the statements aloud is to help you articulate aspects of your self-awareness and to receive reactions to them from others.

1. In taking the assessment instruments, I was surprised by . . .

2. Some of my dominant characteristics captured by the instruments are . . .

3. Among my greatest strengths are . . .

4. Among my greatest weaknesses are . . .

5. The time I felt most successful was . . .

6. The time I felt least competent was . . .

7. My three highest priorities in life are . . .

8. The way in which I differ most from other people is . . .

9. I get along best with people who . . .

10. The best analogy that captures how I think of myself is . . .

11. From what you've said, I have noticed about you . . .

Exercise for Identifying Aspects of Personal Culture

Family Lineage and Autobiography

Not only do our experiences and interactions affect our self-concept, but each person enters this world with certain inclinations and talents, sometimes called "temperament" by psychologists. This temperament may be developed both socially by our close family interactions and as a result of genetic factors. This exercise helps you identify and analyze the major family influences that may have had an important impact on your values, attitudes, styles, and personality. Not only is each person's physiology different, but each person's family culture varies as well. This exercise can help you highlight important aspects of your family culture.

The outcome of this exercise will be a written autobiography. In order to help you prepare such a document, the following four steps should be completed. Then use the results to construct an autobiography.

Step 1: On the chart in Figure 5, plot the points in each area of self-awareness that correspond to where you would like to have scored. The vertical axis in the figure ranges from Very Satisfied to Very Unsatisfied. Your plots will represent your level of satisfaction with the scores you received on each instrument. For example, if you are satisfied with the score on the Defining Issues Test, make a mark near the top for 1. If you are dissatisfied with your score on FIRO-B, make a mark near the bottom on 5. Connect each point so you have a "self-awareness satisfaction profile."

Step 2: On the chart in Figure 6, draw your lifeline, plotting the major activities and events of your life. The vertical axis represents the importance or significance of events in terms of their impact on who you are today and how you think. The horizontal axis represents time in years. Your line should identify times that had major impact on forming your values, styles, and orientations. Label each of these "peak" experiences on your lifeline.

Step 3: On the chart in Figure 7, complete as much of your family tree as you can. Below each name, identify the major traits you associate with the person and the major way in which the person influenced your life. Then identify the way in which your family differs from other families you know.

Step 4: Now combine all the information you have generated in steps 1 through 3 and write an autobiography, which is essentially an answer to the question, "Who am I?" Include in the autobiography your answers to the five questions on page 79. Your analysis should include more than just the answers to these questions, but be sure to include them.

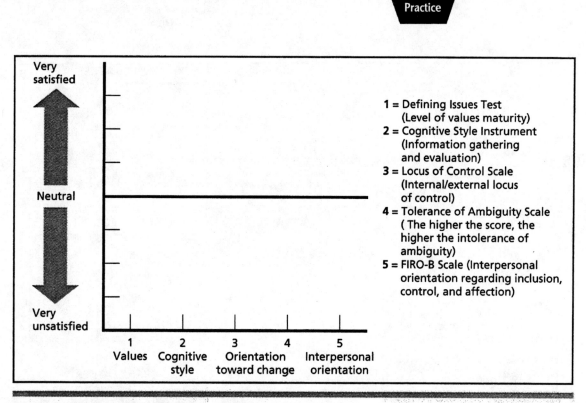

Very
satisfied

Neutral

Very
unsatisfied

1 = Defining Issues Test
(Level of values maturity)
2 = Cognitive Style Instrument
(Information gathering
and evaluation)
3 = Locus of Control Scale
(Internal/external locus
of control)
4 = Tolerance of Ambiguity Scale
(The higher the score, the
higher the intolerance of
ambiguity)
5 = FIRO-B Scale (Interpersonal
orientation regarding inclusion,
control, and affection)

| 1 | 2 | 3 | 4 | 5 |
| Values | Cognitive style | Orientation toward change | | Interpersonal orientation |

Figure 5   Satisfaction with Self-Awareness Scores

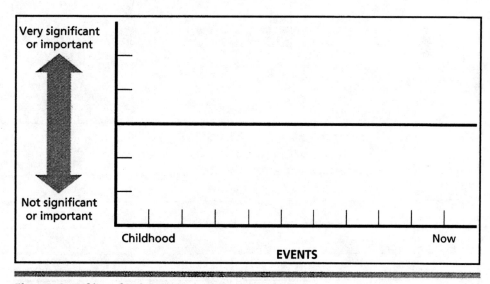

Very significant
or important

Not significant
or important

Childhood

Now

EVENTS

Figure 6   Lifeline of Peak Experiences

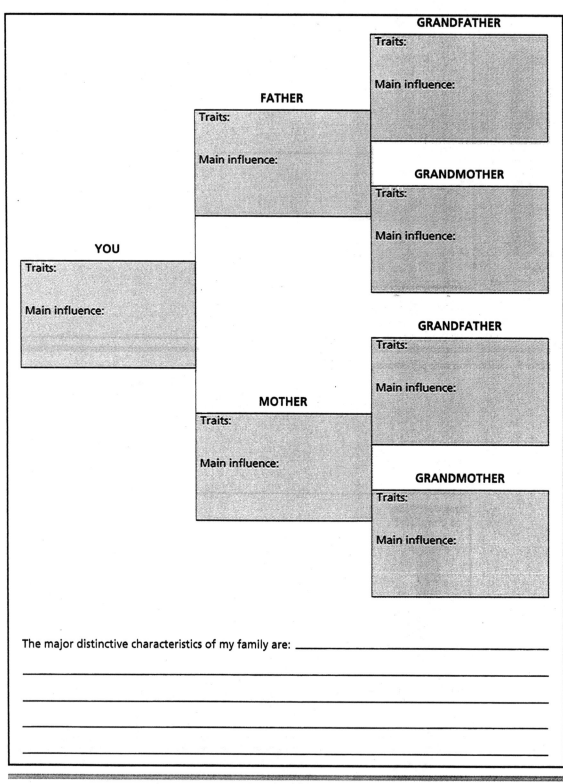

Figure 7 Family Genealogy with Important Influences Identified

Assignment

1. How would you describe your personal style?

2. What are your main strengths and weaknesses?

3. What behavioral principles lie at the center of your life?

4. What do you want to achieve in the next five years?

5. What legacy do you want to leave?

Skill Application

Activities for Developing Self-Awareness

Suggested Assignments

1. Keep a journal for at least the remainder of this course. Record significant discoveries, insights, learnings, and personal recollections, not just daily activities. Write in your journal at least twice a week. Give yourself some feedback.

2. Write down the comprehensive, consistent, and universal principles that guide your behavior under all circumstances and that you will rarely violate.

3. After completing these personal assessment instruments and discussing their implications with someone else, write a statement or an essay responding to the following four questions: (1) Who am I? (2) What are my main strengths and weaknesses? (3) What do I want to achieve in my life? (4) What legacy do I want to leave?

4. Spend an evening with a close friend or relative discussing your values, cognitive style, attitude toward change, and interpersonal orientation. You may want to have that person complete the instruments, giving his or her impressions of you, so you can compare and contrast your scores. Discuss implications for your future and for your relationship.

5. Teach someone else the value of self-awareness in managerial success and explain the relevance of values maturity, cognitive style, attitudes toward change, and interpersonal orientation. Describe the experience in your journal.

Application Plan and Evaluation

The intent of this exercise is to help you apply this cluster of skills in a real-life, out-of-class setting. Now that you have become familiar with the behavioral guidelines that form the basis of effective skill performance, you will improve most by trying out those guidelines in an everyday context. Unlike a classroom activity, in which feedback is immediate and others can assist you with their evaluations, this skill application activity is one you must accomplish and evaluate on your own. There are two parts to this activity. Part 1 helps prepare you to apply the skill. Part 2 helps you evaluate and improve on your experience. Be sure to write down answers to each item. Don't short-circuit the process by skipping steps.

Part 1. Planning

1. Write down the two or three aspects of this skill that are most important to you. These may be areas of weakness, areas you most want to improve, or areas that are most salient to a problem you face right now. Identify the specific aspects of this skill that you want to apply.

2. Now identify the setting or the situation in which you will apply this skill. Establish a plan for performance by actually writing down a description of the situation. Who else will be involved? When will you do it? Where will it be done?

   Circumstances:

   Who else?

   When?

   Where?

3. Identify the specific behaviors you will engage in to apply this skill. Operationalize your skill performance?

4. What are the indicators of successful performance? How will you know you have been effective? What will indicate you have performed competently?

Part 2. Evaluation

5. After you have completed your implementation, record the results. What happened? How successful were you? What was the effect on others?

6. How can you improve? What modifications can you make next time? What will you do differently in a similar situation in the future?

7. Looking back on your whole skill practice and application experience, what have you learned? What has been surprising? In what ways might this experience help you in the long term?

Solving Problems Creatively

OBJECTIVES

Increase proficiency in

▶ Rational problem solving

▶ Recognizing personal conceptual blocks

▶ Enhancing creativity by overcoming conceptual blocks

▶ Fostering innovation among others

Skill Assessment

Diagnostic Surveys for Creative Problem Solving

Problem Solving, Creativity, and Innovation

Step 1: Before you read the material in this chapter, please respond to the following statements by writing a number from the rating scale below in the left-hand column (Preassessment). Your answers should reflect your attitudes and behavior as they are now, not as you would like them to be. Be honest. This instrument is designed to help you discover your level of competency in problem solving and creativity so you can tailor your learning to your specific needs. When you have completed the survey, use the scoring key in Appendix I to identify the skill areas discussed in this chapter that are most important for you to master.

Step 2: After you have completed the reading and the exercises in this chapter and, ideally, as many as you can of the Skill Application assignments at the end of this chapter, cover up your first set of answers. Then respond to the same statements again, this time in the right-hand column (Postassessment). When you have completed the survey, use the scoring key in Appendix I to measure your progress. If your score remains low in specific skill areas, use the behavioral guidelines at the end of the Skill Learning section to guide further practice.

Rating Scale

1	Strongly disagree	4	Slightly agree
2	Disagree	5	Agree
3	Slightly disagree	6	Strongly agree

Assessment

Pre-   Post-   *When I encounter a routine problem:*

_____ _____ 1. I state clearly and explicitly what the problem is. I avoid trying to solve it until I have defined it.

_____ _____ 2. I always generate more than one alternative solution to the problem, instead of identifying only one obvious solution.

_____ _____ 3. I keep in mind both long-term and short-term consequences as I evaluate various alternative solutions.

_____ _____ 4. I gather as much information as I can about what the problem is before trying to solve it.

_____ _____ 5. I keep steps in the problem-solving process distinct; that is, I define the problem before proposing alternative solutions, and I generate alternatives before selecting a single solution.

When faced with an ambiguous or difficult problem that does not have an easy solution:

_____ _____ 6. I try out several definitions of the problem. I don't limit myself to just one way to define it.

_____ _____ 7. I try to be flexible in the way I approach the problem by trying out several different alternatives rather than relying on conventional approaches.

_____ _____ 8. I try to find underlying patterns among elements in the problem so that I can uncover underlying dimensions or principles that help me understand the problem.

_____ _____ 9. I try to unfreeze my thinking by asking lots of questions about the nature of the problem before considering ways to solve it.

_____ _____ 10. I try to think about the problem from both the left (logical) side of my brain and the right (intuitive) side of my brain.

_____ _____ 11. To help me understand the problem and generate alternative solutions, I use analogies and metaphors that help me identify what else this problem is like.

_____ _____ 12. I frequently try to reverse my initial definition of the problem to consider whether or not the exact opposite is also true.

_____ _____ 13. I do not evaluate the merits of an alternative solution to the problem before I have generated a list of alternatives. That is, I avoid selecting one solution until I have developed several possible solutions.

_____ _____ 14. I often break down the problem into smaller components and analyze each one separately.

_____ _____ 15. I have some specific techniques that I use to help develop creative and innovative solutions to problems.

When trying to foster more creativity and innovation among those with whom I work:

_____ _____ 16. I help arrange opportunities for individuals to work on their ideas outside the constraints of normal procedures.

_____ _____ 17. I make sure there are divergent points of view represented in every problem-solving group.

_____ _____ 18. I sometimes make outrageous suggestions, even demands, to stimulate people to find new ways of approaching problems.

_____ _____ 19. I try to acquire information from customers regarding their preferences and expectations.

_____ _____ 20. I sometimes involve outsiders (e.g., customers or recognized experts) in problem-solving discussions.

_____ _____ 21. I provide recognition not only to those who are idea champions but also to those who support others' ideas and who provide resources to implement them.

_____ _____ 22. I encourage informed rule-breaking in pursuit of creative solutions.

How Creative Are You?© (REVISED)

How creative are you? The following test helps you determine if you have the personality traits, attitudes, values, motivations, and interests that characterize creativity. It is based on several years' study of attributes possessed by men and women in a variety of fields and occupations who think and act creatively.

For each statement, write in the appropriate letter:

A   Agree

B   Undecided or Don't Know

C   Disagree

Be as frank as possible. Try not to second-guess how a creative person might respond. Turn to Appendix I to find the answer key and an interpretation of your scores.

_____	1.	I always work with a great deal of certainty that I am following the correct procedure for solving a particular problem.
_____	2.	It would be a waste of time for me to ask questions if I had no hope of obtaining answers.
_____	3.	I concentrate harder on whatever interests me than do most people.
_____	4.	I feel that a logical step-by-step method is best for solving problems.
_____	5.	In groups I occasionally voice opinions that seem to turn some people off.
_____	6.	I spend a great deal of time thinking about what others think of me.
_____	7.	It is more important for me to do what I believe to be right than to try to win the approval of others.
_____	8.	People who seem uncertain about things lose my respect.
_____	9.	More than other people, I need to have things interesting and exciting.
_____	10.	I know how to keep my inner impulses in check.
_____	11.	I am able to stick with difficult problems over extended periods of time.
_____	12.	On occasion I get overly enthusiastic.
_____	13.	I often get my best ideas when doing nothing in particular.
_____	14.	I rely on intuitive hunches and the feeling of "rightness" or "wrongness" when moving toward the solution of a problem.
_____	15.	When problem solving, I work faster when analyzing the problem and slower when synthesizing the information I have gathered.
_____	16.	I sometimes get a kick out of breaking the rules and doing things I am not supposed to do.
_____	17.	I like hobbies that involve collecting things.
_____	18.	Daydreaming has provided the impetus for many of my more important projects.
_____	19.	I like people who are objective and rational.
_____	20.	If I had to choose from two occupations other than the one I now have, I would rather be a physician than an explorer.

_____ 21. I can get along more easily with people if they belong to about the same social and business class as myself.

_____ 22. I have a high degree of aesthetic sensitivity.

_____ 23. I am driven to achieve high status and power in life.

_____ 24. I like people who are sure of their conclusions.

_____ 25. Inspiration has nothing to do with the successful solution of problems.

_____ 26. When I am in an argument, my greatest pleasure would be for the person who disagrees with me to become a friend, even at the price of sacrificing my point of view.

_____ 27. I am much more interested in coming up with new ideas than in trying to sell them to others.

_____ 28. I would enjoy spending an entire day alone, just "chewing the mental cud."

_____ 29. I tend to avoid situations in which I might feel inferior.

_____ 30. In evaluating information, the source is more important to me than the content.

_____ 31. I resent things being uncertain and unpredictable.

_____ 32. I like people who follow the rule "business before pleasure."

_____ 33. Self-respect is much more important than the respect of others.

_____ 34. I feel that people who strive for perfection are unwise.

_____ 35. I prefer to work with others in a team effort rather than solo.

_____ 36. I like work in which I must influence others.

_____ 37. Many problems that I encounter in life cannot be resolved in terms of right or wrong solutions.

_____ 38. It is important for me to have a place for everything and everything in its place.

_____ 39. Writers who use strange and unusual words merely want to show off.

_____ 40. Below is a list of terms that describe people. Choose 10 words that best characterize you.

_____ energetic	_____ persuasive	_____ observant
_____ fashionable	_____ self-confident	_____ persevering
_____ original	_____ cautious	_____ habit-bound
_____ resourceful	_____ egotistical	_____ independent
_____ stern	_____ predictable	_____ formal
_____ informal	_____ dedicated	_____ forward-looking
_____ factual	_____ open-minded	_____ tactful
_____ inhibited	_____ enthusiastic	_____ innovative
_____ poised	_____ acquisitive	_____ practical
_____ alert	_____ curious	_____ organized
_____ unemotional	_____ clear-thinking	_____ understanding

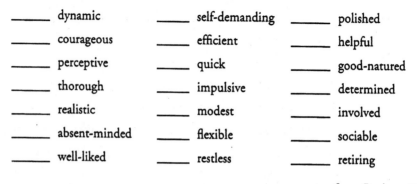

_____ dynamic	_____ self-demanding	_____ polished
_____ courageous	_____ efficient	_____ helpful
_____ perceptive	_____ quick	_____ good-natured
_____ thorough	_____ impulsive	_____ determined
_____ realistic	_____ modest	_____ involved
_____ absent-minded	_____ flexible	_____ sociable
_____ well-liked	_____ restless	_____ retiring

Source: Raudsepp, 1981.

Innovative Attitude Scale

Indicate the extent to which each of the following statements is true of either your actual behavior or your intentions at work. That is, describe the way you are or the way you intend to be on the job. Use the scale for your responses.

Rating Scale

5	Almost always true		2	Seldom true
4	Often true		1	Almost never true
3	Not applicable			

Scoring: To score the "Innovative Attitude Scale" turn to Appendix I to find the answer key and an interpretation of your score.

_____ 1. I openly discuss with my boss how to get ahead.

_____ 2. I try new ideas and approaches to problems.

_____ 3. I take things or situations apart to find out how they work.

_____ 4. I welcome uncertainty and unusual circumstances related to my tasks.

_____ 5. I negotiate my salary openly with my supervisor.

_____ 6. I can be counted on to find a new use for existing methods or equipment.

_____ 7. Among my colleagues and coworkers, I will be the first or nearly the first to try out a new idea or method.

_____ 8. I take the opportunity to translate communications from other departments for my work group.

_____ 9. I demonstrate originality.

_____ 10. I will work on a problem that has caused others great difficulty.

_____ 11. I provide critical input toward a new solution.

_____ 12. I provide written evaluations of proposed ideas.

_____ 13. I develop contacts with experts outside my firm.

_____ 14. I use personal contacts to maneuver into choice work assignments.

	15.	I make time to pursue my own pet ideas or projects.
_____	16.	I set aside resources for the pursuit of a risky project.
_____	17.	I tolerate people who depart from organizational routine.
_____	18.	I speak out in staff meetings.
_____	19.	I work in teams to try to solve complex problems.
_____	20.	If my coworkers are asked, they will say I am a wit.

Source: Ettlie & O'Keefe, 1982.

■ Skill Learning

Problem Solving, Creativity, and Innovation

Problem solving is a skill that is required of every person in almost every aspect of life. Seldom does an hour go by without an individual's being faced with the need to solve some kind of problem. The manager's job is inherently a problem-solving job. If there were no problems in organizations, there would be no need for managers. Therefore, it is hard to conceive of an incompetent problem solver succeeding as a manager.

In this chapter we offer specific guidelines and techniques for improving problem-solving skills. Two kinds of problem solving—rational and creative—are addressed. Effective managers are able to solve problems both rationally and creatively, even though different skills are required for each type of problem. First we discuss rational problem solving—the kind of problem solving that managers use many times each day. Then we turn to creative problem solving, a kind of problem solving that occurs less frequently. Yet this creative problem-solving ability often separates career successes from career failures, the heroes from the goats, and the achievers from the derailed executives. It can also produce a dramatic impact on organizational effectiveness. The chapter provides guidelines for how one can become a more effective problem solver, both rational and creative, and concludes with a brief discussion of how managers can foster creative problem solving and innovation among the people with whom they work.

Steps in Rational Problem Solving

Most people, including managers, don't particularly like problems. Problems are time consuming, they create stress, and they never seem to go away. In fact, most people try to get rid of problems as soon as they can. Their natural tendency is to select the first reasonable solution that comes to mind (March & Simon, 1958). Unfortunately, that first solution is often not the best one. In typical problem solving, most people implement a marginally acceptable or merely satisfactory solution instead of the optimal or ideal solution. In fact, many observers have attributed the decline in U.S. quality and competitiveness in the 1970s and 1980s primarily to the abandonment of correct problem-solving principles. Short cuts, they argue, had a major negative effect on the American economy. Effective problem solving, on the other hand, approaches problems from a rational or logical perspective. It involves at least four steps, which are explained next.

Defining the Problem

The most widely accepted model of rational problem solving is summarized in Table 1. This method is well known and lies at the heart of the quality movement.

It is widely asserted that to improve quality as individuals and as organizations, an essential step is to learn and apply this rational method of problem solving (see, for example, Juran, 1988; Ichikawa, 1986; Greene, 1993). Many large organizations (e.g., Ford Motor, General Electric, Dana) spend hundreds of thousands of dollars to teach their managers this type of problem solving as part of their quality improvement process.

The first step is to define a problem. This involves diagnosing a situation so that the focus is on the real problem, not just its symptoms. For example, suppose you must deal with an employee who consistently fails to get work done on time. Slow work might be the problem, or it might be only a symptom of another underlying problem such as bad health, low morale, lack of training, or inadequate rewards. Defining the problem, therefore, requires a wide search for information. The more information that is acquired, the more likely it is that the problem will be defined accurately. As Charles Kettering put it, "It ain't the things you don't know that'll get you in trouble, but the things you know for sure that ain't so."

Following are some attributes of good problem definition:

1. Factual information is differentiated from opinion or speculation. Objective data are separated from perceptions and suppositions.

2. All individuals involved are tapped as information sources. Broad participation is encouraged.

3. The problem is stated explicitly. This often helps point out ambiguities in the definition.

4. The problem definition clearly identifies what standard or expectation has been violated. Problems, by their very nature, involve the violation of some standard or expectation.

STEP	CHARACTERISTICS
1. Define the problem.	• Differentiate fact from opinion. • Specify underlying causes. • Tap everyone involved for information. • State the problem explicitly. • Identify what standard is violated. • Determine whose problem it is. • Avoid stating the problem as a disguised solution.
2. Generate alternative solutions.	• Postpone evaluating alternatives. • Be sure all involved individuals generate alternatives. • Specify alternatives that are consistent with goals. • Specify both short-term and long-term alternatives. • Build on others' ideas. • Specify alternatives that solve the problem.
3. Evaluate and select an alternative.	• Evaluate relative to an optimal standard. • Evaluate systematically. • Evaluate relative to goals. • Evaluate main effects and side effects. • State the selected alternative explicitly.
4. Implement and follow up on the solution.	• Implement at the proper time and in the right sequence. • Provide opportunities for feedback. • Engender acceptance of those who are affected. • Establish an ongoing monitoring system. • Evaluate based on problem solution.

Table 1   A Model of Problem Solving

5. The problem definition must address the question "Whose problem is this?" No problems are completely independent of people.

6. The definition is not simply a disguised solution. Saying "The problem is that we need to motivate slow employees" is inappropriate because the problem is stated as a solution.

Managers often propose a solution before an adequate definition of a problem has been given. This may lead to solving the "wrong" problem. The definition step in problem solving, therefore, is extremely important.

Generating Alternatives

The second step is to generate alternative solutions. This requires postponing the selection of any one solution until several alternatives have been proposed. Maier (1970) found that the quality of solutions can be significantly enhanced by considering multiple alternatives. Judgment and evaluation, therefore, must be postponed so the first acceptable solution suggested isn't the one immediately selected. As Broadwell (1972, p. 121) noted:

> The problem with evaluating [an alternative] too early is that we may rule out some good ideas by just not getting around to thinking about them. We hit on an idea that sounds good and we go with it, thereby never even thinking of alternatives that may be better in the long run.

Many alternative solutions should be generated before any of them are evaluated. A common problem in managerial decision making is that alternatives are evaluated as they are proposed, so the first acceptable (although frequently not optimal) one is chosen.

Some attributes of good alternative generation follow:

1. The evaluation of each proposed alternative is postponed. All alternatives should be proposed before evaluation is allowed.

2. Alternatives are proposed by all individuals involved in the problem. Broad participation in alternative proposals improves solution quality and group acceptance.

3. Alternative solutions are consistent with organizational goals or policies. Subversion and criticism

are detrimental to both the organization and the alternative generation process.

4. Alternatives take into consideration both short-term and long-term consequences.

5. Alternatives build on one another. Bad ideas may become good ones if they are combined with or modified by other ideas.

6. Alternatives solve the problem that has been defined. Another problem may also be important, but it should be ignored if it does not directly affect the problem being considered.

Evaluating Alternatives

The third problem-solving step is to evaluate and select an alternative. This step involves careful weighing of the advantages and disadvantages of the proposed alternatives before making a final selection. In selecting the best alternative, skilled problem solvers make sure that alternatives are judged in terms of the extent to which they will solve the problem without causing other unanticipated problems; the extent to which all individuals involved will accept the alternative; the extent to which implementation of the alternative is likely; and the extent to which the alternative fits within organizational constraints (e.g., is consistent with policies, norms, and budget limitations). Care is taken not to short-circuit these considerations by choosing the most conspicuous alternative without considering others. As March and Simon (1958, p. 141) point out:

> Most human decision making, whether individual or organizational, is concerned with the discovery and selection of satisfactory alternatives; only in exceptional cases is it concerned with the discovery and selection of optimal alternatives. To optimize requires processes several orders of magnitude more complex than those required to satisfy. An example is the difference between searching a haystack to find the sharpest needle in it and searching the haystack to find a needle sharp enough to sew with.

Given the natural tendency to select the first satisfactory solution proposed, this step deserves particular attention in problem solving.

Some attributes of good evaluation are:

1. Alternatives are evaluated relative to an optimal, rather than a satisfactory standard.

2. Evaluation of alternatives occurs systematically so each alternative is given due consideration. Short-circuiting evaluation inhibits selection of optimal alternatives.

3. Alternatives are evaluated in terms of the goals of the organization and the individuals involved. Organizational goals should be met, but individual preferences should also be considered.

4. Alternatives are evaluated in terms of their probable effects. Both side-effects and direct effects on the problem are considered.

5. The alternative ultimately selected is stated explicitly. This can help uncover latent ambiguities.

Implementing the Solution

The final step is to implement and follow up on the solution. Implementation of any solution requires sensitivity to possible resistance from those who will be affected by it. Almost any change engenders some resistance. Therefore, the best problem solvers are careful to select a strategy that maximizes the probability that the solution will be accepted and fully implemented. This may involve ordering that the solution be implemented by others, "selling" the solution to others, or involving others in the implementation. Tannenbaum and Schmidt (1958) and Vroom and Yetton (1973) provide guidelines for managers to determine which of these implementation behaviors is most appropriate under which circumstances. Generally speaking, participation by others in the implementation of a solution will increase its acceptance and decrease resistance.

Effective implementation also requires follow-up to prevent negative side-effects and ensure solution of the problem. Follow-up not only helps ensure effective implementation but also serves a feedback function by providing information that can be used to improve future problem solving. Drucker (1974, p. 480) explained:

A feedback has to be built into the decision to provide continuous testing, against actual events, of the expectations that underlie the decision. Few decisions work out the way they are intended to. Even the best decision usually runs into snags, unexpected obstacles, and all kinds

of surprises. Even the most effective decision eventually becomes obsolete. Unless there is feedback from the results of the decision, it is unlikely to produce the desired results.

Some attributes of effective implementation and follow-up are these:

1. Implementation occurs at the right time and in the proper sequence. It does not ignore constraining factors, and it does not come before steps 1, 2, and 3 in the problem-solving process.

2. The implementation process includes opportunities for feedback. How well the selected solution works needs to be communicated.

3. Implementation engenders support and acceptance by those affected by a decision. Participation is often the best way to ensure acceptance by others.

4. An ongoing monitoring system is set up for the implemented solution. Long-term as well as short-term effects should be assessed.

5. Evaluation of success is based on problem solution, not on side benefits. Although the solution may provide some positive outcomes, it is unsuccessful unless it solves the problem being considered.

Limitations of the Rational Problem-Solving Model

Most experienced problem solvers are familiar with the preceding steps in rational problem solving, which are based on empirical research results and sound rationale (Maier, 1970; Huber, 1980; Elbing, 1978; Filley, House, & Kerr, 1976). Unfortunately, managers do not always practice these steps. The demands of their jobs often pressure managers into circumventing some steps, and problem solving suffers as a result. When these four steps (defining the problem, generating alternatives, evaluating alternatives, and implementing the solution) are followed, however, effective problem solving is markedly enhanced.

On the other hand, simply learning about and practicing these four steps does not guarantee that an individual will effectively solve all types of problems. These problem-solving steps are useful mainly when the problems faced are straightforward, when alternatives are readily definable, when relevant information is available, and when a clear standard exists against which to judge the correctness of a solution. Thompson and Tuden (1959) call problems with these characteristics "computational problems," for which the main tasks are to gather information, generate alternatives, and make an informed choice. But many managerial problems are not of this type. Definitions, information, alternatives, and standards are seldom unambiguous or readily available. Hence, knowing the steps in problem solving and being able to implement them are not necessarily the same thing. For example, problems such as discovering why morale is so low, determining how to implement downsizing without antagonizing employees, developing a new process that will double productivity and eliminate all errors, or identifying ways to overcome resistance to change are common—and often very complicated—problems faced by most managers. Such problems may not always have an easily identifiable definition or set of alternative solutions available. It may not be clear how much information is needed, what the complete set of

alternatives is, or how one knows if the information being obtained is accurate. Rational problem solving may help, but something more is needed to address these problems successfully.

Table 2 summarizes some reasons why rational problem solving is not always effective in day-to-day managerial situations. Constraints exist on each of these four steps and stem from other individuals or from organizational processes that make it difficult to follow the prescribed model.

Another reason why the rational problem-solving model is not always effective for managers is that some problems are not amenable to systematic or rational analysis. Sufficient and accurate information may not be available, outcomes may not be predictable, or means-ends connections may not be evident. In order to solve such problems, a new way of thinking may be required, multiple or conflicting definitions may be needed, and unprecedented alternatives may have to be generated. In short, creative problem solving must be used.

STEP	CONSTRAINTS
1. Define the problem.	• There is seldom consensus as to the definition of the problem. • There is often uncertainty as to whose definition will be accepted. • Problems are usually defined in terms of the solutions already possessed.
2. Generate alternative solutions.	• Solution alternatives are usually evaluated one at a time as they are proposed. • Few of the possible alternatives are usually known. • The first acceptable solution is usually accepted. • Alternatives are based on what was successful in the past.
3. Evaluate and select an alternative.	• Limited information about each alternative is usually available. • Search for information occurs close to home—in easily accessible places. • The type of information available is constrained by factors such as primacy versus recency, extremity versus centrality, expected versus surprising, and correlation versus causation. • Gathering information on each alternative is costly. • Preferences of which is the best alternative are not always known. • Satisfactory solutions, not optimal ones, are usually accepted. • Solutions are often selected by oversight or default. • Solutions often are implemented before the problem is defined.
4. Implement and follow up on the solution.	• Acceptance by others of the solution is not always forthcoming. • Resistance to change is a universal phenomenon. • It is not always clear what part of the solution should be monitored or measured in follow-up. • Political and organizational processes must be managed in any implementation effort. • It may take a long time to implement a solution.

Table 2 Some Constraints on the Rational Problem-Solving Model

Impediments to Creative Problem Solving

Most people have trouble solving problems creatively. They have developed certain conceptual blocks in their problem-solving activities of which they are not even aware. These blocks inhibit them from solving certain problems effectively. The blocks are largely personal, as opposed to interpersonal or organizational, so skill development is required to overcome them.

Conceptual blocks are mental obstacles that constrain the way problems are defined and limit the number of alternative solutions thought to be relevant (Allen, 1974). Every individual has conceptual blocks, but some people have more numerous and more intense ones. These blocks are largely unrecognized or unconscious, so the only way individuals can be made aware of them is to be confronted with problems that are unsolvable because of them. Conceptual blocks result largely from the thinking processes that problem solvers use when facing problems. Everyone develops some conceptual blocks over time. In fact, we need some of them to cope with everyday life. Here's why.

At every moment, each of us is bombarded with far more information than we can possibly absorb. For example, you are probably not conscious right now of the temperature of the room, the color of your skin, the level of illumination overhead, or how your toes feel in your shoes. All of this information is available to you and is being processed by your brain, but you have tuned out some things and focused on others. Over time, you must develop the habit of mentally filtering out some of the information to which you are exposed; otherwise, information overload would drive you crazy. These filtering habits eventually become conceptual blocks. Though you are not conscious of them, they inhibit you from registering some kinds of information and, therefore, from solving certain kinds of problems.

Paradoxically, the more formal education individuals have, and the more experience they have in a job, the less able they are to solve problems in creative ways. It has been estimated that most adults over 40 display less than 2 percent of the creative problem-solving ability of a child under 5 years old. That's because formal education often prescribes "right" answers, analytic rules, or thinking boundaries. Experience in a job leads to "proper" ways of doing things, specialized knowledge, and rigid expectation of appropriate actions. Individuals lose the ability to experiment, improvise, or take mental detours. Consider the following example:

> If you place in a bottle half a dozen bees and the same number of flies, and lay the bottle down horizontally, with its base to the window, you will find that the bees will persist, till they die of exhaustion or hunger, in their endeavor to discover an issue through the glass; while the flies, in less than two minutes, will all have sallied forth through the neck on the opposite side. . . . It is [the bees'] love of light, it is their very intelligence, that is their undoing in this experiment. They evidently imagine that the issue from every prison must be there when the light shines clearest; and they act in accordance, and persist in too logical an action. To them glass is a supernatural mystery they never have met in nature; they have had no experience of this suddenly impenetrable atmosphere; and the greater their intelligence, the more inadmissible, more incomprehensible, will the strange obstacle appear. Whereas the feather-brained flies, careless of logic as of the enigma of crystal, disregarding the call of the light, flutter wildly, hither and thither, meeting here the good fortune that often waits on the simple, who find salvation where the wiser will perish, necessarily end by discovering the friendly opening that restores their liberty to them (Sill, 1968, p. 189).

This illustration identifies a paradox inherent in learning to solve problems creatively. On the one hand, more education and experience may inhibit creative problem solving and reinforce conceptual blocks. Like the bees in the story, individuals may not find solutions because the problem requires less "educated," more "playful" approaches. On the other hand, as several researchers have found, training directed toward improving thinking significantly enhances creative problem-solving abilities and managerial effectiveness (Barron, 1963; Taylor & Barron, 1963; Torrance, 1965).

Parnes (1962), for example, found that training in thinking increased the number of good ideas produced in problem solving by 125 percent. Bower (1965) recorded numerous examples of organizations that increased profitability and efficiency through training their employees to improve their thinking skills. Many organizations such as IBM, General Electric, and AT&T now send their executives to creativity workshops in order to improve their creative-thinking abilities. Creative problem-solving experts are currently hot property on the consulting circuit, and about a million copies of books on creativity are sold each year in North America. Several well-known products have been produced as a direct result of this kind of training, for example, NASA's Velcro snaps, G.E.'s self-diagnostic dishwashers, Mead's carbonless copy paper, and Kodak's Trimprint film.

Resolving this paradox is not just a matter of more exposure to information or education. Rather, one must master the process of thinking about certain problems in a creative way. As John Gardner (1965, p. 21) stated, people must learn to use their minds, rather than merely filling them up.

> All too often we are giving our young people cut flowers when we should be teaching them to grow plants. We are stuffing their heads with the products of earlier innovation rather than teaching them to innovate. We think of the mind as a storehouse to be filled when we should be thinking of it as an instrument to be used.

In the next section, we focus on problems that require creative rather than rational solutions. These are problems for which no acceptable alternative seems to be available, all reasonable solutions seem to be blocked, or no obvious best answer is accessible. This situation may exist because conceptual blocks inhibit the implementation of rational problem solving. Our focus, therefore, must be on tools and techniques that help overcome conceptual blocks and unlock problem-solving creativity.

Two examples help illustrate the kinds of problems that require creative problem-solving skills. They also illustrate several conceptual blocks that inhibit problem solving and several techniques and tools you can use to overcome such blocks.

Percy Spencer's Magnetron

During World War II, the British developed one of the best-kept military secrets of the war, a special radar detector based on a device called the magnetron. This radar was credited with turning the tide of battle in the war between Britain and Germany and helping the British withstand Hitler's Blitzkrieg. In 1940, Raytheon was one of several U.S. firms invited to produce magnetrons for the war effort.

The workings of magnetrons were not well understood, even by sophisticated physicists. Even among the firms that made magnetrons, few understood what made them work. A magnetron was tested, in those early days, by holding a neon tube next to it. If the neon tube got bright enough, the magnetron tube passed the test. In the process of conducting the test, the hands of the scientist holding the neon tube got warm. It was this phenomenon that led to a major creative breakthrough that eventually transformed lifestyles throughout the world.

At the end of the war, the market for radar essentially dried up, and most firms stopped producing magnetrons. At Raytheon, however, a scientist named Percy Spencer had been fooling around with magnetrons, trying to think of alternative uses for the devices. He was convinced that magnetrons could be used to cook food by using the heat produced in the neon tube. But Raytheon was in the defense business. Next to its two prize products—the Hawk and Sparrow missiles—cooking devices seemed odd and out of place. Percy Spencer was convinced that Raytheon should continue to produce magnetrons, even though production costs were prohibitively high. But Raytheon had lost money on the devices, and now there was no available market for magnetrons. The consumer product Spencer had in mind did not fit within the bounds of Raytheon's business.

As it turned out, Percy Spencer's solution to Raytheon's problem produced the microwave oven and a revolution in cooking methods throughout the world. Later, we will analyze several problem-solving techniques illustrated by Spencer's creative triumph.

Spence Silver's Glue

A second example of creative problem solving began with Spence Silver's assignment to work on a temporary project team within the 3M company. The team was searching for new adhesives, so Silver obtained some material from AMD, Inc., that had potential for a new polymer-based adhesive. He described one of his experiments in this way: "In the course of this exploration, I tried an experiment with one of the monomers in which I wanted to see what would happen if I put a lot of it into the reaction mixture. Before, we had used amounts that would correspond to conventional wisdom" (Nayak & Ketteringham, 1986). The result was a substance that failed all the conventional 3M tests for adhesives. It didn't stick. It preferred its own molecules to the molecules of any other substance. It was more cohesive than adhesive. It sort of "hung around without making a commitment." It was a "now-it-works, now-it-doesn't" kind of glue.

For five years, Silver went from department to department within the company trying to find someone interested in using his newly found substance in a product. Silver had found a solution; he just couldn't find a problem to solve with it. Predictably, 3M showed little interest. The company's mission was to make adhesives that adhered ever more tightly. The ultimate adhesive was one that formed an unbreakable bond, not one that formed a temporary bond.

After four years the task force was disbanded, and team members were assigned to other projects. But Silver was still convinced that his substance was good for something. He just didn't know what. As it turned out, Silver's solution has become the prototype for innovation in American firms, and it has spawned a half-billion dollars in annual revenues for 3M—in a unique product called Post-It Notes.

These two examples are positive illustrations of how solving a problem in a unique way can lead to phenomenal business success. Creative problem solving can have remarkable effects on individuals' careers and on business success. To understand how to solve problems creatively, however, we must first consider the blocks that inhibit creativity.

Conceptual Blocks

Table 3 summarizes four types of conceptual blocks that inhibit creative problem solving. Each is discussed and illustrated below with problems or exercises. We encourage you to complete the exercises and solve the problems as you read the chapter, because doing so will help you become aware of your own conceptual blocks. Later, we shall discuss in more detail how you can overcome those blocks.

Constancy

Constancy, in the present context, means that an individual becomes wedded to one way of looking at a problem or to using one approach to define, describe, or solve it. It is easy to see why constancy is common in problem solving. Being constant, or consistent, is a highly valued attribute for most of us. We like to appear at least moderately consistent in our approach to life, and constancy is often associated with maturity, honesty, and even intelligence. We judge lack of constancy as untrustworthy, peculiar, or airheaded. Several prominent psychologists theorize, in fact, that a need for constancy is the primary motivator of human behavior (Festinger, 1957; Heider, 1946; Newcomb, 1954). Many psychological studies have shown that once individuals take a stand or employ a particular approach to a problem, they are highly likely to pursue

1. Constancy		
	Vertical thinking	Defining a problem in only one way without considering alternative views.
	One thinking language	Not using more than one language to define and assess the problem.
2. Commitment		
	Stereotyping based on past experience	Present problems are seen only as the variations of past problems.
	Ignoring commonalities	Failing to perceive commonalities among elements that initially appear to be different.
3. Compression		
	Distinguishing figure from ground	Not filtering out irrelevant information or finding needed information.
	Artificial constraints	Defining the boundaries of a problem too narrowly.
4. Complacency		
	Noninquisitiveness	Not asking questions.
	Nonthinking	A bias toward activity in place of mental work.

Table 3 Conceptual Blocks That Inhibit Creative Problem Solving

that same course without deviation in the future (see Cialdini, 1988, for multiple examples).

On the other hand, constancy can inhibit the solution of some kinds of problems. Consistency sometimes drives out creativity. Two illustrations of the constancy block are vertical thinking and using only one thinking language.

Vertical Thinking

The term **vertical thinking** was coined by Edward deBono (1968). It refers to defining a problem in a single way and then pursuing that definition without deviation until a solution is reached. No alternative definitions are considered. All information gathered and all alternatives generated are consistent with the original definition. In a search for oil, for example, vertical thinkers determine a spot for the hole and drill the hole deeper and deeper until they strike oil. Lateral thinkers, on the other hand, generate alternative ways of viewing a problem and produce multiple definitions. Instead of drilling one hole deeper and deeper, lateral thinkers drill a number of holes in different places in search of oil. The vertical-thinking conceptual block arises from not being able to view the problem from multiple perspectives—to drill several holes—or to think laterally as well as vertically in problem solving. Problem definition is restricted.

Plenty of examples exist of creative solutions that occurred because an individual refused to get stuck with a single problem definition. Alexander Graham Bell was trying to devise a hearing aid when he shifted definitions and invented the telephone. Harland Sanders was trying to sell his recipe to restaurants when he shifted definitions and developed his Kentucky Fried Chicken business. Karl Jansky was studying telephone static when he shifted definitions, discovered radio waves from the Milky Way galaxy, and developed the science of radio astronomy.

In the development of the microwave industry described earlier, Percy Spencer shifted the definition of the problem from "How can we save our military radar business at the end of the war?" to "What other applications can be made for the magnetron?" Other problem definitions followed, such as: "How can we make magnetrons cheaper?" "How can we mass-produce magnetrons?" "How can we convince someone besides the military to buy magnetrons?" "How can we enter a consumer products market?" "How can we make microwave ovens practical and safe?" And so on. Each

new problem definition led to new ways of thinking about the problem, new alternative approaches, and, eventually, to a new microwave oven industry.

Spence Silver at 3M is another example of someone who changed problem definitions. He began with "How can I get an adhesive that has a stronger bond?" but switched to "How can I find an application for an adhesive that doesn't stick firmly?" Eventually, other problem definitions followed: "How can we get this new glue to stick to one surface but not another (e.g., to notepaper but not normal paper)?" "How can we replace staples, thumbtacks, and paperclips in the workplace?" "How can we manufacture and package a product that uses nonadhesive glue?" "How can we get anyone to pay $1.00 a pad for scratch paper?" And so on.

Shifting definitions is not easy, of course, because it is not natural. It requires individuals to deflect their tendency toward constancy. Later, we will discuss some hints and tools that can help overcome the constancy block while avoiding the negative consequences of inconsistency.

A Single Thinking Language

A second manifestation of the constancy block is the use of only one thinking language. Most people think in words—that is, they think about a problem and its solution in terms of verbal language. Rational problem solving reinforces this approach. Some writers, in fact, have argued that thinking cannot even occur without words (Vygotsky, 1962). Other thought languages are available, however, such as nonverbal or symbolic languages (e.g., mathematics), sensory imagery (e.g., smelling or tactile sensation), feelings and emotions (e.g., happiness, fear, or anger), and visual imagery (e.g., mental pictures). The more languages available to problem solvers, the better and more creative will be their solutions. As Koestler (1967) puts it, "[Verbal] language can become a screen which stands between the thinker and reality. This is the reason that true creativity often starts where [verbal] language ends."

Percy Spencer at Raytheon is a prime example of a visual thinker:

> One day, while Spencer was lunching with Dr. Ivan Getting and several other Raytheon scientists, a mathematical question arose. Several men, in a familiar reflex, pulled out their slide rules, but before any could complete the equation, Spencer gave the answer. Dr. Getting was

astonished. "How did you do that?" he asked. "The root," said Spencer shortly. "I learned cube roots and squares by using blocks as a boy. Since then, all I have to do is visualize them placed together." (Scott, 1974, p. 287).

The microwave oven depended on Spencer's command of multiple thinking languages. Furthermore, the new oven would never have gotten off the ground without a critical incident that illustrates the power of visual thinking. By 1965, Raytheon was just about to give up on any consumer application of the magnetron when a meeting was held with George Foerstner, president of the recently acquired Amana Refrigeration Company. In the meeting, costs, applications, manufacturing obstacles, and so on were discussed. Foerstner galvanized the entire microwave oven effort with the following statement, as reported by a Raytheon vice president.

George says, "It's no problem. It's about the same size as an air conditioner. It weighs about the same. It should sell for the same. So we'll price it at $499." Now you think that's silly, but you stop and think about it. Here's a man who really didn't understand the technologies. But there is about the same amount of copper involved, the same amount of steel as an air conditioner. And these are basic raw materials. It didn't make a lot of difference how you fit them together to make them work. They're both boxes; they're both made out of sheet metal; and they both require some sort of trim. (Nayak & Ketteringham, 1986, p. 181).

In several short sentences, Foerstner had taken one of the most complicated military secrets of World War II and translated it into something no more complex than a room air conditioner. He had painted a picture of an application that no one else had been able to capture by describing a magnetron visually, as a familiar object, not as a set of calculations, formulas, or blueprints.

A similar occurrence in the Post-It Note chronology also led to a breakthrough. Spence Silver had been trying for years to get someone in 3M to adopt his unsticky glue. Art Fry, another scientist with 3M, had heard Silver's presentations before. One day while singing in North Presbyterian Church in St. Paul, Minnesota, Fry was fumbling around with the slips of paper that marked the various hymns in his book. Suddenly, a visual image popped into his mind.

I thought, "Gee, if I had a little adhesive on these bookmarks, that would be just the ticket." So I decided to check into that idea the next week at work. What I had in mind was Silver's adhesive. . . . I knew I had a much bigger discovery than that. I also now realized that the primary application for Silver's adhesive was not to put it on a fixed surface like bulletin boards. That was a secondary application. The primary application concerned paper to paper. I realized that immediately." (Nayak & Ketteringham, 1986, pp. 63–64).

Years of verbal descriptions had not led to any applications for Silver's glue. Tactile thinking (handling the glue) also had not produced many ideas. However, thinking about the product in visual terms, as applied to what Fry initially called "a better bookmark," led to the breakthrough that was needed.

This emphasis on using alternative thinking languages, especially visual thinking, is now becoming the new frontier in scientific research. With the advent of supercomputers, scientists are more and more working with pictures and simulated images rather than with numerical data. "Scientists who are using the new computer graphics say that by viewing images instead of numbers, a fundamental change in the way researchers think and work is occurring. People have a lot easier time getting an intuition from pictures than they do from numbers and tables or formulas. In most physics experiments, the answer used to be a number or a string of numbers. In the last few years the answer has increasingly become a picture" (Markoff, 1988, p. D3).

To illustrate the differences among thinking languages, consider the following two simple problems:

1. Below is the Roman numeral 9. By adding only a single line, turn it into a 6.

IX

2. Figure 1 shows seven matchsticks. By moving only one matchstick, make the figure into a true equality (i.e., the value on one side equals the value on the other side). Before looking up the answers in Appendix I, try defining the problems differently, and try using different thinking languages. How many answers can you find?

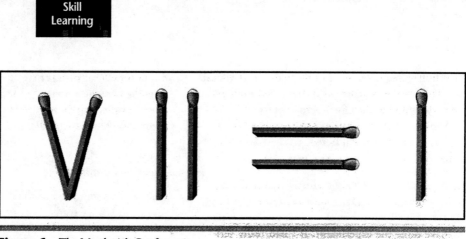

Figure 1 The Matchstick Configuration

Commitment

Commitment can also serve as a conceptual block to creative problem solving. Once individuals become committed to a particular point of view, definition, or solution, it is likely that they will follow through on that commitment. Freedman and Fraser (1966), for example, found that only 17 percent of a sample of Californians agreed to have a large, poorly lettered DRIVE CAREFULLY sign placed on their front lawn. However, in another study, another group of Californians were asked to sign a petition favoring "keeping California beautiful." Two weeks later, a full 76 percent of them were then willing to put up the DRIVE CAREFULLY sign. By signing a petition, they had become committed to the idea that they were responsible citizens. The large, unsightly sign became the visible evidence of their commitment.

A host of other studies have demonstrated the same phenomenon: that commitment can sometimes lead to dysfunctional or foolish decisions, rigidly defended. Two forms of commitment that produce conceptual blocks are *stereotyping based on past experiences* and *ignoring commonalities*.

Stereotyping Based on Past Experiences

March and Simon (1958) point out that a major obstacle to innovative problem solving is that individuals tend to define present problems in terms of problems they have faced in the past. Current problems are usually seen as variations on some past situation, so the alternatives proposed to solve the current problem are ones that have proven successful in the past. Both problem definitions and proposed solutions are therefore restricted by past experience. This restriction is referred to as **perceptual**

stereotyping (Allen, 1974). That is, certain preconceptions formed on the basis of past experience determine how an individual defines a situation.

When individuals receive an initial cue regarding the definition of a problem, all subsequent problems are frequently framed in terms of the initial cue. Of course, this is not all bad, because perceptual stereotyping helps organize problems on the basis of a limited amount of data, and the need to consciously analyze every problem encountered is eliminated. On the other hand, perceptual stereotyping prevents individuals from viewing a problem in novel ways.

The creation of microwave ovens and of Post-It Notes provide examples of overcoming stereotyping based on past experiences. Scott (1974) described the first meeting of John D. Cockcroft, technical leader of the British radar system that invented magnetrons, and Percy Spencer of Raytheon.

> Cockcroft liked Spencer at once. He showed him the magnetron, and the American regarded it thoughtfully. He asked questions—very intelligent ones—about how it was produced, and the Britisher answered at length. Later Spencer wrote, "The technique of making these tubes, as described to us, was awkward and impractical." *Awkward and impractical!* Nobody else dared draw such a judgment about a product of undoubted scientific brilliance, produced and displayed by the leaders of British science.

Despite his admiration for Cockcroft and the magnificent magnetron, Spencer refused to abandon his curious and inquisitive stance. Rather than adopting the position of other scientists and assuming that since the

British invented it and were using it, they surely knew how to produce a magnetron, Spencer broke out of the stereotypes and pushed for improvements.

Similarly, Spence Silver at 3M described his invention in terms of breaking stereotypes based on past experience.

> The key to the Post-It adhesive was doing the experiment. If I had sat down and factored it out beforehand, and thought about it, I wouldn't have done the experiment. If I had really seriously cracked the books and gone through the literature, I would have stopped. The literature was full of examples that said you can't do this (Nayak & Ketteringham, 1986, p. 57).

This is not to say that one should avoid learning from past experience or that failing to learn the mistakes of history does not doom us to repeat them. Rather, it is to say that commitment to a course of action based on past experience can sometimes inhibit viewing problems in new ways, and can even prevent us from solving some problems at all. Consider the following problem as an example.

There are four volumes of Shakespeare on the shelf (see Figure 2). The pages of each volume are exactly two inches thick. The covers are each one-sixth of an inch thick. A bookworm started eating at page 1 of Volume 1 and ate straight through to the last page of Volume IV. What distance did the worm cover? (See Appendix I for the answer.) Solving this problem is relatively simple, but it requires that you overcome a stereotyping block to get the correct answer.

Ignoring Commonalities

A second manifestation of the commitment block is failure to identify similarities among seemingly disparate pieces of data. This is among the most commonly identified blocks to creativity. It means that a person becomes committed to a particular point of view, to the fact that elements are different, and, consequently, becomes unable to make connections, identify themes, or perceive commonalities.

The ability to find one definition or solution for two seemingly dissimilar problems is a characteristic of creative individuals (Dellas & Gaier, 1970; Steiner, 1978). The inability to do this can overload a problem solver by requiring that every problem encountered be solved individually. The discovery of penicillin by Sir Alexander Fleming resulted from his seeing a common theme among seemingly unrelated events. Fleming was working with some cultures of staphylococci that had accidentally become contaminated. The contamination, a growth of fungi, and isolated clusters of dead staphylococci led Fleming to see a relationship no one else had ever seen previously and thus to discover a wonder drug

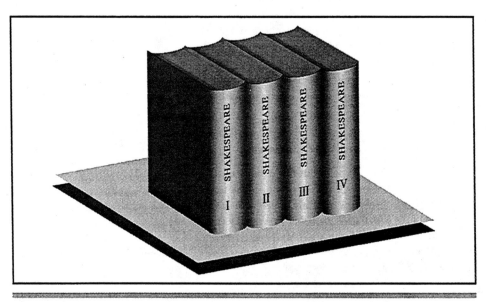

Figure 2   Shakespeare Riddle.
Source: Raudsepp & Hough, 1977.

(Beveridge, 1960). The famous chemist Friedrich Kekule saw a relationship between his dream of a snake swallowing its own tail and the chemical structure of organic compounds. This creative insight led him to the discovery that organic compounds such as benzene have closed rings rather than open structures (Koestler, 1967).

For Percy Spencer at Raytheon, seeing a connection between the heat of a neon tube and the heat required to cook food was the creative connection that led to his breakthrough in the microwave industry. One of Spencer's colleagues recalled: "In the process of testing a bulb [with a magnetron], your hands got hot. I don't know when Percy really came up with the thought of microwave ovens, but he knew at that time—and that was 1942. He [remarked] frequently that this would be a good device for cooking food." Another colleague described Spencer this way: "The way Percy Spencer's mind worked is an interesting thing. He had a mind that allowed him to hold an extraordinary array of associations on phenomena and relate them to one another" (Nayak & Ketteringham, 1986, pp. 184, 205). Similarly, the connection Art Fry made between a glue that wouldn't stick tightly and marking hymns in a choir book was the final breakthrough that led to the development of the revolutionary Post-It Note business.

To test your own ability to see commonalities, answer the following three questions: (1) What are some common terms that apply to both water and finance? (2) What is humorous about the following story? "Descartes, the philosopher, walked into a university class. Recognizing him, the instructor asked if he would like to lecture. Descartes replied, 'I think not,' and promptly disappeared." (3) What does the single

piece of wood look like that will pass through each hole in the block in Figure 3 but that will perfectly fill each hole as it passes through? (Answers are in Appendix I.)

Compression

Conceptual blocks also occur as a result of compression of ideas. Looking too narrowly at a problem, screening out too much relevant data, and making assumptions that inhibit problem solution are common examples. Two especially cogent examples of compression are *artificially constraining problems* and *not distinguishing figure from ground.*

Artificial Constraints

Sometimes people place boundaries around problems, or constrain their approach to them, in such a way that the problems become impossible to solve. Such constraints arise from hidden assumptions people make about problems they encounter. People assume that some problem definitions or alternative solutions are off-limits, so they ignore them. For an illustration of this conceptual block, look at Figure 4. Without lifting your pencil from the paper, draw four straight lines that pass through all nine dots. Complete the task before reading further.

By thinking of the figure as more constrained than it actually is, the problem becomes impossible to solve. Try to break out of your own limiting assumptions on the problem. (One four-line answer is presented in Appendix I.) Now that you have been cued, can you do the same task with only three lines? Work on this problem for a minute. If you are successful, try to do

Figure 3 A Block Problem
Source: McKim, 1972.

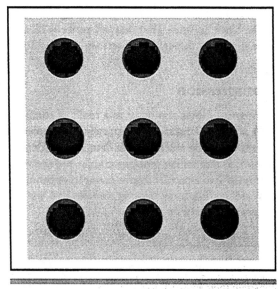

Figure 4 The Nine-Dot Problem

the task with only one line. Can you determine how to put a single straight line through all nine dots without lifting your pencil from the paper? Both the three-line solution and some one-line solutions are in the Appendix.

Artificially constraining problems means that the problem definition and the possible alternatives are limited more than the problem requires. Creative problem solving requires that individuals become adept at recognizing their hidden assumptions and expanding the alternatives they consider.

Separating Figure from Ground

Another illustration of the compression block is the reverse of artificial constraints. It is the inability to constrain problems sufficiently so that they can be solved. Problems almost never come clearly specified, so problem solvers must determine what the real problem is. They must filter out inaccurate, misleading, or irrelevant information in order to define the problem correctly and generate appropriate alternative solutions. The inability to separate the important from the unimportant, and to compress problems appropriately, serves as a conceptual block because it exaggerates the complexity of a problem and inhibits a simple definition.

How well do you filter out irrelevant information? Consider Figure 5. For each pair, find the pattern on the left that is embedded in the more complex pattern

on the right. On the complex pattern, outline the embedded pattern. Now try to find at least two figures in each pattern. (See Appendix I for a solution.)

This compression block—separating figure from ground and artificially constraining problems—played an important role in the microwave oven and Post-It Note breakthroughs. George Foerstner's contribution to the development and manufacture of the microwave oven was to compress the problem, that is, to separate out all the irrelevant complexity that constrained others. Whereas the magnetron was a device so complicated that few people understood it, Foerstner focused on its basic raw materials, its size, and its functionality. By comparing it to an air conditioner, he eliminated much of the complexity and mystery, and, as described by two analysts, "He had seen what all the researchers had failed to see, and they knew he was right" (Nayak & Ketteringham, 1986, p. 181).

On the other hand, Spence Silver had to *add* complexity, to *overcome* compression, in order to find an application for his product. Because the glue had failed every traditional 3M test for adhesives, it was categorized as a useless configuration of chemicals. The potential for the product was artificially constrained by traditional assumptions about adhesives—more stickiness, stronger bonding is best—until Art Fry visualized some unconventional applications—a better bookmark, a bulletin board, scratch paper, and, paradoxically, a replacement for 3M's main product, tape.

Complacency

Some conceptual blocks occur not because of poor thinking habits or inappropriate assumptions but because of fear, ignorance, insecurity, or just plain mental laziness. Two especially prevalent examples of the complacency block are a *lack of questioning* and a *bias against thinking*.

Noninquisitiveness

Sometimes the inability to solve problems results from an unwillingness to ask questions, obtain information, or search for data. Individuals may think they will appear naive or ignorant if they question something or attempt to redefine a problem. Asking questions puts them at risk of exposing their ignorance. It also may be threatening to others because it implies that what they accept may not be correct. This may create resistance, conflict, or even ridicule by others.

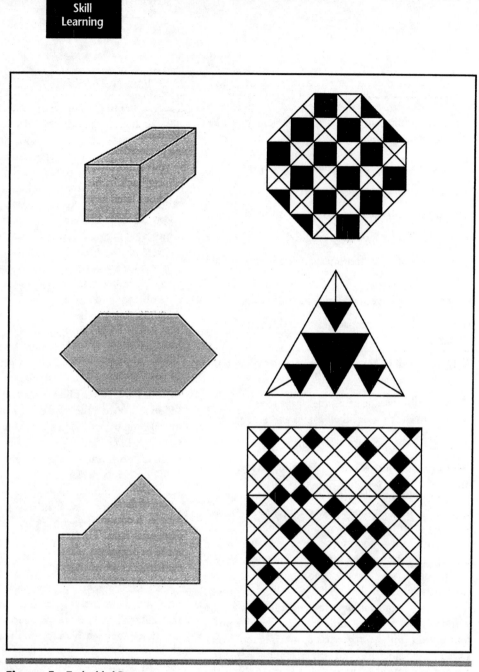

Figure 5 Embedded Pattern

Creative problem solving is inherently risky, therefore, because it potentially involves interpersonal conflict. It is risky also because it is fraught with mistakes. As Linus Pauling, the Nobel laureate, said, "If you want to have a good idea, have a lot of them, because most of them will be bad ones." Years of nonsupportive socialization, however, block the adventuresome and inquisitive stance in most people. Most of us are not rewarded for bad ideas. To illustrate, answer the following questions for yourself:

1. When would it be easier to learn a new language, when you were 5 years old or now? Why?

2. How many times in the last month have you tried something for which the probability of success was less than 50 percent?

3. When was the last time you asked three "why" questions in a row?

David Feldman authored a 1988 book in which he asks and answers more than 100 questions such as:

Why are people immune to their own body odor?

Why are there 21 guns in a 21-gun salute?

What happens to the tread that wears off tires?

Why doesn't sugar spoil or get moldy?

Why doesn't a two-by-four measure two inches by four inches?

Why doesn't postage-stamp glue have flavoring?

Why is a telephone keypad arranged differently from that of a calculator?

Why do hot dogs come 10 in a package while buns come 8 in a package?

How do military cadets find their caps after throwing them in the air at football games and graduation?

Why is Jack the nickname for John?

How do they print "M&M" on M&M candies?

Most of us are a little too complacent to even ask such questions, let alone find out the answers. We often stop being inquisitive as we get older because we learn that it is good to be intelligent, and being intelligent is interpreted as already knowing the answers, instead of asking good questions. Consequently, we learn less well at 35 than at 5, take fewer risks, avoid asking why, and function in the world without trying to understand it. Creative problem solvers, on the other hand, are frequently engaged in inquisitive and experimental behavior. Spence Silver at 3M described his attitude about the complacency block this way:

> People like myself get excited about looking for new properties in materials. I find that very satisfying, to perturb the structure slightly and just see what happens. I have a hard time talking people into doing that—people who are more highly trained. It's been my experience that people are reluctant just to try, to experiment—just to see what will happen (Nayak & Ketteringham, 1986, p. 58).

Bias Against Thinking

A second manifestation of the complacency block is in an inclination to avoid doing mental work. This block, like most of the others, is partly a cultural bias as well as a personal one. For example, assume that you passed by your subordinate's office one day and noticed him leaning back in his chair, staring out the window. A half-hour later, as you passed by again, he had his feet up on the desk, still staring out the window. And 20 minutes later, you noticed that his demeanor hadn't changed much. What would be your conclusion? Most of us would assume that the fellow was not doing any work. We would assume that unless we saw action, he wasn't being productive.

When was the last time you heard someone say, "I'm sorry. I can't go to the ball game (or concert, dance, party, or movie) because I have to think"? Or, "I'll do the dishes tonight. I know you need to catch up on your thinking"? That these statements sound humorous illustrates the bias most people develop toward action rather than thought, or against putting their feet up, rocking back in their chair, looking off into space, and engaging in solitary mental activity. This does not mean daydreaming or fantasizing, but *thinking*.

There is a particular conceptual block in our culture against the kind of thinking that uses the right hemisphere of the brain. **Left-hemisphere thinking,** for most people, is concerned with logical, analytical, linear, or sequential tasks. Thinking using the left hemisphere is apt to be organized, planned, and precise. Language and mathematics are left-hemisphere activities. **Right-hemisphere thinking,** on the other hand, is concerned with intuition, synthesis, playfulness, and qualitative judgment. It tends to be more spontaneous, imaginative, and emotional than left-hemisphere thinking. The emphasis in most formal education is toward left-hemisphere thought development. Problem solving on the basis of reason, logic, and utility is generally rewarded, while problem solving based on sentiment, intuition, or pleasure is frequently considered tenuous and inferior.

A number of researchers have found that the most creative problem solvers are **ambidextrous** in their thinking. That is, they use both left- and right-hemisphere thinking and easily switch from one to the other (Bruner, 1966; Hermann, 1981; Martindale, 1975). Creative ideas arise most frequently in the right hemisphere but must be processed and interpreted by the left, so creative problem solvers use both hemispheres equally well.

Try the exercise in Table 4, the idea for which came from von Oech (1986). It illustrates this ambidextrous principle. There are two lists of words. Take a minute to memorize the first list. Then, on a piece of paper, write down as many words as you can remember. Now take a minute and memorize the words in the second list. Repeat the process of writing down as many words as you can remember.

Most people remember more words from the second list than from the first. This is because the second list contains words that relate to visual perceptions. They connect with right-brain activity as well as left-brain activity. People can draw mental pictures or fantasize about them. The same is true for creative ideas. The more both sides of the brain are used, the more creative the ideas.

Review of Conceptual Blocks

So far, we have suggested that certain conceptual blocks prevent individuals from solving problems creatively. These blocks, summarized in Table 3, narrow the scope of problem definition, limit the consideration of alternative solutions, and constrain the selection of an optimal solution. Unfortunately, many of these conceptual blocks are unconscious, and it is only by being confronted with problems that are unsolvable because of conceptual blocks that individuals

become aware that they exist. We have attempted to make you aware of your own conceptual blocks by asking you to solve problems that require you to overcome these mental barriers. These conceptual blocks are not all bad, of course; not all problems can be addressed by creative problem solving. But research has shown that individuals who have developed creative problem-solving skills are far more effective with complex problems that require a search for alternative solutions than others who are conceptually blocked (Dauw, 1976; Basadur, 1979; Guilford, 1962; Steiner, 1978).

In the next section, we provide some techniques and tools that help overcome these blocks and improve creative problem-solving skills.

Conceptual Blockbusting

Conceptual blocks cannot be overcome all at once because most blocks are a product of years of habit-forming thought processes. Overcoming them requires practice in thinking in different ways over a long period of time. You will not become a skilled creative problem solver just by reading this chapter. On the other hand, by becoming aware of your conceptual blocks and practicing the following techniques, you can enhance your creative problem-solving skills.

Stages in Creative Thought

A first step in overcoming conceptual blocks is recognizing that creative problem solving is a skill that can be developed. Being a creative problem solver is not an inherent ability that some people naturally have and others do not have. As Dauw (1976, p. 19) has noted,

> Research results [show] . . . that nurturing creativity is not a question of increasing one's ability to score high on an IQ test, but a matter of improving one's mental attitudes and habits and cultivating creative skills that have lain dormant since childhood.

Researchers generally agree that creative problem solving involves four stages: preparation, incubation, illumination, and verification. (See Haefele, 1962, for

LIST 1	LIST 2
decline	sunset
very	perfume
ambiguous	brick
resources	monkey
term	castle
conceptual	guitar
about	pencil
appendix	computer
determine	umbrella
forget	radar
quantity	blister
survey	chessboard

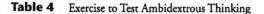

Table 4   Exercise to Test Ambidextrous Thinking

literature reviews of the stages of creative problem solving.) The **preparation** stage includes gathering data, defining the problem, generating alternatives, and consciously examining all available information. The primary difference between skillful creative problem solving and rational problem solving is in how this first step is approached. Creative problem solvers are more flexible and fluent in data gathering, problem definition, alternative generation, and examination of options. In fact, it is in this stage that training in creative problem solving can significantly improve effectiveness (Allen, 1974; Basadur, 1979; McKim, 1972) because the other three steps are not amenable to conscious mental work. The following discussion, therefore, is limited primarily to improving functioning in this first stage. The **incubation** stage involves mostly unconscious mental activity in which the mind combines unrelated thoughts in pursuit of a solution. Conscious effort is not involved. **Illumination,** the third stage, occurs when an insight is recognized and a creative solution is articulated. **Verification** is the final stage, which involves evaluating the creative solution relative to some standard of acceptability.

In the preparation stage, two types of techniques are available for improving creative problem-solving abilities. One technique helps individuals think about and define problems more creatively; the other helps individuals gather information and generate more alternative solutions to problems.

One major difference between effective, creative problem solvers and other people is that creative problem solvers are less constrained. They allow themselves to be more flexible in the definitions they impose on problems and the number of solutions they identify. They develop a large repertoire of approaches to problem solving. In short, they do what Karl Weick (1979, p. 261) prescribes for unblocking decision making: "Complicate yourself!" That is, generate more conceptual options. As Interaction Associates (1971, p. 15) explained:

> Flexibility in thinking is critical to good problem solving. A problem solver should be able to conceptually dance around the problem like a good boxer, jabbing and poking, without getting caught in one place or "fixated." At any given moment, a good problem solver should be able to apply a large number of strategies [for generating alternative definitions and solutions].

Moreover, a good problem solver is a person who has developed, through his understanding of strategies and experiences in problem solving, a sense of appropriateness of what is likely to be the most useful strategy at any particular time.

As a perusal through any bookstore will show, the number of books suggesting ways to enhance creative problem solving is enormous. We now present a few tools and hints that we have found to be especially effective and relatively simple for business executives and students to apply. Although some of them may seem game-like or playful, a sober pedagogical rationale underlies all of them. They help to unfreeze you from your normal skeptical, analytical approach to problems and increase your playfulness.

Methods for Improving Problem Definition

Problem definition is probably the most critical step in creative problem solving. Once a problem is properly defined, solving it is often relatively simple. However, Campbell (1952), Medawar (1967), and Schumacher (1977) point out that individuals tend to define problems in terms with which they are familiar. Medawar (1967, Introduction) notes, "Good scientists study the most important problems they think they can solve." When a problem is faced that is strange or does not appear to have a solution (Schumacher calls these "divergent problems"), the problem either remains undefined or is redefined in terms of something familiar. Unfortunately, new problems may not be the same as old problems, so relying on past definitions may impede the process of solving current problems, or lead to solving the wrong problem. Applying hints for creative problem definition can help individuals see problems in alternative ways so their definitions are less narrowly constrained. Three such hints for improving and expanding the definition process are discussed below.

Make the Strange Familiar and the Familiar Strange

One well-known technique for improving creative problem solving is called **synectics** (Gordon, 1961). The goal of synectics is to help you put something you don't know in terms of something you do know and vice versa. By analyzing what you know and applying it to what you don't know, you can develop new insights and perspectives.

First you form a definition of a problem (make the strange familiar). Then you try to make that definition out of focus, distorted, or transposed in some way (make the familiar strange). Use synectics—analogies and metaphors—to create this distortion. Postpone the original definition of the problem while you analyze the analogy or metaphor. Then impose the analysis on the original problem to see what new insights you can uncover.

For example, suppose you have defined a problem as low morale among members of your team. You may form an analogy or metaphor by answering questions such as the following about the problem: What does this remind me of? What does this make me feel like? What is this similar to? What isn't this similar to? (Your answers, for example, might be: This problem reminds me of trying to turn a rusty bolt. It makes me feel like I do when visiting a hospital ward. This is similar to the loser's locker room after a basketball game. And so on.) Metaphors and analogies should connect what you are less sure about (the original problem) to what you are more sure about (the metaphor). By analyzing the metaphor or analogy, you may identify attributes of the problem that were not evident before. New insights can occur.

Many creative solutions have been generated by such a technique. For example, William Harvey was the first to apply the "pump" analogy to the heart, which led to the discovery of the body's circulatory system. Niels Bohr compared the atom to the solar system and supplanted Rutherford's prevailing "raisin pudding" model of matter's building blocks. Creativity consultant Roger von Oech (1986) helped turn around a struggling computer company by applying a restaurant analogy to the company's operations. The real problems emerged when the restaurant, rather than the company, was analyzed. Major contributions in the field of organizational behavior have occurred by applying analogies to other types of organization, such as machines, cybernetic or open systems, force fields, clans, and so on. Probably the most effective analogies (called parables) were used by Jesus of Nazareth to teach principles that otherwise were difficult for individuals to grasp.

Some hints to keep in mind when constructing analogies are these: (1) Include action or motion in the analogy (e.g., driving a car, cooking a meal, attending a funeral); (2) include things that can be visualized or pictured in the analogy (e.g., stars, football games, crowded shopping malls); (3) pick familiar events or situations (e.g., families, kissing, bedtime); and (4) try to relate things that are not obviously similar (e.g., saying an organization is like a crowd is not nearly so rich a simile as saying an organization is like a psychic prison or a poker game).

Four types of analogies are recommended as part of synectics: **personal analogies,** where individuals try to identify themselves as the problem ("If I were the problem, how would I feel, what would I like, what could satisfy me?"); **direct analogies,** where individuals apply facts, technology, and common experience to the problem (e.g., Brunel solved the problem of underwater construction by watching a shipworm tunneling into a tube); **symbolic analogies,** where symbols or images are imposed on the problem (e.g., modeling the problem mathematically or diagramming the logic flow); and **fantasy analogies,** where individuals ask the question "In my wildest dreams, how would I wish the problem to be resolved?" (e.g., "I wish all employees would work with no supervision.").

Elaborate on the Definition

There are a variety of ways to enlarge, alter, or replace a problem definition once it has been specified. One way is to force yourself to generate at least two alternative hypotheses for every problem definition. That is, specify at least two plausible definitions of the problem in addition to the one originally accepted. Think in plural rather than singular terms. Instead of asking, "What is the problem?" "What is the meaning of this?" "What is the result?" ask instead questions such as: "What are the problems?" "What are the meanings of this?" "What are the results?"

As an example, look at Figure 6. Select the figure that is different from all the others. A majority of people select B first. If you did, you're right. It is the only figure that has all straight lines. On the other hand, quite a few people pick A. If you are one of them, you're also right. It is the only figure with a continuous line and no points of discontinuity. Alternatively, C can also be right, with the rationale that it is the only figure with two straight and two curved lines. Similarly, D is the only one with one curved and one straight line, and E is the only figure that is nonsymmetrical or partial. The

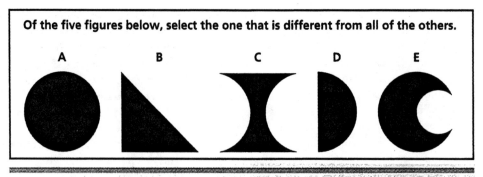

Figure 6 The Five-Figure Problem

point is, there can often be more than one problem definition, more than one right answer, and more than one perspective from which to view a problem.

Another way to elaborate definitions is to use a question checklist. This is a series of questions designed to help individuals think of alternatives to their accepted definitions. Several creative managers have shared with us some of their most fruitful questions:

1. Is there anything else?

2. Is the reverse true?

3. Is there a more general problem?

4. Can it be stated differently?

5. Who sees it differently?

6. What past experience is this like?

As an exercise, take a minute now to think of a problem you are currently experiencing. Write it down so it is formally specified. Now manipulate that definition by answering each of the six questions in the checklist. If you can't think of a problem, try the exercise with this one: "I am not as attractive as I would like to be."

Reverse the Definition

A third tool for improving and expanding problem definition is to reverse the definition of the problem. That is, turn the problem upside down, inside out, or back to front. Reverse the way in which you think of the problem. For example, consider the following problem:

A tradition in Sandusky, Ohio, for as long as anyone could remember was the Fourth of July Parade. It was one of the largest and most popular events on the city's annual calendar. Now, in 1988, the city mayor was hit with some startling and potentially disastrous news. The State of Ohio was mandating that liability insurance be carried on every attraction—floats, bands, majorettes—that participated in the parade. To protect against the possibility of injury or accident of any parade participant, each had to be covered by liability insurance.

The trouble, of course, was that taking out a liability insurance policy for all parade participants would require far more expense than the city could afford. The amount of insurance required for that large a number of participants and equipment made it impossible for the city to carry the cost. On the one hand, the mayor hated to cancel an important tradition that everyone in town looked forward to. On the other hand, to hold the event would break the city budget. If you were a consultant to the mayor, what would you suggest?

Commonly suggested alternatives in this problem include the following:

1. Try to negotiate with an insurance company for a lower rate. (However, the risk is merely being transferred to the insurance company.)

2. Hold fund raising events to generate enough money to purchase the insurance policy, or find a wealthy donor to sponsor the parade. (However, this may deflect potential donations away from, or may compete with, other community service agencies such as

United Way, Red Cross, or local churches who also sponsor fund raisers and require donations.)

3. Charge a "participation fee" to parade participants to cover the insurance expense. (However, this would likely eliminate most high school, junior high school, and elementary school bands and floats. It would also reduce the amount of money float builders and sponsoring organizations could spend on the actual float. Such a requirement would likely be a parade killer.)

4. Charge a fee to spectators of the parade. (However, this would require restricted access to the parade, an administrative structure to coordinate fee collection and ticketing, and the destruction of the sense of community participation that characterized this traditional event.)

Each of these suggestions is good, but each maintains a single definition of the problem. Each assumes that the solution to the problem is associated with solving the financial problem associated with the liability insurance requirement. Each suggestion, therefore, brings with it some danger of damaging the traditional nature of the parade or eliminating it altogether. If the problem is reversed, other answers normally not considered become evident. That is, the need for liability insurance at all could be addressed.

Here is an excerpt from a newspaper report of how the problem was addressed:

Sandusky, Ohio (AP) The Fourth of July parade here wasn't canceled, but it was immobilized by liability insurance worries. The band marched in place to the beat of a drum, and a country fair queen waved to her subjects from a float moored to the curb.

The Reverse Community Parade began at 10:00 a.m. Friday along Washington Row at the north end of the city and stayed there until dusk. "Very honestly, it was the issue of liability," said Gene Kleindienst, superintendent of city schools and one of the celebration's organizers. "By not having a mobile parade, we significantly reduced the issue of liability," he said.

The immobile parade included abut 20 floats and displays made by community groups. Games, displays, and food booths were in an adjacent park. Parade chairman Judee Hill said

some folks didn't understand, however. "Someone asked me if she was too late for the parade, and she had a hard time understanding the parade is here all day," she said.

Those who weren't puzzled seemed to appreciate the parade for its stationary qualities. "I like this. I can see more," said 67-year-old William A. Sibley. "I'm 80 percent blind. Now I know there's something there," he said pointing to a float.

Spectator Emmy Platte preferred the immobile parade because it didn't go on for "what seemed like miles," exhausting participants. "You don't have those little drum majorettes passing out on the street," she commented.

Baton twirler Tammy Ross said her performance was better standing still. "You can throw better. You don't have to worry about dropping it as much," she explained.

Mr. Kleindienst said community responses were favorable. "I think we've started a new tradition," he said.

By reversing the definition, Sandusky not only eliminated the problem without damaging the tradition and without shifting the risk to insurance companies or other community groups, it added a new dimension that allowed at least some people to enjoy the event more than ever.

This reversal is similar to what Rothenberg (1979) refers to as "Janusian thinking." Janus was the Roman god with two faces that looked in opposite directions. **Janusian thinking** means thinking contradictory thoughts at the same time: that is, conceiving two opposing ideas to be true concurrently. Rothenberg claimed, after studying 54 highly creative artists and scientists (e.g., Nobel Prize winners), that most major scientific breakthroughs and artistic masterpieces are products of Janusian thinking. Creative people who actively formulate antithetical ideas and then resolve them produce the most valuable contributions to the scientific and artistic worlds. Quantum leaps in knowledge often occur.

An example is Einstein's account (1919, p. 1) of having "the happiest thought of my life." He developed the concept that, "for an observer in free fall from the roof of a house, there exists, during his fall, no gravitational field . . . in his immediate vicinity. If the observer releases any objects, they will remain, relative to him, in a state of rest. The [falling] observer is therefore justified in considering his state as one of rest." Einstein concluded, in other words, that two seemingly contradictory states could be present simultaneously: motion and rest. This realization led to the development of his revolutionary general theory of relativity.

In another study of creative potential, Rothenberg (1979) found that when individuals were presented with a stimulus word and asked to respond with the word that first came to mind, highly creative students, Nobel scientists, and prize-winning artists responded with antonyms significantly more often than did individuals with average creativity. Rothenberg argued, based on these results, that creative people think in terms of opposites more often than do other people.

For our purposes, the whole point is to reverse or contradict the currently accepted definition in order to expand the number of perspectives considered. For instance, a problem might be that morale is too high instead of (or in addition to) too low in our team, or that employees need less motivation instead of more motivation to increase productivity. Opposites and backward looks often enhance creativity.

These three techniques for improving creative problem definition are summarized in Table 5. Their purpose is not to help you generate alternative definitions just for the sake of alternatives but to broaden your perspectives, to help you overcome conceptual blocks, and to produce more elegant (i.e., high-quality and parsimonious) solutions.

Ways to Generate More Alternatives

A common tendency is to define problems in terms of available solutions (i.e., the problem is defined as a solution already possessed or the first acceptable alternative, e.g., March & Simon, 1958). This tendency leads to consideration of a minimal number and narrow range of alternatives in problem solving. However, Guilford (1962), a pioneer in the study of creative problem solving, asserted that the primary characteristics of effective creative problem solvers are their fluency and their flexibility of thought. **Fluency** refers to the number of ideas or concepts produced in a given length of time. **Flexibility** refers to the diversity of ideas or concepts generated. While most problem solvers consider a few homogeneous alternatives, creative problem solvers consider many heterogeneous alternatives. The follow-

1. Make the strange familiar and the familiar strange.
2. Elaborate on the definition.
3. Reverse the definition.

Table 5   Techniques for Improving Problem Definition

ing techniques are designed to help you improve your ability to generate many varied alternatives when faced with problems. They are summarized in Table 6.

Defer Judgment

Probably the most common method of generating alternatives is the technique of **brainstorming** developed by Osborn (1953). This tool is powerful because most people make quick judgments about each piece of information or each alternative solution they encounter. This technique is designed to help people generate alternatives for problem solving without prematurely evaluating, and hence discarding, them. Four main rules govern brainstorming:

1. No evaluation of any kind is permitted as alternatives are being generated. Individual energy is spent on generating ideas, not on defending them.
2. The wildest possible ideas are encouraged. It is easier to tighten alternatives up than to loosen them.
3. The quantity of ideas takes precedence over the quality. Emphasizing quality engenders judgment and evaluation.
4. Participants should build on or modify the ideas of others. Poor ideas that are added to or altered often become good ideas.

1. Defer judgment.
2. Expand current alternatives.
3. Combine unrelated attributes.

Table 6   Techniques for Generating More Alternatives

Brainstorming techniques are best used in a group setting so individuals can stimulate ideas in one another. In fact, generating alternatives in a group setting produces more and better ideas than can be produced alone (Maier, 1967). One caution about brainstorming should be noted, however. Often, after a rush of alternatives is produced at the outset of a brainstorming session, the quantity of ideas rapidly subsides. But to stop there is an ineffective use of brainstorming. When no easily identifiable solutions are available, truly creative alternatives are often produced in brainstorming groups. So keep working!

The best way to get a feel for the power of brainstorming groups is to participate in one. Try the following exercise based on an actual problem faced by a group of students and university professors. Spend at least 20 minutes in a small group, brainstorming ideas.

A request had been made for a faculty member to design an executive education program for mid-level managers at a major automobile company. It was to focus on enhancing creativity and innovation among managers. The trouble was, the top human resource executive indicated that he did not want to approach the subject with "brain-teaser" examples. Instead, he wanted some other approaches that would help these managers become more creative personally and more effective at fostering innovation among others.

What ideas can you come up with for teaching this subject of creative problem solving to mid-level managers in an organization? How could you help them learn to be more creative? Generate as many ideas as you can following the rules of brainstorming. After at least 20 minutes, assess the fluency and flexibility of the ideas generated.

Expand Current Alternatives

Sometimes, brainstorming in a group is not possible or is too costly in terms of the number of people involved and hours required. Managers pursuing a hectic organizational life may sometimes find brainstorming an unusable alternative. Moreover, people sometimes need an external stimulus or blockbuster to help them generate new ideas. One useful and readily available technique for expanding alternatives is **subdivision,** or dividing a problem into smaller parts. March and

Simon (1958, p. 193) suggest that subdivision improves problem solving by increasing the speed with which alternatives can be generated and selected. As they explain,

The mode of subdivision has an influence on the extent to which planning can proceed simultaneously on the several aspects of the problem. The more detailed the factorization of the problem, the more simultaneous activity is possible, hence, the greater the speed of problem solving.

To see how subdivision helps develop more alternatives and speeds the process of problem solving, consider the problem, common in the creativity literature, of listing alternative uses for a familiar object. For example, in five minutes, how many uses can you list for a ping-pong ball? The more uses you list, the greater is your fluency in thinking. The more variety in the list, the greater is your flexibility in thinking. You might include the following in your list: bob for a fishing line, Christmas ornament, toy for a cat, gearshift knob, model for a molecular structure, wind gauge when hung from a string, head for a finger puppet, miniature basketball. Your list will be much longer.

After you generate your list, apply the technique of subdivision by identifying the specific characteristics of a ping-pong ball, that is, dividing it into its component attributes. For example, weight, color, texture, shape, porosity, strength, hardness, chemical properties, and conduction potential are all attributes of ping-pong balls that help expand the uses you might think of. By dividing an object mentally into more specific attributes, you can arrive at many more alternative uses (e.g., reflector, holder when cut in half, bug bed, ball for lottery drawing, and so on).

One exercise we have used with students and executives to illustrate this technique is to have them write down as many of their managerial strengths as they can think of. Most people list 10 or 12 attributes relatively easily. Then we analyze the various dimensions of the manager's role, the activities that managers engage in, the challenges that most managers face from inside and outside the organization, and so on. We then ask these same people to write down another list of their strengths as managers. The list is almost always twice as long or more. By identifying the subcomponents of any problem, far more alternatives can be generated than by considering the problem as a whole.

One final illustration. Divide the figure in Figure 7 into exactly four pieces equal in size, shape, and area. Try to do it in a minute or less. The problem is easy if you use subdivision. It is more difficult if you don't. One of the answers to the problem is in Appendix I.

Combine Unrelated Attributes

A third technique focuses on helping problem solvers expand alternatives by forcing the integration of seemingly unrelated elements. Research into creative problem solving has shown that an ability to see common relationships among disparate factors is a major factor differentiating creative from noncreative individuals (see Dellas & Gaier, 1970, for a review of the literature). Two ways to do this are through *morphological forced connections* (Koberg & Bagnall, 1974) and the *relational algorithm* (Crovitz, 1970).

With **morphological forced connections,** a four-step procedure is involved. First, the problem is written down. Second, attributes of the problem are listed. Third, alternatives to each attribute are listed. Fourth,

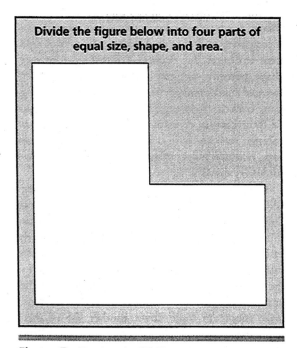

Figure 7 Fractionation Problem

different alternatives from the attributes list are combined together.

To illustrate this procedure, suppose you are faced with the problem of a secretary who takes an extended lunch break almost every day despite your reminders to be on time. Think of alternative ways to solve this problem. The first solution that comes to mind for most people is to sit down and have a talk with (or threaten) the secretary. If that doesn't work, most of us would just fire or transfer the person. However, look at what other alternatives can be generated by using morphological connections (see Table 7).

You can see how many more alternatives come to mind when you force together attributes that aren't obviously connected. The matrix of attributes can create a very long list of possible solutions. In more complicated problems—for example, how to improve quality, how to serve customers better, how to improve the reward system—the potential number of alternatives is even greater, and, hence, more creativity is required to analyze them.

The second technique for combining unrelated attributes in problem solving, the **relational algorithm,** involves applying connecting words that force a relationship between two elements in a problem. For example, the following is a list of some relational words:

about	across	after
against	opposite	or
out	among	and
as	at	over
round	still	because
before	between	but
so	then	though
by	down	for
from	through	till
to	if	in
near	not	under
up	when	now
of	off	on
where	while	with

To illustrate the use of this technique, suppose you are faced with the following problem: Our customers are dissatisfied with our service. The two major elements in this problem are *customers* and *service*. They are connected by the phrase *are dissatisfied with*. With the relational algorithm technique, the relational words in the problem statement are removed and replaced with other

Step 1. Problem statement: The secretary takes extended lunch breaks every day with friends in the cafeteria.

Step 2. Major attributes of the problem:

Amount of time	Start time	Place	With whom	Frequency
More than 1 hour	12 noon	Cafeteria	Friends	Daily

Step 3. Alternative attributes:

Amount of time	Start time	Place	With whom	Frequency
30 minutes	11:00	Office	Coworkers	Weekly
90 minutes	11:30	Conference Room	Boss	Twice a Week
45 minutes	12:30	Restaurant	Management Team	Alternate Days

Step 4. Combining Attributes:

1. A 30-minute lunch beginning at 12:30 in the conference room with the boss once a week.
2. A 90-minute lunch beginning at 11:30 in the conference room with coworkers twice a week.
3. A 45-minute lunch beginning at 11:00 in the cafeteria with the management team every other day.
4. A 30-minute lunch beginning at 12:00 alone in the office on alternate days.

Table 7 Morphological Forced Connections

relational words to see if new ideas for alternative solutions can be identified. For example, consider the following connections where new relational words are used:

- Customers *among* service (e.g., Customers interact with service personnel).

- Customers *as* service (e.g., Customers deliver service to other customers).

- Customers *and* service (e.g., Customers and service personnel work together).

- Customers *for* service (e.g., Customer focus groups help improve our service).

- Service *near* customers (e.g., Change the location of the service).

- Service *before* customers (e.g., Prepare service before the customer arrives).

- Service *through* customers (e.g., Use customers to provide additional service).

- Service *when* customers (e.g., Provide timely service).

By connecting the two elements of the problem in different ways, new possibilities for problem solution can be formulated.

Hints for Applying Problem-Solving Techniques

Not every problem is amenable to these techniques and tools for conceptual blockbusting, of course. Our intent in presenting these six is to help you expand the number of options available to you for defining problems and generating additional potential solutions. They are most useful with problems that require a new approach or perspective. All of us have enormous creative potential, but the stresses and pressures of daily life, coupled with the inertia of conceptual habits, tend to submerge that potential. These hints are ways to help unlock it again.

Reading about techniques or wanting to be creative won't improve your creativity, of course. These techniques and tools are not magic in themselves. They depend on your ability to actually generate new ideas and to think different thoughts. Because that is so difficult for most of us, here are six practical hints to help prepare you to create more conceptual flexibility and better apply these techniques.

1. Give yourself some relaxation time. The more intense your work, the more your need for complete breaks. Break out of your routine sometimes. This

frees up your mind and gives room for new thoughts.

2. Find a place (physical space) where you can think. It should be a place where interruptions are eliminated, at least for a time. Reserve your best time for thinking.

3. Talk to other people about ideas. Isolation produces far fewer ideas than does conversation. Make a list of people who stimulate you to think. Spend some time with them.

4. Ask other people for their ideas about your problems. Find out what others think about them. Don't be embarrassed to share your problems, but don't become dependent on others to solve them for you.

5. Read a lot. Read at least one thing regularly that is outside your field of expertise. Keep track of new thoughts from your reading.

6. Protect yourself from idea-killers. Don't spend time with "black holes"—that is, people who absorb all of your energy and light but give nothing in return. Don't let yourself or others negatively evaluate your ideas too soon.

You'll find these hints useful not only for enhancing creative problem solving but for rational problem solving as well. Figure 8 summarizes the two problem-solving processes—rational and creative—and the factors you should consider when determining how to approach each type of problem. In brief, when you encounter a problem that is straightforward—that is, outcomes are predictable, sufficient information is available, and means-ends connections are clear—rational problem-solving techniques are most appropriate. You should apply the four distinct, sequential steps. On the other hand, when the problem is not straightforward— that is, information is ambiguous or unavailable and alternative solutions are not apparent—you should apply creative problem-solving techniques in order to improve problem definition and alternative generation.

Fostering Innovation

Unlocking your own creative potential is not enough, of course, to make you a successful manager. A major challenge is to help unlock it in other people as well. Fostering innovation and creativity among those with whom you work is at least as great a challenge as increasing your own creativity. In this last section of the chapter, we briefly discuss some principles that will help you better accomplish the task of fostering innovation.

Management Principles

Neither Percy Spencer nor Spence Silver could have succeeded in his creative ideas had there not been a managerial support system present that fostered creative problem solving and the pursuit of innovation. In each case, certain characteristics were present in their organizations, fostered by managers around them, that made their innovations possible. In this section we will not discuss the macro-organizational issues associated with innovation (e.g., organization design, strategic orientation, and human resource systems). Excellent discussions of those factors are reviewed in sources such as Galbraith (1982), Kanter (1983), McMillan (1985), Tichy (1983), and Amabile (1988). Instead, we'll focus on activities in which individual managers can engage that foster innovation. Table 8 summarizes three management principles that help engender innovativeness and creative problem solving.

Pull People Apart; Put People Together

Percy Spencer's magnetron project involved a consumer product closeted away from Raytheon's main-line business of missiles and other defense-contract work. Spence Silver's new glue resulted when a polymer adhesive task force was separated from 3M's normal activities. The Macintosh computer was developed by a task force taken outside the company and given space and time to work on an innovative computer. Many new ideas come from individuals being given time and resources and allowed to work apart from the normal activities of the organization. Establishing bullpens, practice fields, or sandlots is as good a way to develop new skills in business as it has proven to be in athletics. Because most businesses are designed to produce the 10,000th part correctly or to service the 10,000th customer efficiently, they do not function well at producing the first part. That is why pulling people apart is often necessary to foster innovation and creativity.

On the other hand, forming teams (putting people together) is almost always more productive than having people work by themselves. Such teams should be characterized by certain attributes, though. For example,

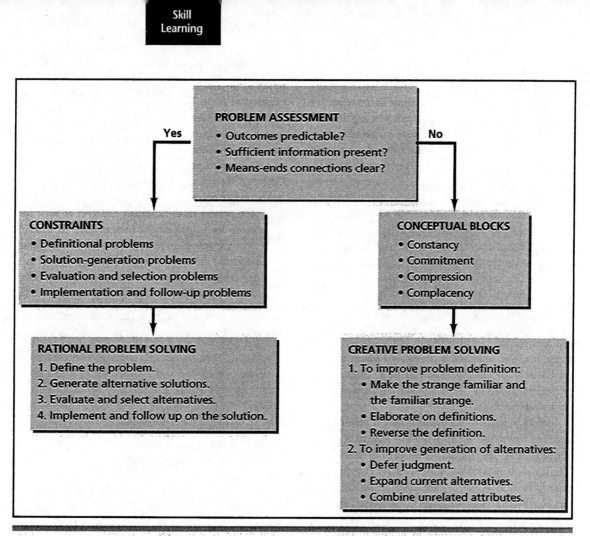

Figure 8   A Model of Rational and Creative Problem Solving

PRINCIPLE	EXAMPLES
1. Pull people apart; Put people together.	• Let individuals work alone as well as with teams and task forces.
	• Encourage minority reports and legitimize "devil's advocate" roles.
	• Encourage heterogeneous membership in teams.
	• Separate competing groups or subgroups.
2. Monitor and prod.	• Talk to customers.
	• Identify customer expectations both in advance and after the sale.
	• Hold people accountable.
	• Use "sharp-pointed" prods.
3. Reward multiple roles.	• Idea champion
	• Sponsor and mentor
	• Orchestrator and facilitator
	• Rule breaker

Table 8   Three Principles for Fostering Innovativeness

Nemeth (1986) found that creativity increased markedly when minority influences were present in the team, for example, when "devil's advocate" roles were legitimized, a formal minority report was always included in final recommendations, and individuals assigned to work on a team had divergent backgrounds or views. "Those exposed to minority views are stimulated to attend to more aspects of the situation, they think in more divergent ways, and they are more likely to detect novel solutions or come to new decisions" (Nemeth, 1986, p. 25). Nemeth found that those positive benefits occur in groups even when the divergent or minority views are wrong. Similarly, Janis (1971) found that narrow-mindedness in groups (dubbed "groupthink") was best overcome by establishing competing groups working on the same problem, participation in groups by outsiders, assigning a role of critical evaluator in the group, having groups made up of cross-functional participants, and so on. The most productive groups are those characterized by fluid roles, lots of interaction among members, and flat power structures.

Innovativeness can be fostered when individuals are placed in teams and when they are at least temporarily separated from the normal pressures of organizational life. Teams, however, are most effective at generating innovative ideas when they are characterized by attributes of minority influence, competition, heterogeneity, and interaction. You can help foster innovation among people you manage, therefore, by pulling people apart (e.g., giving them a bullpen) as well as putting people together (e.g., putting them on a team).

Monitor and Prod

Neither Percy Spencer nor Spence Silver was allowed to work on their projects with no accountability. Both men eventually had to report on the results they accomplished with their experimentation and imagination. At 3M, for example, people are expected to allocate 15 percent of their time away from company business to work on new, creative ideas. They can even appropriate company materials and resources to work on them. However, individuals are always held accountable for their decisions. They need to show results for their "play time."

Holding people accountable for outcomes, in fact, is an important motivator for improved performance. Two innovators in the entertainment industry captured this principle with these remarks: "The ultimate inspi-

ration is the deadline. That's when you have to do what needs to be done. The fact that twice a year the creative talent of this country is working until midnight to get something ready for a trade show is very good for the economy. Without this kind of pressure, things would turn to mashed potatoes" (von Oech, 1986, p. 119). One way Woody Morcott, DEO at Dana Corporation, holds people accountable for innovation is to require that each person in the company submit at least two suggestions for improvement each month. At least 70 percent of the new ideas must be implemented. Woody admitted that he stole the idea during a visit to a Japanese company where he noticed workers huddled around a table scribbling notes on how some ideas for improvement might work. At Dana, this requirement is part of every person's job assignment. Rewards are associated with such ideas as well. A plant in Chihuahua, Mexico, for example, rewards employees with $1.89 for every idea submitted and another $1.89 if the idea is used. "We drill into people that they are responsible for keeping the plant competitive through innovation," Morcott said (personal communication).

In addition to accountability, innovativeness is stimulated by what Gene Goodson at Johnson Controls called "sharp-pointed prods." After taking over the automotive group at that company, Goodson found that he could stimulate creative problem solving by issuing certain mandates that demanded innovativeness. One such mandate was, "There will be no more forklift trucks allowed in any of our plants." At first hearing, that mandate sounds absolutely outrageous. Think about it. You have a plant with tens of thousands of square feet of floor space. The loading docks are on one side of the building, and many tons of heavy raw materials are unloaded weekly and moved from the loading docks to work stations throughout the entire facility. The only way it can be done is with forklifts. Eliminating forklift trucks would ruin the plant, right? Wrong. This sharp-pointed prod demanded that individuals working in the plant find ways to move the work stations closer to the raw materials, to move the unloading of the raw materials closer to the work stations, or to change the size and amounts of material being unloaded. The innovations that resulted from eliminating forklifts saved the company millions of dollars in materials handling and wasted time, dramatically improved quality, productivity, and efficiency, and made it possible for Johnson Controls to capture some business from their Japanese competitors.

One of the best methods for generating useful prods is regularly to monitor customer preferences, expectations, and evaluations. Many of the most creative ideas have come from customers, the recipients of goods and services. Identifying their preferences in advance and monitoring their evaluations of products or services later are good ways to get ideas for innovation and to be prodded to make improvements. All employees should be in regular contact with their own customers, asking questions and monitoring performance.

By customers, we don't mean just the end-users of a business product or service. In fact, all of us have customers, whether we are students in school, members of a family, players on a basketball team, or whatever. Customers are simply those for whom we are trying to produce something or whom we serve. Students, for example, can count their instructors, class members, and potential employers as customers whom they serve. A *priori* and *post hoc* monitoring of their expectations and evaluations is an important way to help foster new ideas for problem solving. This monitoring is best done through one-on-one meetings (see Chapter 4, which discusses the Personal Management Interview Program), but it can also be done through follow-up calls, surveys, customer complaint cards, suggestion systems, and so on.

In summary, you can foster innovativeness by holding people accountable for new ideas and by stimulating them with periodic prods. The most useful prods generally come from customers.

Reward Multiple Roles

The success of the sticky yellow notes at 3M is more than a story of the creativity of Spence Silver. It also illustrates the necessity of people playing multiple roles in innovation and the importance of recognizing and rewarding those who play such roles. Without a number of people playing multiple roles, Spence Silver's glue would probably still be on a shelf somewhere.

Four crucial roles in the innovative process are the *idea champion* (the person who comes up with innovative problem solutions), the *sponsor* or *mentor* (the person who helps provide the resources, environment, and encouragement for the idea champion to work on his idea), the *orchestrator* or *facilitator* (the person who brings together cross-functional groups and necessary political support to facilitate implementation of creative ideas), and the *rule breaker* (the person who goes beyond organizational boundaries and barriers to ensure

success of the innovation). Each of these roles is present in most important innovations in organizations, and all are illustrated by the Post-It Note example below.

This story has four major parts.

1. Spence Silver, while fooling around with chemical configurations that the academic literature indicated wouldn't work, invented a glue that wouldn't stick. Silver spent years giving presentations to any audience at 3M that would listen, trying to pawn off his glue on some division that could find a practical application for it. But nobody was interested.

2. Henry Courtney and Roger Merrill developed a coating substance that allowed the glue to stick to one surface but not to others. This made it possible to produce a permanently temporary glue, that is, one that would peel off easily when pulled but would otherwise hang on forever.

3. Art Fry found a problem that fit Spence Silver's solution. He found an application for the glue as a "better bookmark" and as a note pad. No equipment existed at 3M to coat only a part of a piece of paper with the glue. Fry therefore carried 3M equipment and tools home to his own basement, where he designed and made his own machine to manufacture the forerunner of Post-It Notes. Because the working machine became too large to get out of his basement, he blasted a hole in the wall to get the equipment back to 3M. He then brought together engineers, designers, production managers, and machinists to demonstrate the prototype machine and generate enthusiasm for manufacturing the product.

4. Geoffrey Nicholson and Joseph Ramsey began marketing the product inside 3M. They also submitted the product to the standard 3M market tests. The product failed miserably. No one wanted to pay $1.00 for a pad of scratch paper. But when Nicholson and Ramsey broke 3M rules by personally visiting test market sites and giving away free samples, the consuming public became addicted to the product.

In this scenario, Spence Silver was both a rule breaker and an idea champion. Art Fry was also an idea champion, but more importantly, he orchestrated the coming together of the various groups needed to get the innovation off the ground. Henry Courtney and Roger Merrill helped sponsor Silver's innovation by providing him with the coating substance that would allow his idea to work. Geoff Nicholson and Joe Ramsey were both rule breakers and sponsors in their bid to get the product accepted by the public. In each case, not only did all these people play unique roles, but they did so with tremendous enthusiasm and zeal. They were confident of their ideas and willing to put their time and resources on the line as advocates. They fostered support among a variety of constituencies, both within their own areas of expertise as well as among outside groups. Most organizations are inclined to give in to those who are sure of themselves, persistent in their efforts, and savvy enough to make converts of others.

Not everyone can be an idea champion. But when managers reward and recognize those who sponsor and orchestrate the ideas of others, innovation increases in organizations. Teams form, supporters replace competitors, and creativity thrives. Facilitating multiple role development is the job of the innovative manager.

Summary

In the last 15 years, the growth rate of new patent applications in this country has declined by 25 percent. Last year almost half of the patents issued in America were given to foreigners. One major U.S. corporation reported that five years ago over 70 percent of its licensing agreements consisted of patents it sold to other countries. Now it purchases over half its products using licensing agreements from foreign countries. America marketed 82 percent of the world's inventions 25 years ago, but it now ranks behind several other countries in new-product introductions. Despite the well-developed medical and pharmaceutical school system existing in the United States, Japan has still led the world in the introductions of new drugs for the last five years. One U.S. automobile manufacturer bragged of receiving over 30,000 suggestions for improvement from employees in one year; then a Japanese rival opened a plant 50 miles away and received over 3 million suggestions from employees in a single year. In short, the United States has experienced a decline in creativity and innovation in the last several years. Flexibility in thinking and effective management problem solving seem to have taken a nose-dive.

As we have pointed out, a well-developed model exists for solving problems. It consists of four separate and sequential stages: defining a problem; generating alternative solutions; evaluating and selecting the best solution; and implementing the chosen solution. This model, however, is mainly useful for solving straightforward problems. Many problems faced by managers are not of this type, and frequently managers are called on to exercise creative problem-solving skills. That is, they must broaden their perspective of the problem and develop alternative solutions that are not immediately obvious.

We have discussed and illustrated eight major conceptual blocks that inhibit most people's creative problem-solving abilities. Conceptual blocks are mental obstacles that artificially constrain problem definition and solution and that keep most people from being effective creative problem solvers. The four major conceptual blocks are summarized in Table 3.

Overcoming these conceptual blocks is a matter of skill development and practice in thinking, not a matter of innate ability. Everyone can become a skilled creative problem solver with practice. Becoming aware of these thinking inhibiters helps individuals overcome them. We also discussed three major principles for improving creative problem definition and three major principles for improving the creative generation of alternative solutions. Certain techniques were described that can help implement these six principles.

We concluded by offering some hints about how to foster creativity and innovativeness among other people. Becoming an effective problem solver yourself is important, but effective managers can also enhance this activity among their subordinates, peers, and superiors.

Behavioral Guidelines

Below are specific behavioral action guidelines to help your skill practice in problem solving, creativity, and fostering innovation.

1. Follow the four-step procedure outlined in Table 1 when solving straightforward problems. Keep the steps separate, and do not take shortcuts.

2. When approaching a difficult problem, try to overcome your conceptual blocks by consciously doing the following mental activities:

▶ Use lateral thinking in addition to vertical thinking.

- Use several thought languages instead of just one.

- Challenge stereotypes based on past experiences.

- Identify underlying themes and commonalities in seemingly unrelated factors.

- Delete superfluous information and fill in important missing information when studying the problem.

- Avoid artificially constraining problem boundaries.

- Overcome any unwillingness to be inquisitive.

- Use both right- and left-brain thinking.

3. When defining a problem, make the strange familiar and the familiar strange by using metaphor and analogy, first to focus and then to distort and refocus the definition.

4. Elaborate problem definitions by developing at least two alternative (opposite) definitions and by applying a checklist.

5. Reverse problem definitions by beginning with end results and working backwards.

6. In generating potential problem solutions, defer any judgment until many solutions have been proposed. Use the four rules of brainstorming:

- Do not evaluate.

- Encourage "wild ideas."

- Encourage quantity.

- Build on others' ideas.

7. Expand the list of current alternative solutions by subdividing the problem into its attributes.

8. Increase the number of possible solutions by combining unrelated problem attributes. Morphological connections and relational algorithms may be helpful.

9. Foster innovativeness among those with whom you work by doing the following:

- Find a "practice field" where individuals can experiment and try out ideas, and assign them responsibility for fostering innovation.

- Put people holding different perspectives in teams to work on problems.

- Hold people accountable for innovation.

- Use sharp-pointed prods to stimulate new thinking.

- Recognize, reward, and encourage the participation of multiple players, including idea champions, sponsors, orchestrators, and rule breakers.

Skill Analysis

Cases Involving Problem Solving

Admiral Kimmel's Failure at Pearl Harbor

In the summer of 1941, as relations between the United States and Japan were rapidly deteriorating, Admiral Kimmel, Commander in Chief of the Pacific Fleet, received many warnings concerning the imminence of war. During this period he worked out a plan in collaboration with his staff at Pearl Harbor, which gave priority to training key personnel and supplying basic equipment to U.S. outposts in the Far East. The plan took account of the possibility of a long, hard war with Japan and the difficulties of mobilizing scarce resources in manpower and material. At that time, Admiral Kimmel and his staff were keenly aware of the risks of being unprepared for war with Japan, as well as the high costs and risks involved in preparing for war. They appear to have been relatively optimistic about being able to develop a satisfactory military plan and about having sufficient time in which to implement it. In short, all the conditions were present for vigilance, and it seems likely that this coping pattern characterized their planning activity.

But during the late fall of 1941, as warnings became increasingly more ominous, a different pattern of coping behavior emerged. Admiral Kimmel and his staff continued to cling to the policy to which they had committed themselves, discounting each fresh warning and failing to note that more and more signs were pointing to Pearl Harbor as a possible target for a surprise air attack. They repeatedly renewed their decision to continue using the available resources primarily for training green sailors and soldiers and for supplying bases close to Japan, rather than instituting an adequate alert that would give priority to defending Pearl Harbor against enemy attack.

Knowing that neither their own sector nor the rest of the U.S. military organization was ready for a shooting war, they clung to an unwarranted set of rationalizations. The Japanese, they thought, would not launch an attack against any American possession; and if by some remote chance they decided to do so, it certainly wouldn't be at Pearl Harbor. Admiral Kimmel and his staff acknowledged that Japan could launch a surprise attack in any direction, but remained convinced that it would not be launched in their direction. They saw no reason to change their course. Therefore, they continued to give peacetime weekend leave to the majority of the naval forces in Hawaii and allowed the many warships in the Pacific Fleet to remain anchored at Pearl Harbor, as sitting ducks. Kimmel regularly discussed each warning with members of his staff. At times he became emotionally aroused and obtained reassurance from the members of his in-group. He shared with them a number of rationalizations that bolstered his decision to ignore the warnings. On November 27, 1941, for example, he received an explicit "war warning" from the chief of naval operations in Washington, which stirred up his concern but did not impel him to take any new protective action. This message was intended as a strong follow-up to an earlier warning, which Kimmel had received only three days earlier, stating that war with Japan was imminent and that "a surprise aggressive movement in any direction, including attack on Philippines or Guam, is a possibility." The new warning asserted that "an aggressive move by Japan is expected within the next few days" and instructed Kimmel to "execute appropriate defensive deployment" preparatory to carrying out the naval war plan.

The threat conveyed by this warning was evidently strong enough to induce Kimmel to engage in prolonged discussion with his staff about what should be done. But their vigilance seems to have been confined to paying careful attention to the way the warning was worded. During the meeting, members of the staff pointed out to Kimmel that Hawaii was not specifically mentioned as a possible target in either of the two war warnings, whereas other places—the Philippines, Malaya, and other remote areas—were explicitly named. Kimmel went along with the interpretation that the ambiguities they had detected in the wording must have meant that Pearl Harbor was not supposed to be regarded as a likely target, even though the message seemed to be saying that it was. The defensive quality that entered into this judgment is revealed by the fact that Kimmel made no effort to use his available channels of communication in Washington to find out what really had been meant. He ended up agreeing with the members of his advisory group that there was no chance of a surprise air attack on Hawaii at that particular time.

Since he judged Pearl Harbor not to be vulnerable, Kimmel decided that the limited-alert condition that had been instituted months earlier would be sufficient. He assumed, however, that all U.S. Army units in Hawaii had gone on full alert in response to this war warning, so that antiaircraft and radar units under army control would be fully activated. But, again, reflecting his defensive lack of interest in carrying out tasks that required acknowledging the threat, Kimmel failed to inquire of Army headquarters exactly what was being done. As a result, he did not discover until after the disaster on December 7 that the Army, too, was on only limited alert, designed exclusively to protect military installations against local sabotage.

On December 3, 1941, Kimmel engaged in intensive discussion with two members of his staff upon receiving a fresh warning from naval headquarters in Washington stating that U.S. cryptographers had decoded a secret message from Tokyo to all diplomatic missions in the United States and other countries, ordering them to destroy their secret codes. Kimmel realized that this type of order could mean that Japan was making last-minute preparations before launching an attack against the United States. Again, he and his advisors devoted considerable attention to the exact wording of this new, worrisome warning. They made much of the fact that the dispatch said "most" of the codes but not "all." They concluded that the destruction of the codes should be interpreted as a routine precautionary measure and not as a sign that Japan was planning to attack an American possession. Again, no effort was made to find out from Washington how the intelligence units there interpreted the message. But the lengthy discussions and the close attention paid to the wording of these messages imply that they did succeed in at least temporarily inducing decisional conflict.

By December 6, 1941, the day before the attack, Kimmel was aware of a large accumulation of extremely ominous signs. In addition to receiving the official war warnings during the preceding week, he had received a private letter three days earlier from Admiral Stark in Washington stating that both President Roosevelt and Secretary of State Hull now thought that the Japanese were getting ready to launch a surprise attack. Then on December 6, Kimmel received another message from Admiral Stark containing emergency war orders pertaining to the destruction of secret and confidential documents in American bases on outlying Pacific islands. On that same day, the FBI in Hawaii informed Kimmel that the local Japanese consulate had been burning its papers for the last two days. Furthermore, Kimmel's chief naval intelligence officer had reported to him that day, as he had on the preceding days, that despite fresh efforts to pick up Japanese naval signal calls, the whereabouts of all six of Japan's aircraft carriers still remained a mystery. (U.S. Naval Combat Intelligence had lost track of the Japanese aircraft carriers in mid-November, when they started to move toward Hawaii for the planned attack on Pearl Harbor.)

Although the various warning signs, taken together, clearly indicated that Japan was getting ready to launch an attack against the United States, they remained ambiguous as to exactly where the attack was likely to be. There was also considerable "noise" mixed in with the warning signals, including intelligence reports that huge Japanese naval forces were moving toward Malaya. But, inexplicably, there was a poverty of imagination on the part of Kimmel and his staff with regard to considering the possibility that Pearl Harbor itself might be one of the targets of a Japanese attack.

The accumulated warnings, however, were sufficiently impressive to Kimmel to generate considerable concern. On the afternoon of December 6, as he was pondering alternative courses of action, he openly expressed his anxiety to two of his staff officers. He told them he was worried about the safety of the fleet at Pearl Harbor in view of all the disturbing indications that Japan was getting ready for a massive attack somewhere. One member of the staff immediately reassured him that "the Japanese could not possibly be able to proceed in force against Pearl Harbor when they had so much strength concentrated in their Asiatic operations." Another told him that the limited-alert condition he had ordered many weeks earlier would certainly be sufficient and nothing more was needed. "We finally decided," Kimmel subsequently recalled, "that what we had [already] done was still good and we would stick to it." At the end of the discussion, Kimmel "put his worries aside" and went off to a dinner party.

Source: Janis & Mann, 1977, pp. 120–123.

Discussion Questions

1. What conceptual blocks are illustrated in this case?

2. Outline the problem-solving steps followed by Kimmel and his advisors. What steps in rational problem solving were skipped or short-circuited?

3. What kinds of conceptual blockbusters could have been useful to Kimmel? If you were his advisor, what would you have suggested to help his problem-solving processes?

4. If you knew then what you know now, how would you have redesigned Kimmel's structures and processes so that effective problem solving could occur?

The Sony Walkman

They had been disappointed at first, but it wasn't something that was going to keep them awake nights. Mitsuro Ida and a group of electronics engineers in Sony Corporation's Tape Recorder Division in Tokyo had tried to redesign a small, portable tape recorder, called "Pressman," so that it gave out stereophonic sounds. A year or so before, Ida and his group had been responsible for inventing the first Pressman, a wonderfully compact machine—ideal for use by journalists—which had sold very well.

But the sound in that tape machine was monaural. The next challenge for Sony's tape recorder engineers was to make a portable machine just as small, but with stereophonic sound. The very first stereo Pressman they made, in the last few months of 1978, didn't succeed. When Ida and his colleagues got the stereo circuits into the Pressman chassis (5.25 inches by 3.46 inches and only 1.14 inches deep), they didn't have any space left to fit in the recording mechanism. They had made a stereophonic tape recorder that couldn't record anything. Ida regarded this as a good first try but a useless product. But he didn't throw it away. The stereo Pressman was a nice little machine. So the engineers found a few favorite music cassettes and played them while they worked.

After Ida and his fellow designers had turned their nonrecording tape recorder into background music, they didn't entirely ignore it. They had frequent discussions about how to fit the stereo function and the recording mechanism into that overly small space. It was not an easy problem to solve, but that made it all the more fascinating and attractive to Ida and his group of inveterate problem solvers. Their focus on the problem of the stereo Pressman [to the solution—to a different problem—that was in their hands.

"And then one day," said Takichi Tezuka, manager of product planning for the Division, "into our room came Mr. Ibuka, our honorary chairman. He just popped room, saw us listening to this, and thought it was very interesting."

It is the province of honorary chairmen everywhere, because their status is almost invariably ceremonial, to putter about the plant looking in on this group and that, nodding over the latest incomprehensible gadget. To this mundane task, Masaru Ibuka brought an undiminished intelligence and an active imagination. When he happened into the Tape Recorder Division and saw Ida's incomplete tape recorder, he admired the quality of its stereophonic sound. He also remembered an entirely unrelated project going on elsewhere in the building, where an engineer named Yoshiyuki Kamon was working to develop lightweight portable headphones.

What if you combined them? asked Ibuka. At the very least, he said, the headphones would use battery power much more efficiently than stereo speakers. Reduce power requirements and you can reduce battery consumption. But another idea began to form in his mind. If you added the headphones, wouldn't you dramatically increase the quality of what the listener hears? Could you leave out the recorder entirely and make a successful product that just plays music?

In the world of tape recorders, Ibuka's thought was heresy. He was mixing up functions. Headphones traditionally were supposed to extend the usefulness of tape recorders, not be essential to their success. This idea was so well established that if Ibuka had not made an association between a defective tape recorder design and the unfinished headphone design, Walkman may well have remained a little byway in musical history. Design groups within Sony tend to be very close-knit and remain focused on short-term task completion. Even when things were less busy, there was never any reason for tape-recorder people to communicate with headphone people. They had nothing to do with each other. Tezuka, the man later described as "the secretariat of the Walkman project," said, "No one dreamed that a headphone would ever come in a package with a tape recorder. We're not very interested in what they do in the Headphone Division."

But, even without this insularity, there is no assurance that someone else at Sony would have made the connection that Ibuka made. To people today, the relationship between a cassette player and a set of headphones is self-evident. But to people at Sony, and at virtually every consumer electronics company, that connection was invisible in 1978.

Ibuka got a predictable response from the researchers in the electronics lab and from others in the Tape Recorder and Headphone Divisions. They were painfully polite but noncommittal. Ibuka might be right that the headphones would improve Pressman's efficiency, but nobody could guess how much of an improvement that would be. No one wanted to tell Ibuka that the idea of removing the speaker in favor of headphones was crazy. But it was! What if the owner of the device wanted to play back a tape so that more than one person could listen?

When Ibuka ventured further into illogic by suggesting a playback machine with no speaker and no recorder, he lost everybody. Who would want to buy such a thing? Who in Sony Corporation would support even 10 minutes of development on such a harebrained scheme?

In a way, they were right and Ibuka was wrong. This was an idea that violated most industries' well-established criteria for judging the natural increments of product development. It only makes sense that a new product prototype should be better than the previous generation of product. Ida's nonrecording prototype seemed worse. The idea had no support from the people who eventually would be responsible for funding its development, carrying out the research, and trying to sell it to a consumer market. The idea should have been killed. The system made sense and the people who worked within the system were making sense.

For Honorary Chairman Ibuka, the handwriting was on the wall. Even though he was a revered man at Sony, he had no authority to order such a project undertaken against the wishes of the division's leaders. It was clear that the only way to sell a bad idea to a group of cautious, reasonable businessmen was to find an ally. So, in his enthusiasm, his next step was straight to the office of his partner and friend, Akio Morita.

Source: Nayak and Ketteringham, 1986.

Discussion Questions

1. What principles of rational problem solving and creative problem solving were used in this case?

2. How was innovativeness fostered within Sony by top managers?

3. What roles were played by the various characters in the case that led to the success of the Walkman?

4. If you were a consultant to Sony, what would you advise to help foster this kind of innovation more frequently and more broadly throughout the company?

⬡ Skill Practice

Exercises for Applying Conceptual Blockbusting

Creative problem solving is most applicable to problems that have no obvious solutions. Most problems people face can be solved relatively easily with a systematic analysis of alternatives. But other problems are ambiguous enough that obvious alternatives are not workable; such problems require nontraditional approaches to find reasonable alternatives. Following are two such problems. They are real, not fictitious, and it probably characterizes your own college or university or public library and many local restaurants. Apply the principles of creative problem solving in the chapter to come up with realistic, cost-effective, creative solutions to these problems. Don't stop at the first solutions that come to mind because there are no obvious right answers.

Assignment

Form small groups to engage in the following problem-solving exercises. Each group should generate solutions to the cases. Each case is factual, not fictitious. Try to be as creative in your solutions as possible. The creativity of those solutions should be judged by an independent observer, and the best group's solution should be given recognition. In defining and solving the problems, use the following five steps. Do not skip steps.

1. Generate a single statement that accurately defines the problem. Make sure that all group members agree with the definition of the problem.

2. Propose alternative solutions to the problem. Write these down and prepare to report them to the larger group.

3. All small groups should report their top three alternatives to the large group. The top three are the ones that most group members agree would produce the best solution to the problem.

4. Now, in each small group, generate at least five plausible alternative definitions of the problem. Use any of the techniques for expanding problem definition discussed in the text. Each problem statement should differ from the others in its definition, not just in its attributions of causes of the problem.

5. After each group has agreed on the wording of the five statements, identify at least 10 new alternatives for solving the problems you have defined in step 4. Apply the techniques for expanding alternatives discussed in the text.

As a result of steps 4 and 5, your group should have identified some new alternatives as well as more alternatives than you did in steps 1 and 2. Report to the large group the three alternatives that your small group judges to be the most creative.

An observer should provide feedback on the extent to which each group member applied these principles effectively, using the Observer's Feedback Form in Appendix I.

The Bleak Future of Knowledge

Libraries throughout the world are charged with the responsibility of preserving the accumulated wisdom of the past and gathering information in the present. They serve as sources of information and resources, alternate schools, and places of exploration and discovery. No one would question the value of libraries to societies and cultures throughout the world. The materials housed there are the very foundation of civilization. But consider the following two problems.

1. In America alone (and the problem is much worse in Eastern Europe and the former Soviet-bloc countries), hundreds of thousands of books are in states of decay so advanced that when they are touched they fall into powder. Whereas parchments seem to survive better when they are handled, and books printed before 1830 on rag paper stay flexible and tough, books printed since the mid 19th century on wood-pulp paper are being steadily eaten away by natural acids. At the Library of Congress, about 77,000 books out of the stock of 13 million enter the endangered category every year. Fairly soon, about 40 percent of the books in the biggest research collections in America will be too fragile to handle. At the Bibliothèque Nationale in France, more than 600,000 books require treatment immediately. The largest library in England, the British Library, has a backlog of 1.6 million urgent cases.

2. The Library of Congress estimates that it will take 25 years to work through the backlog of cases. But of more concern is the fact that it costs about $200 in time and labor to treat a single volume. It costs more if it is to be put on another medium (e.g., microfiche, CD-ROM). The budget for most large libraries in the United States, including the Library of Congress, has been cut during the 1980s and 1990s, and with pressure to raise taxes to fund social programs ever present on a national level and the cost of higher education rising beyond the inflation rate in universities, it is doubtful that book preservation will receive high funding priority in the near future.

Source: The Economist, December 23, 1989.

Keith Dunn and McGuffey's Restaurant

Keith Dunn knew exactly what to expect. He knew how his employees felt about him. That's why he had sent them the questionnaire in the first place. He needed a shot of confidence, a feeling that his employees were behind him as he struggled to build McGuffey's Restaurants, Inc., beyond two restaurants and $4 million in annual sales.

Gathering up the anonymous questionnaires, Dunn returned to his tiny corporate office in Asheville, North Carolina. With one of his partners by his side, he ripped open the first envelope as eagerly as a Broadway producer checking the reviews on opening night. His eyes zoomed directly to the question where employees were asked to rate the three owners' performance on a scale of 1 to 10.

A zero. The employee had scrawled in a big, fat zero. "Find out whose handwriting this is," he told his partner, Richard Laibson.

He ripped open another: zero again. And another. A two. "We'll fire these people," Dunn said to Laibson coldly.

Another zero.

A one.

"Oh, go work for somebody else, you jerk!" Dunn shouted.

Soon he had moved to fire 10 of his 230 employees. "Plenty of people seemed to hate my guts," he says.

Over the next day, though, Dunn's anger subsided. "You think, I've done all this for these people and they think I'm a total jerk who doesn't care about them," he says. "Finally, you have to look in the mirror and think, 'Maybe they're right.'"

For Dunn, that realization was absolutely shattering. He had started the company three years earlier, in 1983, out of frustration over all the abuse he had suffered while working at big restaurant chains. If Dunn had one overriding mission at McGuffey's, it was to prove that restaurants didn't have to mistreat their employees.

He thought he had succeeded. Until he opened those surveys, he had believed that McGuffey's was a place where employees felt valued, involved, and appreciated. "I had no idea we were treating people so badly," he says. Somewhere along the way, in the day-to-day running of the business, he had lost his connection with them and left behind the employee-oriented company he thought he was running.

Dunn's 13-year odyssey through some big restaurant chains left him feeling as limp as a cheeseburger after a day under the heat lamps. Ponderosa in Georgia. Bennigan's in Florida and Tennessee. TGI Friday's in Texas, Tennessee, and Indiana. Within one six-month period at Friday's, he got two promotions, two bonuses, and two raises; then his boss left, and he got fired. That did it. Dunn was fed up with big chains.

In 1982, at the age of 29, he returned to Atlanta, where he had attended Emory University as an undergraduate and where he began waiting tables at a local restaurant.

There he met David Lynn, the general manager of the restaurant, a similarly jaded 29-year-old who, by his own admission, had "begun to lose faith." Lynn and Dunn started hatching plans to open their own place, where employees would enjoy working as much as customers enjoyed eating. They planned to target the smaller markets that the chains ignored. With financing from a friend, they opened McGuffey's in 1983.

True to their people-oriented goals, the partners tried to make employees feel more appreciated than they themselves had felt at the chains. They gave them a free drink and a meal at the end of every shift, let them give away appetizers and desserts, and provided them a week of paid vacation each year.

A special camaraderie developed among the employees. After all, they worked in an industry in which a turnover rate of 250 percent was something to aspire to. The night before McGuffey's opened, in October 1983, some 75 employees encircled the ficus tree next to the bar, joined hands, and prayed silently for two minutes. "The tree had a special energy," says Dunn.

Maybe so. By the third night of operation, the 230-seat McGuffey's had a waiting list. The dining room was so crowded that after three months the owners decided to add a 58-seat patio. Then they had to rearrange the kitchen to handle the volume. In its first three and a half months, McGuffey's racked up sales of about $415,000, ending 1983 just over $110,000 in the red, mostly because the partners paid back the bulk of their $162,000 debt right away.

Word of the restaurant's success reached Hendersonville, North Carolina, a town of 30,000 about 20 miles away. The managing agent of a mall there—*the* mall there—even stopped by to recruit the partners. They made some audacious requests, asking him to spend $300,000 on renovations, including the addition of a patio and upgraded equipment. The agent agreed. With almost no market research, they opened the second McGuffey's in April 1985; the first, in Asheville, was still roaring, having broken the $2 million mark in sales its first year, with a marginal loss of just over $16,000.

By midsummer, the 200-seat Hendersonville restaurant was hauling in $35,000 a week. "Gee, you guys must be getting rich," the partners heard all around town. "When are you going to buy your own jets?" "Everyone was telling us we could do no wrong," says Dunn. The Asheville restaurant, though, was developing some problems. Right after the Hendersonville McGuffey's opened, sales at Asheville fell 15 percent. But the partners shrugged it off; some Asheville customers lived closer to Hendersonville, so one restaurant was probably pulling some of the other's customers. Either way, the customers were still there. "We're just spreading our market a little thinner," Dunn told his partners. When Asheville had lost another 10 percent and Hendersonville 5 percent, Dunn blamed the fact that the drinking age had been raised to 21 in Asheville, cutting into liquor sales.

By 1985 the company recorded nearly $3.5 million in sales, with nominal losses of about $95,000. But the adulation and the expectation of big money and fancy cars were beginning to cloud the real reason they had started the business. "McGuffey's was born purely out of frustration," says Dunn. Now, the frustration was gone. "You get pulled in so many directions that you just lose touch," says Laibson. "There are things that you simply forget."

What the partners forgot, in the warm flush of success, were their roots.

"Success breeds ego," says Dunn, "and ego breeds contempt." He would come back from trade shows or real-estate meetings all pumped up. "Isn't this exciting?" he'd ask an employee. "We're going to open a new restaurant next year." When the employee stared back blankly, Dunn felt resentful. "I didn't understand why they weren't thrilled," he says. He didn't see that while his world was constantly growing and expanding, his employees' world was sliding downhill. They were still busing tables or cooking burgers and thinking, "Forget the new restaurant; you haven't said hello to me in months; and by the way, why don't you fix the tea machine?"

"I just got too good, and too busy, to do orientation," he says. So he decided to tape orientation sessions for new employees, to make a film just like the one he had been subjected to when he worked at Bennigan's. On tape, Dunn told new employees one of his favorite stories, the one about the customer who walks into a chain restaurant and finds himself asking questions of a hostess sign because he can't find a human. The moral: "McGuffey's will never be so impersonal as to make people talk to a sign." A film maybe, but never a sign.

Since Dunn wasn't around the restaurants all that much, he didn't notice that employees were leaving in droves. Even the departure of Tom Valdez, the kitchen manager in Asheville, wasn't enough to take the shine off his "glowing ego," as he calls it.

Valdez had worked as Dunn's kitchen manager at TGI Friday's. When the Hendersonville McGuffey's was opening up, Dunn recruited him as kitchen manager. A few months later, Valdez marched into Dunn's office and announced that he was heading back to Indianapolis. "There's too much b.s. around here," he blurted out. "You don't care about your people." Dunn was shocked. "As soon as we get this next restaurant opened, we'll make things the way they used to be," he replied. But Valdez wouldn't budge. "Keith," he said bitterly, "you are turning out to be like all the other companies." Dunn shrugged. "We're a big company, and we've got to do big-company things," he replied.

Valdez walked out, slamming the door. Dunn still didn't understand that he had begun imitating the very companies that he had so loathed. He stopped wanting to rebel against them; under the intense pressure of growing a company, he just wanted to master their tried-and-true methods. "I was allowing the company to become like the companies we hated because I thought it was inevitable," he says.

Three months later, McGuffey's two top managers announced that they were moving to the West Coast to start their own company. Dunn beamed, "Our employees learn so much," he would boast, "that they are ready to start their own restaurants."

Before they left, Dunn sat down with them in the classroom at Hendersonville. "So," he asked casually, "how do you think we could run the place better?" Three hours later, he was still listening. "The McGuffey's we fell in love with just doesn't exist anymore," one of them concluded sadly.

Dunn was outraged. How could his employees be so ungrateful? Couldn't they see how everybody was sharing the success? Who had given them health insurance as soon as the partners could afford it? Who had given them dental insurance this year? And who—not that anyone would appreciate it—planned to set up profit sharing next year?

Sales at both restaurants were still dwindling. This time, there were no changes in the liquor laws or new restaurants to blame. With employees feeling ignored, resentful, and abandoned, the rest rooms didn't get scrubbed as thoroughly, the food didn't arrive quite as piping hot, the servers didn't smile so often. But the owners, wrapped up in themselves, couldn't see it. They were mystified. "It began to seem like what made our company great had somehow gotten lost," says Laibson.

Shaken by all the recent defections, Dunn needed a boost of confidence. So he sent out the one-page survey, which asked employees to rate the owners' performance. He was crushed by the results. Out of curiosity, Dunn later turned to an assistant and asked a favor. Can you calculate our turnover rate? Came the reply: "220 percent, sir."

Keith Dunn figured he would consult the management gurus through their books, tapes, and speeches. "You want people-oriented management?" he thought. "Fine. I'll give it to you."

Dunn and Laibson had spent a few months visiting 23 of the best restaurants in the Southeast. Driving for hours, they'd listen to tapes on management, stop them at key points, and ask, "Why don't we do something like this?" At night, they read management books, underlining significant passages, looking for answers.

"They were all saying that people is where it's at," says Dunn. "We've got to start thinking of our people as an asset," they decided. "And we've got to increase the value of that asset." Dunn was excited by the prospect of forming McGuffey's into the shape of a reverse pyramid, with employees on top. Keeping employees, he now knew, meant keeping employees involved.

He heard consultant Don Beveridge suggest that smart companies kept managers involved by tying their compensation to their performance. McGuffey's had been handing managers goals every quarter; if they hit half the goals, they pocketed half their bonus. Sound reasonable? No, preached Beveridge, you can't reward managers for a halfhearted job. It has to be all or nothing. "From now on," Dunn told his managers firmly, "there's no halfway."

Dunn also launched a contest for employees. Competition, he had read, was a good way of keeping employees motivated.

So the CUDA (Customer Undeniably Deserves Attention) contest was born. At Hendersonville and Asheville, he divided the employees into six teams. The winning team would win $1,000, based on talking to customers, keeping the restaurant clean, and collecting special tokens for extra work beyond the call of duty.

Employees came in every morning, donned their colors, and dug in for battle. Within a few weeks, two teams pulled out in front. Managers also seemed revitalized. To Dunn, it seemed like they would do anything, *anything*, to keep their food costs down, their sales up, their profit margins in line. This was just what Tom Peters, Kenneth Blanchard, Don Beveridge, Zig Ziglar, and the others had promised.

But after about six months, only one store's managers seemed capable of winning those all-or-nothing bonuses. At managers' meetings and reviews, Dunn started hearing grumblings. "How come your labor costs are so out of whack?" he'd ask. "Heck, I can't win the bonus anyway," a manager would answer, "so why try?" "Look, Keith," another would say, "I haven't seen a bonus in so long, I've forgotten what they look like." Some managers wanted the bonus so badly that they worked understaffed, didn't fix equipment, and ran short on supplies.

The CUDA contest deteriorated into jealousy and malaise. Three teams lagged far behind after the first month or so. Within those teams people were bickering and complaining all the time: "We can't win, so what's the use?" The contest, Dunn couldn't help but notice, seemed to be having a reverse effect than the one he had intended. "Some people were really killing themselves," he says. About 12, to be exact. The other 100-plus were utterly demoralized.

Dunn was angry. These were the same employees who, after all, had claimed he wasn't doing enough for them. But OK, he wanted to hear what they had to say. "Get feedback," Tom Peters preached; "find out what your employees think." Dunn announced that the owners would hold informal rap sessions once a month.

"This is your time to talk," Dunn told the employees who showed up—all three of them. That's how it was most times, with three to five employees in attendance, and the owners dragging others away from their jobs in the kitchen. Nothing was sinking in, and Dunn knew it.

Source: Hyatt, 1989.

Skill Application

Activities for Solving Problems Creatively

Suggested Assignments

1. Teach someone else how to solve problems creatively. Record your experience in your journal.

2. Think of a problem that is important to you right now for which there is no obvious solution. Use the principles and techniques discussed in the chapter to work out a creative solution to that problem. Spend the time it takes to do a good job, even if several days are required. Describe the experience in your journal.

3. Help direct a group (your family, roommates, social club, church, etc.) in a creative problem-solving exercise using techniques discussed in the chapter. Record your experience in your journal.

4. Write a letter to a congressional representative, dean, or CEO identifying several alternative solutions to some perplexing problem facing his or her organization, community, or state right now. Write about an issue that you care about. Be sure to offer suggested solutions. This will require that you apply in advance the principles of problem solving discussed in the chapter.

Application Plan and Evaluation

The intent of this exercise is to help you apply this cluster of skills in a real-life, out-of-class setting. Now that you have become familiar with the behavioral guidelines that form the basis of effective skill performance, you will improve most by trying out those guidelines in an everyday context. Unlike a classroom activity, in which feedback is immediate and others can assist you with their evaluations, this skill application activity is one you must accomplish and evaluate on your own. There are two parts to this activity. Part 1 helps prepare you to apply the skill. Part 2 helps you evaluate and improve on your experience. Be sure to write down answers to each item. Don't short-circuit the process by skipping steps.

Part 1. Planning

1. Write down the two or three aspects of this skill that are most important to you. These may be areas of weakness, areas you most want to improve, or areas that are most salient to a problem you face right now. Identify the specific aspects of this skill that you want to apply.

2. Now identify the setting or the situation in which you will apply this skill. Establish a plan for performance by actually writing down a description of the situation. Who else will be involved? When will you do it? Where will it be done?

    Circumstances:

    Who else?

    When?

    Where?

3. Identify the specific behaviors you will engage in to apply this skill. Operationalize your skill performance.

4. What are the indicators of successful performance? How will you know you have been effective? What will indicate you have performed competently?

Part 2. Evaluation

5. After you have completed your implementation, record the results. What happened? How successful were you? What was the effect on others?

6. How can you improve? What modifications can you make next time? What will you do differently in a similar situation in the future?

7. Looking back on your whole skill practice and application experience, what have you learned? What has been surprising? In what ways might this experience help you in the long term?

Interpersonal Skills

Chapter

Communicating Supportively

skill development

Skill Assessment

Diagnostic Surveys for Supportive Communication

Communicating Supportively

Step 1: Before you read the material in this chapter, please respond to the following statements by writing a number from the rating scale below in the left-hand column (Preassessment). Your answers should reflect your attitudes and behavior as they are now, not as you would like them to be. Be honest. This instrument is designed to help you discover your level of competency in communicating supportively so you can tailor your learning to your specific needs. When you have completed the survey, use the scoring key in Appendix I to identify the skill areas discussed in this chapter that are most important for you to master.

Step 2: After you have completed the reading and the exercises in this chapter and, ideally, as many as you can of the Skill Application assignments at the end of this chapter, cover up your first set of answers. Then respond to the same statements again, this time in the right-hand column (Postassessment). When you have completed the survey, use the scoring key in Appendix I to measure your progress. If your score remains low in specific skill areas, use the behavioral guidelines at the end of the Skill Learning section to guide further practice.

Rating Scale

1	Strongly disagree	4	Slightly agree
2	Disagree	5	Agree
3	Slightly disagree	6	Strongly agree

Assessment

Pre-　Post-　*In situations where I have to provide negative feedback or offer corrective advice:*

3 ____ 1. I understand clearly when it is appropriate to offer advice and direction to others and when it is not.

4 ____ 2. I help others recognize and define their own problems when I counsel them.

6 ____ 3. I am completely honest in the feedback that I give to others, even when it is negative.

4 ____ 4. I always give feedback that is focused on problems and solutions, not on personal characteristics.

4 ____ 5. I always link negative feedback to a standard or expectation that has been violated.

4 ____ 6. When I correct someone's behavior, our relationship is almost always strengthened.

5 ____ 7. I am descriptive in giving negative feedback to others. That is, I objectively describe events, their consequences, and my feelings about them.

4 ____ 8. I always suggest specific alternatives to those whose behavior I'm trying to correct.

3 _____ 9. I reinforce other people's sense of self-worth and self-esteem in my communication with them.

6 _____ 10. I convey genuine interest in the other person's point of view, even when I disagree with it.

5 _____ 11. I don't talk down to those who have less power or less information than I.

2 _____ 12. I convey a sense of flexibility and openness to new information when presenting my point of view, even when I feel strongly about it.

3 _____ 13. I strive to identify some area of agreement in a discussion with someone who has a different point of view.

5 _____ 14. My feedback is always specific and to the point, rather than general or vague.

3 _____ 15. I don't dominate conversations with others.

6 _____ 16. I take responsibility for my statements and point of view by saying, "I think" instead of "they think."

2 _____ 17. When discussing someone's problem, I usually respond with a reply that indicates understanding rather than advice.

3 _____ 18. When asking questions of others in order to understand their viewpoints better, I generally ask "what" questions instead of "why" questions.

4 _____ 19. I hold regular, private meetings with people I work with and live with.

3 _____ 20. I am clear about when I should coach someone and when I should provide counseling instead.

Communication Styles

This assessment instrument is divided into two parts.

In Part 1, four people complain about problems they face in their jobs. Following each complaint are five possible responses. Rank three of the responses you would be most likely to make, with 3 being your first choice, 2 being your second choice, and 1 being your third choice.

Part 2 of the assessment describes a particular situation. Several pairs of statements follow. Place a check mark next to the statement in each pair that you would mostly likely use in responding to that situation.

To score the Communication Styles instrument, turn to Appendix I to find the answer key and an interpretation of your scores.

Part 1

1. I've been in this job now for six months, and I hardly know anyone at all in the company. I just can't seem to make friends or to be accepted by other people. Most people are extremely busy and don't take time to socialize. I feel isolated and excluded from what's going on.

   _____ a. Don't be concerned about not making friends so soon. Things will get better the longer you're with the company, you'll see.

   _____ b. When you first meet people, what do you say? Are you the one to be friendly first?

_____ c. Because company employees are so busy, probably no one has time to get close socially. You shouldn't expect too much.

_____ d. So you're feeling that people haven't accepted you in the company?

_____ e. When I first joined the company it took me more than six months to get adjusted. I still don't know some of the people in several departments.

2. I can't stand my boss. He is the most autocratic, demanding person you can imagine. I've never worked around anyone who cared less for his employees than he does. His complete insensitivity and lack of humanity have made this a miserable place to work.

_____ a. You sound as if you're having difficulty dealing with rigid control and authority.

_____ b. I know how you feel because last year we had a woman in our department who would drive anybody crazy. She was the ultimate domineering boss.

_____ c. You're going to have problems unless you work this out. I think you should go to him and tell him how you feel.

_____ d. You really are having a hard time adjusting to your boss, aren't you?

_____ e. Why is it you feel so strongly about him?

3. What I want to know is, what happened on that last promotion decision? I thought I was in line for it. I'm sure no else in the department has my experience, and the scuttlebutt I heard indicated the job was mine for the asking. I'm really disappointed that you brought in someone from the outside over me. I don't think it's fair. What does it take to get promoted around here anyway?

_____ a. What was it that made you think this promotion was yours? Are you aware of the requirements of the job and what kind of person we were looking for?

_____ b. Don't be discouraged. Your work is good, and if you're patient I'm sure other chances will come along. I'll try to help you be ready the next time around.

_____ c. I think you have the wrong impression about this. The criteria were very clear for the new position, and the other person was just a better fit.

_____ d. In other words, you feel kind of puzzled about where you stand with the company.

_____ e. Are you interpreting this promotion decision as a challenge to your technical competence?

4. Hey, what's the idea of not approving my request for a new personal computer? I really need it in the office. We've got far more work to do than one machine can handle, and we're doing things manually that ought to be done on a spreadsheet. And don't give me that old story about tight company resources again. I've been in line for new equipment for a long time now.

_____ a. You sound really upset about not getting your request approved.

_____ b. Why do you need a new computer when you already have one? Can't you schedule work so that one system will handle your load? How about the possibility of borrowing one during the times you really feel the crunch?

_____ c. You know, several other offices are a lot worse off than yours is. Some of them don't have the trained personnel to operate the software. We're having a terrible time trying to get the necessary training accomplished for the existing machines.

_____ d. I know you're upset. But if you'll be patient, I'm sure I can work out a solution to your problem.

_____ e. I'm sorry, but it's true that resources are really tight. That's why we turned you down, so you're just going to have to make do.

Part 2

You are the manager of Carole Schulte, a 58-year-old supervisor who has been with the company for 21 years. She will retire at age 62, the first year she's eligible for a full pension. The trouble is, her performance is sliding, she is not inclined to go the extra mile by putting in extra time when required, and occasionally her work is even a little slipshod. Several line workers and customers have complained that she's treated them rather abruptly and without much sensitivity, even though superior customer service is a hallmark of your organization. She doesn't do anything bad enough to be fired, but she's just not performing up to levels you expect. Assume that you are having your monthly one-on-one meeting with her in your office. Which of the statements in each pair would you be most likely to use?

_____ 1. a. I've received complaints from some of your customers that you have not followed company standards in being responsive to their requests.

    b. You don't seem to be motivated to do a good job anymore, Carole.

_____ 2. a. I know that you've been doing a great job as supervisor, but there's just one small thing I want to raise with you about a customer complaint, probably not too serious.

    b. I have some concerns about several aspects of your performance on the job, and I'd like to discuss them with you.

_____ 3. a. When one of your subordinates called the other day to complain that you had criticized his work in public, I became concerned. I suggest that you sit down with that subordinate to work through any hard feelings that might still exist.

    b. You know, of course, that you're wrong to have criticized your subordinate's work in public. That's a sure way to create antagonism and lower morale.

_____ 4. a. I would like to see the following changes in your performance:

     _____ (1) (2) and (3).

    b. I have some ideas for helping you to improve; but first, what do you suggest?

_____ 5. a. I must tell you that I'm disappointed in your performance.

    b. Several of our employees seem to be unhappy with how you've been performing lately.

◼ Skill Learning

The Importance of Effective Communication

Surveys have consistently shown that the ability to communicate effectively is the characteristic judged by managers to be most critical in determining promotability (see surveys reported by Randle, 1956; Bowman, 1964; Steil, Barker, & Watson, 1983; Brownell, 1986; Brownell, 1990). Frequently, the quality of communication between managers and their employees is fairly low (Schnake, Dumler, Cochran, & Barnett, 1990). This ability may involve a broad array of activities, from writing to speech-making to body language. Whereas skill in each of these activities is important, for most managers it is face-to-face, one-on-one communication that dominates all the other types in predicting managerial success. In a study of 88 organizations, both profit and nonprofit, Crocker (1978) found that, of 31 skills assessed, interpersonal communication skills, including listening, were rated as the most important. Thorton (1966, p. 237) summarized a variety of survey results by stating, "A manager's number-one problem can be summed up in one word: communication."

At least 80 percent of a manager's waking hours are spent in verbal communication, so it is not surprising that serious attention has been given to a plethora of procedures to improve interpersonal communication. Scholars and researchers have written extensively on communicology, semantics, rhetoric, linguistics, cybernetics, syntactics, pragmatics, proxemics, and canalization; and library shelves are filled with books on the physics of the communication process—encoding, decoding, transmission, media, perception, reception, and noise. Similarly, volumes are available on effective public-speaking techniques, making formal presentations, and the processes of organizational communication. Most colleges and universities have academic departments dedicated to the field of speech communication; most business schools provide a business communication curriculum; and many organizations have public communication departments and intra-organizational communication specialists such as newsletter editors and speech writers.

Even with all this available information about the communication process and the dedicated resources in many organizations for fostering better communication, most managers still indicate that poor communication is their biggest problem (Schnake, Dumler, Cochran, & Barnett, 1990). In a study of major manufacturing organizations undergoing large-scale changes, Cameron (1988) asked two key questions: (1) What is your major problem in trying to get organizational changes implemented? and (2) What is the key factor that explains your past success in effectively managing organizational change? To both questions, a large majority of managers gave the same answer: communication. All of them agreed that more communication is better than less communication. Most thought that overcommunicating with employees was more a virtue than a vice. It would seem surprising, then, that in light of this agreement by managers about the importance of communication, communication remains a major problem for managers. Why might this be?

One reason is that most individuals feel that they are very effective communicators. They feel that communication problems are a product of others' weaknesses, not their own (Brownell, 1990; Golen, 1990). Haney (1979, p. 219) reported on a survey of over 8,000 people in universities, businesses, military units, government agencies, and hospitals in which "virtually everyone felt that he or she was communicating at least as well as and, in many cases, better than almost everyone else in the organization. Most people readily admit that their organization is fraught with faulty communication, but it is almost always 'those other people' who are responsible." Thus, while most agree that proficiency in interpersonal communication is critical to managerial success, most individuals don't seem to feel a strong need to improve their own skill level.

Focus on Accuracy

Much of the writing on interpersonal communication focuses on the *accuracy* of the information being communicated. The emphasis is generally on making certain that messages are transmitted and received with little alteration or variation from original intent. The communication skill of most concern is the ability to transmit clear, precise messages. The following incidents illustrate problems that result from inaccurate communication:

A motorist was driving on the Merritt Parkway outside New York City when his engine stalled. He quickly determined that his battery was dead and managed to stop another driver who consented to push his car to get it started.

"My car has an automatic transmission," he explained, "so you'll have to get up to 30 or 35 miles an hour to get me started."

The second motorist nodded and walked back to his own car. The first motorist climbed back into his car and waited for the good Samaritan to pull up behind him. He waited—and waited. Finally, he turned around to see what was wrong.

There was the good Samaritan—coming up behind his car at about 35 miles an hour!

The damage amounted to $3,800 (Haney, 1979, p. 285).

A woman of 35 came in one day to tell me that she wanted a baby but had been told that she had a certain type of heart disease that, while it might not interfere with a normal life, would be dangerous if she ever had a baby. From her description, I thought at once of mitral stenosis. This condition is characterized by a rather distinctive rumbling murmur near the apex of the heart and especially by a peculiar vibration felt by the examining finger on the patient's chest. The vibration is known as the "thrill" of mitral stenosis.

When this woman had undressed and was lying on my table in her white kimono, my stethoscope quickly found the heart sounds I had expected. Dictating to my nurse, I described them carefully. I put my stethoscope aside and felt intently for the typical vibration which may be found in a small and variable area of the left chest.

I closed my eyes for better concentration and felt long and carefully for the tremor. I did not find it, and with my hand still on the woman's bare breast, lifting it upward and out of the way, I finally turned to the nurse and said: "No thrill."

The patient's black eyes snapped, and with venom in her voice, she said, "Well, isn't that just too bad! Perhaps it's just as well you don't get one. That isn't what I came for."

My nurse almost choked, and my explanation still seems a nightmare of futile words (Loomis, 1939, p. 47).

Because in England a billion is a million million, whereas in the United States and Canada a billion is a thousand million, it is easy to see how misunderstanding can occur regarding financial performance. Similarly, in an American meeting, if you "table" a subject, you postpone its discussion. In a British meeting, to "table" a topic means to discuss it now.

A Confucian proverb states: "Those who speak do not know. Those who know do not speak." It is not difficult to understand why Americans are often viewed as brash and unsophisticated in Asian cultures. A common problem for American business executives has been to announce, upon their return home, that a business deal has been struck, only to discover that no agreement was made at all. Usually it is because Americans assume that when their Japanese colleagues say "hai," the Japanese word for "yes," it means agreement. To the Japanese, it often means "Yes, I am trying to understand you (but I may not necessarily agree with you)."

When accuracy is the primary consideration, attempts to improve communication generally center on improving the mechanics: transmitters and receivers, encoding and decoding, sources and destinations, and noise.

Fortunately, much progress has been made recently in improving the transmission of accurate messages—that is, in improving their clarity and precision. Primarily through the development of a sophisticated information-based technology, major strides have been taken to enhance communication speed and accuracy in organizations. Computer networks with multimedia capabilities now enable members of an organization to transmit messages, documents, video images, and sound almost anywhere in the world. The technology that enables modern companies to share, store, and retrieve information has dramatically changed the nature of business in just a decade. Customers and employees routinely expect information technology to function smoothly and the information it manages to be reliable. Sound decisions and competitive advantage depend on such accuracy.

However, comparable progress has not occurred in the interpersonal aspects of communication. People still become offended at one another, make insulting statements, and communicate clumsily. The interpersonal aspects of communication involve the nature of the relationship between the communicators. Who says what to whom, what is said, why it is said, and how it is said all have an effect on the relationships between people. This has important implications for the effectiveness of the communication, aside from the accuracy of the statement. A statement Josiah Stamp made over 80 years ago illustrates this point.

> The government are very keen on amassing statistics. They collect them, add them, raise them to the nth power, take the cube root and prepare wonderful diagrams. But you must never forget that every one of these figures come in the first instance from the village watchman, who just puts down what he damn pleases.

Similarly, irrespective of the availability of sophisticated information technologies and elaborately developed models of communication processes, individuals still communicate pretty much as they please—often in abrasive, insensitive, and unproductive ways. More often than not, it is the interpersonal aspect of communication that stands in the way of effective message delivery rather than the inability to deliver accurate information (Golen, 1990).

Ineffective communication may lead individuals to dislike each other, be offended by each other, lose confidence in each other, refuse to listen to each other, and disagree with each other, as well as cause a host of other interpersonal problems. These interpersonal problems, in turn, generally lead to restricted communication flow, inaccurate messages, and misinterpretations of meanings. Figure 1 summarizes this process.

To illustrate, consider the following situation. Cal is introducing his new goal-setting program to the organization as a way to overcome some productivity problems. After Cal's carefully prepared presentation in the management council meeting, Jedd raises his hand. "In my opinion, this is a naive approach to solving our productivity issues. The considerations are much more complex than Cal seems to realize. I don't think we should waste our time by pursuing this plan any further." Jedd's opinion may be justified, but the manner in which he delivers the message will probably eliminate any hope of its being dealt with objectively. Instead, Cal will probably hear a message such as, "You're naive," "You're stupid," or "You're incompetent." We wouldn't be surprised if Cal's response were defensive or even hostile. Any good feelings between the two have probably been jeopardized, and their communication will probably be reduced to self-image protection. The merits of the proposal will be smothered by personal defensiveness. Future communication between the two will probably be minimal.

What Is Supportive Communication?

In this chapter, we focus on a kind of interpersonal communication that helps managers communicate accurately and honestly without jeopardizing interpersonal relationships—namely, **supportive communication.** Supportive communication is communication that seeks to preserve a positive relationship between the communicators while still addressing the problem at hand. Supportive communication has eight attributes, which

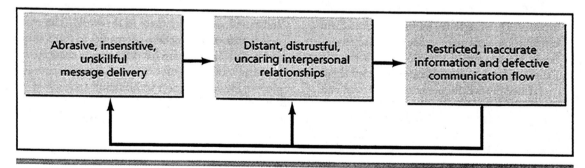

Figure 1 Relationships Between Unskillful Communication and Interpersonal Relationships

are summarized in Table 1. Later in the chapter we expand on each attribute. When supportive communication is used, not only is a message delivered accurately, but the relationship between the two communicating parties is supported, even enhanced, by the interchange. Positive interpersonal relationships result. The goal of supportive communication is not merely to be liked by other people or to be judged to be a nice person, however. Nor is it used merely to produce social acceptance. As pointed out in the introductory chapter, positive interpersonal relationships have practical, instrumental value in organizations. Researchers have found, for example, that organizations fostering these kinds of relationships enjoy higher productivity, faster problem solving, higher-quality outputs, and fewer conflicts and subversive activities than do groups and organizations where relationships are less positive. Moreover, deliver-

ing outstanding customer service is almost impossible without supportive communication. Customer complaints and misunderstandings frequently require supportive communication skills to resolve. Not only must managers be competent in using this kind of communication, therefore, but they must help their subordinates develop this competency as well.

One important lesson that American managers have been taught by foreign competitors is that good relationships among employees, and between managers and employees, produce bottom-line advantages (Ouchi, 1981; Peters, 1988). Hanson (1986) found, for example, that the presence of good interpersonal relationships between managers and subordinates was three times more powerful in predicting profitability in 40 major corporations over a five-year period than the four next most powerful variables—market share,

---

1. **Problem-Oriented, Not Person-Oriented**
"How can we solve this problem?"

Not "Because of you there is a problem."

2. **Congruent, Not Incongruent**
"Your behavior really upset me."

Not "Do I seem upset? No, everything's fine."

3. **Descriptive, Not Evaluative**
"Here is what happened; here is my reaction; here is what I suggest that would be more acceptable to me."

Not "You are wrong for doing what you did."

4. **Validating, Not Invalidating**
"I have some ideas, but do you have any suggestions?"

Not "You wouldn't understand, so we'll do it my way."

5. **Specific, Not Global**
"You interrupted me three times during the meeting."

Not "You're always trying to get attention."

6. **Conjunctive, Not Disjunctive**
"Relating to what you just said, I'd like to discuss this."

Not "I want to discuss this (regardless of what you want to discuss)."

7. **Owned, Not Disowned**
"I've decided to turn down your request because . . ."

Not "You have a pretty good idea, but they just wouldn't approve it."

8. **Supportive Listening, Not One-Way Listening**
"What do you think are the obstacles standing in the way of improvement?"

Not "As I said before, you make too many mistakes. You're just not doing the job."

Table 1   Eight Attributes of Supportive Communication

capital intensity, firm size, and sales growth rate—combined. Supportive communication, therefore, isn't just a "nice-person technique," but a proven competitive advantage for both managers and organizations.

Coaching and Counseling

The principles of supportive communication discussed in this chapter are best understood and most useful when they are applied to the interpersonal communication tasks commonly rated as the most challenging by managers: coaching and counseling subordinates (Ross, 1986). In coaching, managers pass along advice and information or set standards to help subordinates improve their work skills. In counseling, managers help subordinates recognize and address problems involving their state of mind, emotions, or personalities. Thus, coaching focuses on abilities, counseling on attitudes.

The chapter on Motivating Employees provides tools for analyzing and addressing employees' problems in ability and attitude. The current chapter focuses on the communication model and skills that will help you discuss problems with employees and set the stage to resolve them cooperatively. Thus, for example, when you study the six elements of an integrative motivation program in the chapter on Motivating Employees (see Table 1 in that chapter), the coaching and counseling models should be integral to considering how you would implement such a program.

The skills of coaching and counseling also apply to a broader array of activities, of course, such as handling customer complaints, passing critical or negative information upward, handling conflicts between other parties, negotiating for a certain position, and so on. However, coaching and counseling are almost universal managerial activities, and we will use them to illustrate and explain the behavioral principles involved.

Skillful coaching and counseling are especially important in (1) rewarding positive performance and (2) correcting problem behaviors or attitudes. Both of these activities are discussed in more detail in the chapter on Motivating Others. But in that chapter, we discuss the *content* of rewarding and correcting behavior (i.e., *what* to do), whereas in our present discussion we shall focus on the *processes* used by effective managers to coach and counsel employees (i.e., *how* to do it). Coaching and counseling are more difficult to perform effectively when employees are not performing up to expectations, when their attitudes are negative, when their behavior is disruptive, or when their personalities clash with others in the organization. Whenever managers have to help subordinates change their attitudes or behaviors, coaching or counseling is required. In these situations, managers face the responsibility of providing negative feedback to subordinates or getting them to recognize problems that they don't want to acknowledge. Managers must criticize and correct subordinates, but in a way that facilitates positive work outcomes, positive feelings, and positive relationships.

What makes coaching and counseling so challenging is the risk of offending or alienating subordinates. That risk is so high that many managers ignore completely the feelings and reactions of employees by taking a directive, hard-nosed, "shape up or ship out" approach to correcting behavior or attitudes. Or they soft-pedal, avoiding confrontations for fear of hurting feelings and destroying relationships—the "don't worry be happy" approach. The principles we describe in this chapter not only facilitate accurate message delivery in sensitive situations, but their effective use can produce higher levels of motivation, increased productivity, and better interpersonal relationships.

Of course, coaching and counseling skills are also required when negative feedback is not involved, such as when subordinates ask for advice, need someone to listen to their problems, or want to register complaints. Sometimes just listening is the most effective form of coaching or counseling. Although the risk of damaged relationships, defensiveness, or hurt feelings is not as likely as when negative feedback is given, these situations still require competent communication skills. Guidelines for how to implement supportive communication effectively in both negative and positive coaching and counseling situations are discussed in the rest of this chapter.

Consider the two following scenarios:

Tom Nielson is the manager of the division sales force in your firm, which makes and sells components for the aerospace industry. He reports directly to you. Tom's division consistently misses its sales projections, its revenues per salesperson are below the firm average, and Tom's monthly reports are almost always late. You make another appointment to visit with Tom after getting the latest sales figures, but he isn't in his office when you arrive. His secretary tells you that one of Tom's sales managers dropped by a few minutes ago to complain that some employees are coming in late for work in the morning and taking extra-long coffee breaks. Tom had immediately gone with the manager to his sales department to give the salespeople a "pep talk" and to remind them of performance expectations. You wait for 15 minutes until he returns.

Betsy Christensen has an MBA from a prestigious Big Ten school and has recently joined your firm in the financial planning group. She came with great recommendations and credentials. However, she seems to be trying to enhance her own reputation at the expense of others in her group. You have heard increasing complaints lately that Betsy acts arrogant, is self-promotional, and is openly critical of other group members' work. In your first conversation with her about her performance in the group, she denied that there is a problem. She said that, if anything, she was having a positive impact on the group by raising its standards. You schedule another meeting with Betsy after this latest set of complaints from her coworkers.

What are the basic problems in these two cases? How would you approach them so that the problems got solved and, at the same time, your relationships with your subordinates were strengthened? What would you say, and how would you say it, so that the best possible outcomes result? This chapter can help you improve your skill in handling such situations effectively.

Coaching and Counseling Problems

The two cases above help identify the two basic kinds of interpersonal communication problems faced by managers. In the case with Tom Nielson, the basic need is for **coaching.** Coaching situations are those in which managers must pass along advice and information or set standards for subordinates. Subordinates must be advised on how to do their jobs better and to be coached to better performance. Coaching problems are usually caused by lack of ability, insufficient information or understanding, or incompetence on the part of subordinates. In these cases, the accuracy of the information passed along by managers is important. The

subordinate must understand clearly what the problem is and how to overcome it.

In the Tom Nielson case, Tom was accepting upward delegation from his subordinates, and he was not allowing them to solve their own problems. In the chapter on Managing Stress, we learned that upward delegation is one of the major causes of ineffective time management. By not insisting that his subordinates bring recommendations for solutions to him instead of problems, and by intervening directly in the problems of his subordinate's subordinates, Tom became overloaded himself. He didn't allow his subordinates to do their jobs. Productivity almost always suffers in cases where one person is trying to resolve all the problems and run the whole show. Tom needs to be coached regarding how to avoid upward delegation and how to delegate responsibility as well as authority effectively. In the chapter on Motivating Employees, the section Diagnosing Work Performance Problems gives more specific guidelines for diagnosing the reasons for poor performance. Such diagnosis can then help guide the manager in coaching a subordinate.

The Betsy Christensen case illustrates a **counseling** problem. Managers need to counsel subordinates instead of coach them when the problem stems from attitudes, personality clashes, defensiveness, or other factors tied to emotions. Betsy's competency or skill is not a problem, but her unwillingness to recognize that a problem exists or that a change is needed on her part requires counseling by the manager. Betsy is highly qualified for her position, so coaching or giving advice would not be a useful approach. Instead, an important goal of counseling is to help Betsy recognize that a problem exists and to identify ways in which that problem might be addressed. Coaching applies to ability problems, and the manager's approach is, "I can help you do this better." Counseling applies to attitude problems, and the manager's approach is, "I can help you recognize that a problem exists."

Although many problems involve both coaching and counseling, it is important to recognize the difference between these two types of problems because a mismatch of problem with communication approach can aggravate, rather than resolve, a problem. Giving direction or advice (coaching) in a counseling situation often increases defensiveness or resistance to change. For example, advising Betsy Christensen about how to do her job or about the things she should not be doing (such as criticizing others' work) will probably only magnify her defensiveness because she doesn't perceive that she has a problem. Similarly, counseling in a situation that calls for coaching simply side-steps the problem and doesn't resolve it. Tom Nielson knows that a problem exists, for example, but he doesn't know how to resolve it. Coaching, not problem recognition, is needed.

The question that remains, however, is, "How do I effectively coach or counsel another person? What behavioral guidelines help me perform effectively in these situations?" Both coaching and counseling rely on the same set of key supportive communication principles summarized in Table 1, which we'll now examine more closely.

Defensiveness and Disconfirmation

If principles of supportive communication are not followed when coaching or counseling subordinates, two major obstacles result that lead to a variety of negative outcomes (Gibb, 1961; Sieburg, 1978; Brownell, 1986; Steil et al., 1983). These two obstacles are defensiveness and disconfirmation (see in Table 2).

Defensiveness is an emotional and physical state in which one is agitated, estranged, confused, and inclined to strike out (Gordon, 1988). Defensiveness arises when one of the parties feels threatened or punished by the communication. For that person, self-protection becomes more important than listening, so defensiveness blocks both the message and the interpersonal relationship. Clearly a manager's coaching or counseling will not be effective if it creates defensiveness in the other party. But defensive thinking may be pervasive and entrenched within an organization. Overcoming it calls for awareness by managers of their own defensiveness and vigorous efforts to apply the principles of supportive communication described in this chapter (Argyris, 1991).

The second obstacle, **disconfirmation,** occurs when one of the communicating parties feels put down, ineffectual, or insignificant because of the communication. Recipients of the communication feel that their self-worth is being questioned, so they focus more on building themselves up rather than listening. Reactions are often self-aggrandizing or show-off behaviors, loss of motivation, withdrawal, and loss of respect for the offending communicator.

The eight attributes of supportive communication, which we'll explain and illustrate in the following

Supportive communication engenders feelings of support, understanding, and helpfulness. It helps overcome the two main obstacles resulting from poor interpersonal communication:

Defensiveness
- One individual feels threatened or attacked as a result of the communication.
- Self-protection becomes paramount.
- Energy is spent on constructing a defense rather than on listening.
- Aggression, anger, competitiveness, and avoidance are common reactions.

Disconfirmation
- One individual feels incompetent, unworthy, or insignificant as a result of the communication.
- Attempts to reestablish self-worth take precedence.
- Energy is spent trying to portray self-importance rather than on listening.
- Showing off, self-centered behavior, withdrawal, and loss of motivation are common reactions.

Table 2   Two Major Obstacles to Effective Interpersonal Communication

pages, serve as behavioral guidelines for overcoming defensiveness and disconfirmation. Competent coaching and counseling depend on knowing and practicing these guidelines. They also depend on maintaining a balance among the guidelines, as we'll illustrate.

Principles of Supportive Communication

1. Supportive communication is problem-oriented, not person-oriented.
Problem-oriented communication focuses on problems and solutions rather than on personal traits. Person-oriented communication focuses on the characteristics of the individual, not the event. Problem-oriented communication is useful even when personal appraisals are called for because it focuses on behaviors and events, whereas person-oriented communication can send the message that the individual is inadequate.

Statements such as "You are dictatorial" and "You are insensitive" describe the person, while "I am not involved in decisions" and "We don't seem to see things the same way" describe problems. Imputing motives is person oriented ("It's because you want to control other people"), whereas describing overt behaviors is problem oriented ("You made several sarcastic comments in the meeting today").

One problem with person-oriented communication is that, while most people can change their behavior, few can change their basic personalities. Because nothing can generally be done to accommodate person-oriented communication, it leads to a deterioration in the relationship rather than to problem solving. Person-oriented messages often try to persuade the other individual that "this is how you should feel" or "this is what kind of person you are" (e.g., "You are an incompetent manager, a lazy worker, or an insensitive office mate"). But since most individuals accept themselves, their common reaction to person-oriented communication is to defend themselves against it or reject it outright. Even when communication is positive (e.g., "You are a wonderful person"), it may not be viewed as trustworthy if it is not tied to a behavior or an accomplishment. The absence of a meaningful referent is the key weakness in person-oriented communication.

In coaching and counseling, problem-oriented communication should also be linked to accepted standards or expectations rather than to personal opinions. Personal opinions are more likely to be interpreted as person-oriented and arouse defensiveness than statements in which the behavior is compared to an accepted standard. For example, the statement "I don't like the way you dress" is an expression of a personal opinion and will probably create resistance, especially if the listener does not feel that the communicator's opinions are any more legitimate than his or her own. On the other hand, "Your dress is not in keeping with the company dress code," or "Everyone is expected to wear a tie to work," are comparisons to external standards that have some legitimacy. Feelings of defensiveness are less likely to arise since the problem, not the person, is being addressed. In addition, other people are more likely to support a statement based on a common standard.

Effective supportive communicators need not avoid expressing personal opinions or feelings about the behavior or attitudes of others. But when doing so, they should keep in mind the following additional principles.

2. Supportive communication is based on congruence, not incongruence.

Rogers (1961), Dyer (1972), and Schnake et al. (1990) argue that the best interpersonal communications, and the best relationships, are based on **congruence,** that is, exactly matching the communication, verbally and non-verbally, to what an individual is thinking and feeling.

Two kinds of **incongruence** are possible: One is a mismatch between what one is experiencing and what one is aware of. For example, an individual may not even be aware that he or she is experiencing anger toward another person, even though the anger is really present. Therapists must frequently help individuals reach greater congruence between experience and awareness. A second kind of incongruence, and the one more closely related to supportive communication, is a mismatch between what one feels and what one communicates. For example, an individual may be aware of a feeling of anger but deny having that feeling.

When coaching and counseling subordinates, genuine, honest statements are always better than artificial or dishonest statements. Managers who hold back their true feelings or opinions, or who don't express what's really on their minds, create the impression that a hidden agenda exists. Subordinates sense that there is something else not being said. Therefore, they trust the communicator less and focus on trying to figure out what the hidden message is, not on listening or trying to improve. The chapter on Managing Stress discussed Covey's (1989) "emotional bank account" and the importance of mutual trust and respect in establishing collaborative relationships. Communication cannot be genuinely supportive unless it is based on trust and respect and is also *perceived* as trusting and respectful. Otherwise, false impressions and miscommunication result.

Rogers (1961, pp. 344–345) suggests that congruence in communication lies at the heart of a general law of interpersonal relationships.

The greater the congruence of experience, awareness, and communication on the part of one individual, the more the ensuing relationship will involve a tendency toward reciprocal communication with increasing congruence; a tendency toward more mutually accurate understanding of the communications; improved psychological adjustment and functioning in both parties; mutual satisfaction in the relationship.

Conversely, the greater the communicated incongruence of experience and awareness, the more the ensuing relationship will involve further communication with the same quality; disintegration of accurate understanding; less adequate psychological adjustment and functioning in both parties; mutual dissatisfaction in the relationship.

Congruence also relates to matching the content of your words to your manner and tone of voice. "What a nice day" can mean the opposite if muttered sarcastically. "I'm only concerned for your welfare" can mean the opposite if said without sincerity, especially if the history of the relationship suggests otherwise.

Striving for congruence, of course, does not mean that one should blow off steam immediately upon getting upset, nor does it mean that one cannot repress certain inappropriate feelings (e.g., anger, disappointment, aggression). Other principles of supportive communication must also be practiced, and achieving congruence at the expense of all other consideration is not productive. On the other hand, in problematic interactions, when reactive feedback must be given, individuals are more likely to express too little congruence than too much. This is because many people are afraid to respond in a completely honest way or are not sure how to communicate congruently without being offensive. Saying exactly what one feels can sometimes offend the other person.

Consider the problem of a subordinate who is not performing up to expectations and displays a nonchalant attitude when given hints that the division's rating is being negatively affected. What could the superior say that would strengthen the relationship with the subordinate and still resolve the problem? How can one express honest feelings and opinions and still remain problem-focused, not person-focused? How can one be completely honest without offending another person? Other principles of supportive communication provide some guidelines.

3. Supportive communication is descriptive, not evaluative.

Evaluative communication makes a judgment or places a label on other individuals or on their behavior: "You are doing it wrong," "You are incompetent." Such evaluation generally makes the other person feel under attack and respond defensively. Probable responses are, "I'm not doing it wrong," or "I am as competent as you are." Arguments, bad feelings, and a weakening of the interpersonal relationship result.

The tendency to evaluate others is strongest when the issue is emotionally charged or when a person feels personally threatened. Sometimes people try to resolve their own bad feelings or anxieties by placing a label on others: "You are bad" implies "I am good. Therefore, I feel better." They may have such strong feelings that they want to punish the other person for violating their expectations or standards: "What you've done deserves to be punished. You deserve what's coming to you."

The problem with evaluative communication is that it is likely to be self-perpetuating. Placing a label on another generally leads that person to place a label on *you*, which makes you defensive in return. The accuracy of the communication and quality of the relationship deteriorate. Arguments ensue.

An alternative to evaluation is **descriptive communication**. Because it is difficult to avoid evaluating other people without some alternative strategy, descriptive communication reduces the tendency to evaluate and perpetuate a defensive interaction. Descriptive communication involves three steps, summarized in Table 3.

First, *describe objectively the event that occurred or the behavior that needs to be modified*. This description should identify elements of the behavior that could be confirmed by another person. Behavior, as mentioned before, should be compared to accepted standards rather than to personal opinions or preferences. Subjective impressions or attributions to the motives of another person should be avoided. The description "You have finished fewer projects this month than anyone else in the division" can be confirmed by an objective record. It relates strictly to the behavior and to an objective standard, not to the motives or personal characteristics of the subordinate. There is less likelihood of the subordinate's feeling unfairly treated, since no evaluative label is placed on the behavior or the person. Describing a behavior, as opposed to evaluating a behavior, is relatively neutral, as long as the manager's manner is congruent with the message.

Second, *describe reactions to the behavior or its consequences*. Rather than projecting onto another person the cause of the problem, focus on the reactions or consequences the behavior has produced. This requires that communicators be aware of their own reactions and able

Step 1: Describe objectively the event, behavior, or circumstance.
- Avoid accusations.
- Present data or evidence.

Example: Three clients have complained to me this month that you have not responded to their requests.

Step 2: Focus on the behavior and your reaction, not on the other person's attributes.
- Describe your reactions and feelings.
- Describe the objective consequences that have resulted or will result.

Example: I'm worried because each client has threatened to go elsewhere if we aren't more responsive.

Step 3: Focus on solutions.
- Avoid discussing who's right or wrong.
- Suggest an acceptable alternative.
- Be open to other alternatives.

Example: We need both to win back their confidence and to show them you are responsive. For example, you could do a free analysis of their systems.

Table 3 Descriptive Communication

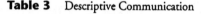

to describe them. Using one-word descriptions for feelings is often the best method: "I'm *concerned* about our productivity." "Your level of accomplishment *frustrates* me." Similarly, the consequences of the behavior can be pointed out: "Profits are off this month," "Department quality ratings are down," or "Two customers have called in to express dissatisfaction." Describing feelings or consequences also lessens the likelihood of defensiveness since the problem is framed in the context of the communicator's feelings or objective consequences, not the attributes of the subordinate. If those feelings or consequences are described in a non-accusing way, the major energies of the communicators can be focused on problem solving rather than on defending against evaluations.

Third, *suggest a more acceptable alternative.* This helps the other person save face (Goffman, 1955) and feel valued (Sieburg, 1978) by separating the individual from the behavior. The self-esteem of the person is preserved; it is just the behavior that should be modified. Care should be taken not to give the message, "I don't like the way things are, so what are you going to do about it?" The change need not be the responsibility of only one of the communicating parties. Rather, the emphasis should be on finding a solution that is acceptable to both, not on deciding who is right and who is wrong or who should change and who shouldn't: "I'd like to suggest that we meet regularly to help you complete six more projects than last month," or "I would like to help you identify the things that are standing in the way of higher performance."

One concern that is sometimes expressed regarding descriptive communication is that these steps may not work unless the other person knows the rules, too. For example, the other person might say, "I don't care how you feel," or "I have an excuse for what happened, so it's not my fault," or "It's too bad if this annoys you. I'm not going to change." Any such lack of concern or a defensive stance now becomes the priority problem, because the problem of low performance will be very difficult to address as long as the more important interpersonal problem between the manager and the subordinate is blocking progress. In effect, the focus has shifted from coaching to counseling, from focusing on ability to focusing on attitude. If the manager and the subordinate cannot work on the problem together, no amount of communication about the consequences of poor performance will be productive. Instead, the focus of the communication should be shifted to the obstacles that inhibit working together to improve performance. Staying focused on the problem, remaining congruent, and using descriptive language become critical.

Effective managers do not abandon the three steps. They simply switch the focus. They might respond, "I'm surprised to hear you say that you don't care how I feel about this problem (step 1). Your response concerns me, and I think it might have important implications for the productivity of our team (step 2). I suggest we spend some time trying to identify the obstacles you feel might be inhibiting our ability to work together on this problem (step 3)."

It has been our experience that few individuals are completely recalcitrant about wanting to improve, and few are completely unwilling to work on problem solving when they believe that the communicator has their interests at heart. A common criticism of American managers, however, is that compared to their Asian competitors, many do not believe in these assumptions. They do not accept the fact that employees are "doing the best that they can" and that "people are motivated by opportunities for improvement." These are core Theory Y assumptions (McGregor, 1960), as opposed to Theory X assumptions such as "employees are to be mistrusted" and "it takes a sharp stick to motivate change." In our experience, however, most people want to do better, to perform successfully, and to be contributors. When managers use supportive communication principles not as manipulative devices but as genuine techniques to foster development and improvement, we have seldom found that people will not accept these genuine, congruent expressions.

It is important to keep in mind, however, that the steps of descriptive communication do not imply that one person should do all the changing. Frequently a middle ground must be reached on which both individuals are satisfied (e.g., one person becomes more tolerant of deliberate work, and the other person becomes more conscious of trying to work faster).

It is important to follow up coaching and counseling sessions with monitoring discussions. A subordinate's performance problems, for example, may stem from poor work habits developed over time. Such habits are not likely to change abruptly even if the coaching sessions goes especially well. If the subordinate doesn't show reasonable improvement, in subsequent coaching discussions the manager may need to be more directive.

When it is necessary to make evaluative statements, the evaluations should be made in terms of some established criteria (e.g., "Your behavior does not meet the prescribed standard"), probable outcomes (e.g., "Continuation of your behavior will lead to worse consequences"), or less appropriate behavior by the same individual (e.g., "This behavior is not as good as your past behavior"). The important point is to avoid disconfirming the other person or arousing defensiveness.

4. Supportive communication validates rather than invalidates individuals.

Communication can be destructive. Barnlund (1968, p. 618) observed:

> People do not take time, do not listen, do not try to understand, but interrupt, anticipate, criticize, or disregard what is said; in their own remarks they are frequently vague, inconsistent,

verbose, insincere, or dogmatic. As a result, people often conclude conversations feeling more inadequate, more misunderstood, and more alienated than when they started.

Validating communication helps people feel recognized, understood, accepted, and valued. Communication that is invalidating arouses negative feelings about self-worth, identity, and relatedness to others. It denies the presence, uniqueness, or importance of other individuals (Sieburg, 1978). Especially important are communications that invalidate people by conveying superiority, rigidity, indifference, and imperviousness (Sieburg, 1978; Galbraith, 1975; Gibb, 1961; Brownell, 1986; Steil et al., 1983).

Communication that is **superiority oriented** gives the impression that the communicator is informed while others are ignorant, adequate while others are inadequate, competent while others are incompetent, or powerful while others are impotent. It creates a barrier between the communicator and those to whom the message is sent.

Superiority-oriented communication can take the form of put-downs, in which others are made to look bad so that the communicator looks good. Or it can take the form of "one-upmanship," in which the communicator tries to elevate himself or herself in the esteem of others. One form of one-upmanship is withholding information, either boastfully ("If you knew what I knew, you would feel differently") or coyly to trip people up ("If you had asked me, I could have told you the executive committee would disapprove of your proposal"). Another common form of superiority-oriented communication is the use of jargon, acronyms, or words used in such a way as to exclude others or to create barriers in a relationship. Doctors, lawyers, government employees, and many other professionals are well known for their use of jargon or acronyms to exclude others or to elevate themselves rather than to clarify a message. Speaking a foreign language in the presence of individuals who don't understand it may also be done to create the impression of superiority. In most circumstances, using words or language that a listener can't understand is bad manners because it invalidates the other person.

Rigidity in communication is the second major type of invalidation: The communication is portrayed as absolute, unequivocal, or unquestionable. No other opinion or point of view could possibly be considered.

Individuals who communicate in dogmatic, "know-it-all" ways often do so in order to minimize others' contributions or to invalidate others' perspectives. It is possible to communicate rigidity, however, in ways other than just being dogmatic. Rigidity is also communicated by:

▶ Reinterpreting all other viewpoints to conform to one's own.

▶ Never saying, "I don't know," but having an answer for everything.

▶ Appearing unwilling to tolerate criticisms or alternative points of view.

▶ Reducing complex issues to simplistic definitions or generalizations.

▶ Placing exclamation points after statements so the impression is created that the statement is final, complete, or unqualified.

Indifference is communicated when the other person's existence or importance is not acknowledged. A person may do this by using silence, by making no verbal response to the other's statements, by avoiding eye contact or any facial expression, by interrupting the other person frequently, by using impersonal words ("one should not" instead of "you should not"), or by engaging in unrelated activity during a conversation. The communicator appears not to care about the other person and gives the impression of being impervious to the other person's feelings or perspectives.

Imperviousness (Sieburg, 1978) means that the communicator does not acknowledge the feelings or opinions of the other person. They are either labeled illegitimate—"You shouldn't feel that way" or "Your opinion is incorrect"—or they are labeled as naive—"You don't understand," "You've been misinformed," or (worse yet) "Your opinion is uninformed."

Communication is invalidating when it denies the other person an opportunity to establish a mutually satisfying relationship or when contributions cannot be made by both parties. When one person doesn't allow the other to finish a sentence, adopts a competitive, win-or-lose stance, sends confusing messages, or disqualifies the other person from making a contribution, communication is invalidating and, therefore, dysfunctional for effective problem solving.

Invalidation is even more destructive in coaching and counseling than criticism or disagreement because criticism and disagreement validate the other person by recognizing that what was said or done is worthy of correction, response, or at least notice (Jacobs, 1973). As William James (1965) stated, "No more fiendish punishment could be devised, even were such a thing physically possible, than that one could be turned loose in a society and remain absolutely unnoticed by all the members thereof." **Validating communication,** on the other hand, helps people feel recognized, understood, accepted, and valued (see also Chapter 8, Empowering and Delegating). It has four attributes: It is egalitarian, flexible, two-way, and based on agreement.

Respectful communication (the opposite of superiority-oriented communication) is especially important when a manager coaches or counsels a subordinate. When a hierarchical distinction exists between coaches or counselors and subordinates, it is easy for subordinates to feel invalidated since they have access to less power and information than their manager. Supportive communicators, however, help subordinates feel that they have a stake in identifying problems and resolving them by communicating an egalitarian stance. They treat subordinates as worthwhile, competent, and insightful and emphasize joint problem solving rather than projecting a superior position. One way they do this is by using flexible (rather than rigid) statements.

Flexibility in communication is the willingness of the coach or counselor to accept that additional data and other alternatives may exist and other individuals may be able to make significant contributions both to the problem solution and to the relationship. It means communicating genuine humility—not self-abasement or weakness—and openness to new insight. As Benjamin Disraeli noted, "To be conscious that you are ignorant is a first great step toward knowledge."

Perceptions and opinions are not presented as facts in flexible communication, but are stated provisionally. No claim is made for the truthfulness of opinions or assumptions. Rather, they are identified as being changeable if more data should become available. Flexible communication conveys a willingness to enter into joint problem solving rather than to control the other person or to assume a master-teacher role. Being flexible is not synonymous with being wishy-washy. "Gee, I can't make up my mind" is wishy-washy, whereas "I have my own opinions, but what do you think?" suggests flexibility.

Two-way communication is an implied result of respectfulness and flexibility. Individuals feel validated when they are asked questions, given "air time" to express their opinions, and encouraged to participate actively in the coaching and counseling process. Two-way interchange communicates the message that subordinates are valued by the manager and that coaching and counseling are best accomplished in an atmosphere of teamwork.

Finally, the manager's communication validates the subordinate when it identifies **areas of agreement** and joint commitment. One way to express validation based on agreement is to identify positive behaviors and positive attitudes as well as negative ones during the process of coaching and counseling. The manager should point out important points made by the subordinate before pointing out trivial ones, areas of agreement before areas of disagreement, advantages of the subordinate's statements before disadvantages, compliments before criticisms, and positive next steps before past mistakes. The point is, validating other people helps create feelings of self-worth and self-confidence that can translate into self-motivation and improved performance. Invalidation, on the other hand, seldom produces such positive outcomes, yet it is a common form of management response to subordinates.

5. Supportive communication is specific (useful), not global (useless).

In general, the more specific a statement is, the more useful it is. For example, the statement "You have trouble managing your time" is too general to be useful, whereas "You spent an hour scheduling meetings today when that could have been done by your assistant" provides specific information that can serve as a basis for behavioral change. "Your communication needs to improve" is not nearly as useful as a more specific "In this role play, you used evaluative statements 60 percent of the time and descriptive statements 10 percent of the time."

Specific statements avoid extremes and absolutes. The following are extreme statements that lead to defensiveness or disconfirmation:

A: "You never ask for my advice."
B: "Yes, I do. I always consult you before making a decision."
A: "You have no consideration for others' feelings."
B: "I do so. I am completely considerate."
A: "This job stinks."
B: "You're wrong. It's a great job."

Another common type of global communication is the either-or statement, such as "You either do what I say or I'll fire you," "Life is either a daring adventure or nothing" (Helen Keller), and "If America doesn't reduce its national debt, our children will never achieve the standard of living we enjoy today."

The problem with extreme and either-or statements is that they deny any alternatives. The possible responses of the recipient of the communication are severely constrained. To contradict or deny it generally leads to defensiveness and arguments. A statement by Adolf Hitler in 1933 illustrates the point: "Everyone in Germany is a National Socialist; the few outside the party are either lunatics or idiots."

Specific statements are more useful in coaching and counseling because they focus on behavioral events and indicate gradations in positions. More useful forms of the examples above are the following:

A: "You made that decision yesterday without asking for my advice."
B: "Yes, I did. While I generally like to get your opinion, I didn't think it was necessary in this case."
A: "By using sarcasm in your response to my request, you gave me the impression you don't care about my feelings."
B: "I'm sorry. I know I am often sarcastic without thinking how it affects others."
A: "The pressure to meet deadlines affects the quality of my work."
B: "Since deadlines are part of our work, let's consider ways to manage the pressure."

Specific statements may not be useful if they focus on things over which another person has no control. "I hate it when it rains," for example, may relieve some personal frustration, but nothing can be done to change the weather. Similarly, communicating the message (even implicitly) "The sound of your voice bothers me" only proves frustrating for the interacting individuals. Such a statement is usually interpreted as a personal attack. Specific communication is useful to the extent that it focuses on an identifiable problem or behavior about which something can be done (e.g., "It bothers me when you talk so loudly in the hall that it disturbs others' concentration").

6. Supportive communication is conjunctive, not disjunctive.

Conjunctive communication is joined to previous messages in some way. It flows smoothly. **Disjunctive communication** is disconnected from what was stated before.

Communication can become disjunctive in at least three ways. First, there can be a lack of equal opportunity to speak. When one person interrupts another, when someone dominates by controlling "air time," or when two or more people try to speak at the same time, the communication is disjunctive. The transitions between exchanges do not flow smoothly. Second, extended pauses are disjunctive. When speakers pause for long periods in the middle of their speeches or when there are long pauses before responses, the communication is disjunctive. Pauses need not be total silence; the space may be filled with "umm," "aaah," or a repetition of something stated earlier, but the communication does not progress. Third, topic control can be disjointed. When one person decides unilaterally what the next topic of conversation will be (as opposed to having it decided bilaterally), the communication is disjunctive. Individuals may switch topics, for example, with no reference to what was just said, or they may control the other person's communication topic by directing what should be responded to. Sieburg (1969) found that more than 25 percent of the statements made in small-group discussions failed to refer to or even acknowledge prior speakers or their statements.

These three factors—taking turns speaking, management of timing, and topic control—contribute to what Wiemann (1977) calls "interaction management." They have been found to be critical to effective supportive communication. In an empirical study of perceived communication competence, Wiemann (1977, p. 104) found that "the smoother the management of the interaction [of the three factors above], the more competent the communicator was perceived to be." In fact, interaction management was concluded to be the most powerful determinant of perceived communication competence in his experimental study. Individuals who used conjunctive communication were rated as being significantly more competent in interpersonal communication than were those whose communication was disjunctive.

This suggests that skilled coaches and counselors use several kinds of behaviors in managing communication situations so they are conjunctive rather than disjunctive. For example, they foster conjunctive communication in an interaction by asking questions that are based directly on the subordinate's previous statement, by waiting for a sentence to be completed before beginning a response (e.g., not finishing a sentence for someone else), and by saying only two or three sentences at a time before pausing to give the other person a chance to add input. In addition, they avoid long pauses; their statements refer to what has been said before; and they take turns speaking. Figure 2 illustrates the continuum of conjunctive and disjunctive statements.

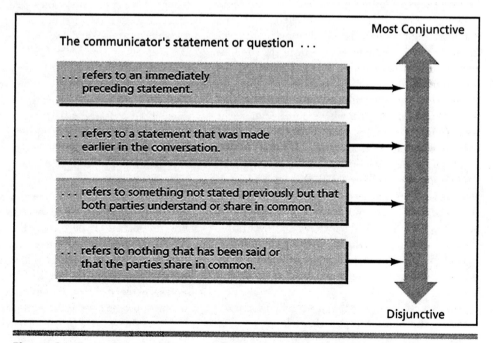

Figure 2 The Continuum of Conjunctive Statements

By using conjunctive communication, managers confirm the worth of the other person's statements, thereby helping to foster joint problem solving and teamwork.

7. Supportive communication is owned, not disowned.

Taking responsibility for one's statements and acknowledging that the source of the ideas is oneself and not another person or group is **owning communication.** Using first-person words, such as "I," "me," "mine," indicates owning communication. **Disowning communication** is suggested by use of third-person or first-person-plural words: "We think," "They said," or "One might say." Disowned communication is attributed to an unknown person, group, or to some external source (e.g., "Lots of people think"). The communicator avoids taking responsibility for the message and therefore avoids investing in the interaction. This conveys the message that the communicator is aloof or uncaring about the receiver or is not confident enough in the ideas expressed to take responsibility for them.

Glasser (1965) based his approach to mental health—reality therapy—on the concept of taking responsibility for, or owning, communication and behavior. According to Glasser, mental health depends on accepting responsibility for one's statements and behaviors. According to reality therapy, taking responsibility for one's communication builds self-confidence and a sense of self-worth in the communicator. It also builds trust in the receiver of the communication.

One result of disowning communication is that the listener is never sure whose point of view the message represents: "How can I respond if I don't know to whom I am responding?" "If I don't understand the message, whom can I ask?" Moreover, an implicit message associated with disowned communication is, "I want to keep distance between you and me." The speaker communicates as a representative rather than as a person, as a message-conveyer rather than an interested individual. Owning communication, on the other hand, indicates a willingness to invest oneself in a relationship and to act as a colleague or helper.

This last point suggests that the coach or counselor encourage the subordinate also to own his or her statements. The manager can do this by example but also by asking the subordinate to restate disowning statements, as in this exchange:

SUBORDINATE: Everyone else says my work is fine.

MANAGER: So no one besides me has ever expressed dissatisfaction with your work or suggested how to improve it?

SUBORDINATE: Well . . . Mark complained that I took shortcuts and left him to clean up after me.

MANAGER: Was his complaint fair?

SUBORDINATE: Yeah, I guess so.

MANAGER: Why did you take shortcuts?

SUBORDINATE: My work was piling up, and I felt I had too much to do.

MANAGER: Does this happen often, that your work builds up and you look for shortcuts?

SUBORDINATE: More than I'd like.

Here the manager has used conjunctive questions to guide the subordinate away from disowning responsibility toward acknowledging a behavior that may be affecting the subordinate's performance.

8. Supportive communication requires listening, not one-way message delivery.

The previous seven attributes of supportive communication all focus on message delivery, where a message is initiated by the coach or counselor. But another aspect of supportive communication—that is, listening and responding effectively to someone else's statements—is at least as important as delivering supportive messages. As Maier, Solem, and Maier (1973, p. 311) stated: "In any conversation, the person who talks the most is the one who learns the least about the other person. The good supervisor therefore must become a good listener." Haas and Arnold (1995) found that about one-third of the characteristics that people in the workplace use to judge communication competence have to do with listening. In short, good listeners are more likely to be seen as skillful communicators.

In a survey of personnel directors in 300 businesses and industries conducted to determine what skills are most important in becoming a manager, Crocker (1978) reported that effective listening was ranked highest. Despite its importance in managerial success, however, and despite the fact that most people spend at least 45 percent of their communication time listening, most people have underdeveloped listening skills. Tests have shown, for example, that individuals are usually about 25 percent effective in listening (Huseman,

Lahiff, & Hatfield, 1976), that is, they listen to and understand only about a fourth of what is being communicated. When asked to rate the extent to which they are skilled listeners, 85 percent of all individuals rate themselves as average or worse. Only 5 percent rate themselves as highly skilled (Steil, 1980). It is particularly unfortunate that listening skills are often poorest when people interact with those closest to them, such as family members and coworkers. They interrupt and jump to conclusions more frequently (i.e., they stop listening) with people close to them than with others.

When individuals are preoccupied with meeting their own needs (e.g., saving face, persuading someone else, winning a point, avoiding getting involved), when they have already made a prior judgment, or when they hold negative attitudes toward the communicator or the message, they can't listen effectively. Because a person listens at the rate of 500 words a minute but speaks at a normal rate of only 125 to 250 words a minute, the listener's mind can dwell on other things half the time. Therefore, being a good listener is neither easy nor automatic. It requires developing the ability to hear and understand the message sent by another person, while at the same time helping to strengthen the relationship between the interacting parties.

Rogers and Farson (1976, p. 99) suggest that this kind of listening conveys the idea that, "I'm interested in you as a person, and I think what you feel is important. I respect your thoughts, and even if I don't agree with them, I know they are valid for you. I feel sure you have a contribution to make. I think you're worth listening to, and I want you to know that I'm the kind of person you can talk to."

People do not know they are being listened to unless the listener makes some type of **response.** Competent managers who must coach and counsel select carefully from a repertoire of response alternatives that clarify the communication as well as strengthen the interpersonal relationship. The mark of a supportive listener is the competence to select appropriate responses to others' statements.

The appropriateness of a response depends largely on whether the focus of the interaction is primarily coaching or counseling. Of course, seldom can these two activities be separated from one another completely—effective coaching often involves counseling and effective counseling sometimes involves coaching—and attentive listening involves the use of a variety of responses. But some responses are more appropriate under certain circumstances than others.

Figure 3 lists four major response types and arranges them on a continuum from most directive and closed to most nondirective and open. Closed responses eliminate discussion of topics and provide direction to

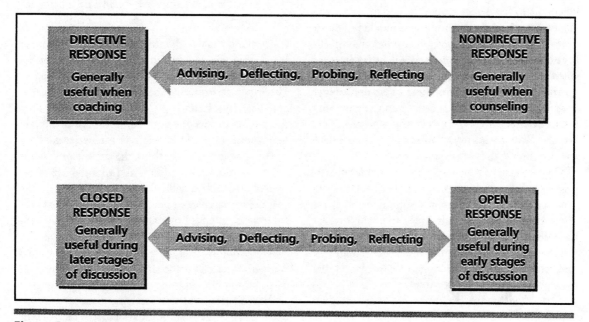

Figure 3   Responsive Types in Supportive Listening

individuals. They represent methods by which the listener can control the topic of conversation. Open responses, on the other hand, allow the communicator, not the listener, to control the topic of conversation. Each of these response types has certain advantages and disadvantages, and none is appropriate all the time under all circumstances.

Most people get in the habit of relying heavily on one or two response types, and they use them regardless of the circumstances. Moreover, most people have been found to rely first and foremost on evaluative or judgmental responses (Rogers, 1961). That is, when they encounter another person's statements, most people tend to agree or disagree, to pass judgment, or to immediately form a personal opinion about the legitimacy or veracity of the statement. On the average, about 80 percent of most people's responses have been found to be evaluative. Supportive listening, however, avoids evaluation and judgment as a first response. Instead, it relies on flexibility in response types and the appropriate match of responses to circumstances. The four response types follow.

Advising.   An **advising response** provides direction, evaluation, personal opinion, or instructions. Such a response imposes on the communicator the point of view of the listener, and it creates listener control over the topic of conversation. The advantages of an advising response are that it helps the communicator understand something that may have been unclear before, it helps identify a problem solution, and it can provide clarity about how the communicator should feel or act in the future. It is most appropriate when the listener has expertise that the communicator doesn't possess or when the communicator is in need of direction. Supportive listening sometimes means that the listener does the talking, but this is usually appropriate only when advice or direction is specifically requested. Most listeners have a tendency to offer much more advice and direction than is appropriate.

One problem with advising is that it can produce dependence. Individuals get used to having someone else generate answers, directions, or clarifications. They are not permitted to figure out issues and solutions for themselves. A second problem is that advising also creates the impression that the communicator is not being understood by the listener. Rogers (1961) found that most people, even when they seem to be asking for advice, mainly desire understanding and acceptance, not advice. They want the listener to share in the communication but not take charge of it. The problem with advising is that it removes from the communicator control of the conversation. A third problem with advising is that it shifts focus from the communicator's issue to the listener's advice. When listeners feel advising is appropriate, they concentrate more on the legitimacy of the advice or on the generation of alternatives and solutions than on simply listening attentively. When listeners are expected to generate advice and direction, they may focus more on their own experience than on the communicator's. A fourth potential problem with advising is that it can imply that communicators don't have sufficient understanding, expertise, insight, or maturity and that they need help because of their incompetence.

One way to overcome the disadvantages of advising in coaching and counseling is to avoid giving advice as a first response. It should follow other responses that allow communicators to have control over the topics of conversation, that show understanding and acceptance, and that encourage self-reliance on the part of communicators. In addition, advice should either be connected to an accepted standard or should be tentative. An accepted standard means that communicators and listeners both acknowledge that the advice will lead to a desired outcome and that it is inherently good, right, or appropriate. When this is impossible, the advice should be communicated as the listener's opinion or feeling, and as only one option (i.e., with flexibility), not as the only option. This permits communicators to accept or reject the advice without feeling that the advisor is being invalidated or rejected if the advice is not accepted.

Deflecting.   A **deflecting response** switches the focus from the communicator's problem to one selected by the listener. The listener changes the subject. Listeners may substitute their own experience for that of the communicator (e.g., "Let me tell you something similar that happened to me") or introduce an entirely new topic (e.g., "That reminds me of [something else]"). The listener may think the current problem is unclear to the communicator and that the use of examples or analogies will help. Or the listener may feel that the communicator needs to be reassured that others have experienced the same problem and that support and understanding are available.

Deflecting responses are most appropriate when a comparison or reassurance is needed. They can provide empathy and support by communicating the message "I understand because of what happened to me (or someone else)." They can also convey the assurance "Things will be fine. Others have also had this experience." Deflection is also often used to avoid embarrassing either the communicator or the listener. Changing the subject when either party gets uncomfortable and answering a question other than the one asked are common examples.

The disadvantages of deflecting responses, however, are that they can imply that the communicator's message is not important or that the experience of the listener is more significant than that of the communicator. It may produce competitiveness or feelings of being one-upped by the listener. Deflection can be interpreted as, "My experience is more worthy of discussion than yours." Or it may simply change the subject from something that is important and central to the communicator to a topic that is not important.

Deflecting responses are most effective when they are conjunctive—that is, when they are clearly connected to what the communicator just said, when the listener's response leads directly back to the communicator's concerns, and when the reason for the deflection is made clear. That is, deflecting can produce desirable outcomes in coaching and counseling if the communicator feels supported and understood, not invalidated, by the change in topic focus.

Probing.   A **probing response** asks a question about what the communicator just said or about a topic selected by the listener. The intent of a probe is to acquire additional information, to help the communicator say more about the topic, or to help the listener foster more appropriate responses. For example, an effective way to avoid being evaluative and judgmental and to avoid triggering defensive reactions is to continue to ask questions. Questioning helps the listener adopt the communicator's frame of reference so that in coaching situations suggestions can be specific (not global) and in counseling situations statements can be descriptive (not evaluative). Questions tend to be more neutral in tone than direct statements.

Questioning, however, can sometimes have the unwelcome effect of switching the focus of attention from the communicator's statement to the reasons behind it. The question "Why do you think that?" for example, might force the communicator to justify a feeling or a perception rather than just report it. Similarly, probing responses can serve as a mechanism for escaping discussion of a topic or for maneuvering the topic around to one the listener wants to discuss (e.g., "Instead of discussing your feelings about your job, tell me why you didn't respond to my memo"). Probing responses can also allow the communicator to lose control of the conversation, especially when difficult subjects need to be addressed (e.g., "I'll talk about only those things you ask me").

Two important hints should be kept in mind to make probing responses more effective. One is that "why" questions are seldom as effective as "what" questions. "Why" questions lead to topic changes, escape, and speculation more often than to valid information. For example, the question "Why do you feel that way?" can lead to statements such as "Because my id is not sufficiently controlled by my ego" or "Because my father was an alcoholic and my mother beat me." These are extreme, even silly, examples, but they illustrate how ineffective "why" questions can be. "What do you mean by that?" is likely to be more fruitful.

A second hint is to tailor the probes to fit the situation. For example, Supplement B in this book summarizes four types of probes that are useful in interviewing. When the communicator's statement does not contain enough information, or part of the message is not understood, an **elaboration probe** should be used (e.g., "Can you tell me more about that?"). When the message is not clear or is ambiguous, a **clarification probe** is best (e.g., "What do you mean by that?"). A **repetition probe** works best when the communicator is avoiding a topic or hasn't answered a previous question (e.g., "Once again, what do you think about that?"). A **reflective probe** is most effective when the communicator is being encouraged to keep pursuing the same topic in greater depth (e.g., "You say you are discouraged?"). Probing responses are especially effective in turning hostile or conflictive conversations into supportive conversations. Asking questions can often turn attacks into consensus, evaluations into descriptions, general statements into specific statements, disowning statements into owning statements, or person-focused declarations into problem-focused declarations. In other words, probes can often be used to help others use supportive communication when they have not been trained in advance to do so.

Reflecting.   The primary purpose of the **reflecting response** is to mirror back to the communicator the message that was heard and to communicate understanding and acceptance of the person. Reflecting the message *in different words* allows the speaker to feel listened to, understood, and free to explore the topic in more depth. Reflective responding involves paraphrasing and clarifying the message. Instead of simply mimicking the communication, supportive listeners contribute meaning, understanding, and acceptance to the conversation while still allowing communicators to pursue topics of their choosing. Athos and Gabarro (1978), Brownell (1986), Steil et al. (1983), and others argue that this response should be used most of the time in coaching and counseling since it leads to the clearest communication and the most supportive relationships.

A potential disadvantage of reflective responses is that communicators can get an impression opposite from the one intended. That is, they can get the feeling that they are not being understood or listened to carefully. If they keep hearing reflections of what they just said, their response might be, "I just said that. Aren't you listening to me?" Reflective responses, in other words, can be perceived as an artificial "technique" or as a superficial response to a message.

The most effective listeners keep the following rules in mind when using reflective responses.

1. Avoid repeating the same response, such as "You feel that . . . ," "Are you saying that . . . ?" or "What I heard you say was. . . ."

2. Avoid an exchange in which listeners do not contribute equally to the conversation, but serve only as mimics. (One can use understanding or reflective responses while still taking equal responsibility for the depth and meaning of the communication.)

3. Respond to the personal rather than the impersonal. For example, to a complaint by a subordinate about close supervision and feelings of incompetence and annoyance, a reflective response would focus on personal feelings rather than on supervision style.

4. Respond to expressed feelings before responding to content. When expressed, feelings are the most important part of the message to the person and may stand in the way of the ability to communicate clearly.

5. Respond with empathy and acceptance. Avoid the extremes of complete objectivity, detachment, or distance on the one hand or over-identification (accepting the feelings as one's own) on the other.

6. Avoid expressing agreement or disagreement with the statements. Use reflective listening and other listening responses to help the communicator explore and analyze the problem. Later you can draw on this information to help fashion a solution.

The Personal Management Interview

Not only are the eight attributes of supportive communication effective in normal discourse and problem-solving situations, but they can be most effectively applied when specific interactions with subordinates are planned and conducted frequently. One important difference between effective and ineffective managers is the extent to which they provide their subordinates with opportunities to receive regular feedback, to feel supported and bolstered, and to be coached and counseled. Providing these opportunities is difficult, however, because of the tremendous time demands most managers face. Many managers want to coach, counsel, and train subordinates, but they simply never find the time. Therefore, one important mechanism for applying supportive communication and for providing subordinates with development and feedback opportunities is to implement a personal management interview program.

A **personal management interview program** is a regularly scheduled, one-on-one meeting between a manager and his or her subordinates. In a study of the performance of intact departments and teams in a variety of organizations, Boss (1983) found that effectiveness increased significantly when managers conducted regular, private meetings with subordinates on a biweekly or monthly basis. These meetings were referred to as "personal management interviews." Figure 4 compares the performance effectiveness of teams and departments that implemented the program versus those that did not.

Instituting a personal management interview program consists of two steps. First, a role-negotiation session is held in which expectations, responsibilities, standards of evaluation, reporting relationships, and so on, are clarified. Unless such a meeting is held, most subordinates do not have a clear idea of exactly what is expected of them or on what basis they will be evaluated. In our own experiences with managers and executives, few have expressed confidence that they know precisely what is expected of them or how they are being evaluated in their jobs. In a role-negotiation session, that uncertainty is overcome; the manager and subordinate negotiate all job-related issues that are not prescribed by policy or by mandate. A written record should be made of the agreements and responsibilities that result from the meeting that can serve as an infor-

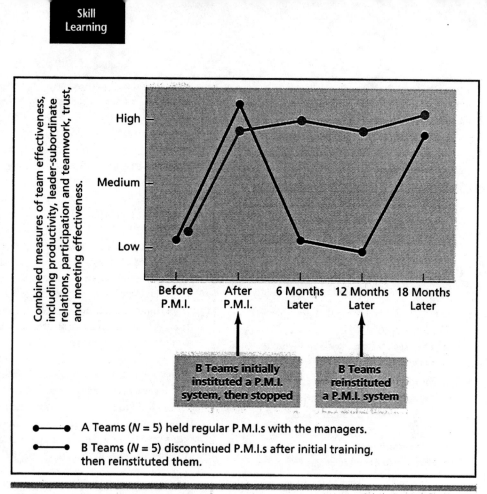

Figure 4   Effects of an Ongoing Personal Management Interview Program
Source: Bass, 1983.

mal contract between the manager and the subordinate. The goal of a role-negotiation session is to obtain clarity between both parties regarding what each expects from the other. Because this role negotiation is not adversarial but rather focuses on supportiveness and team-building, the eight supportive communication principles should characterize the interaction.

The second, and most important, step in a personal management interview plan is a program of ongoing, one-on-one meetings of the manager with each subordinate. These meetings are regular (not just when a mistake is made or a crisis arises) and private (not overheard by others) for good reason. This meeting provides managers with the opportunity to coach and counsel subordinates and to help them improve their own skills and job performance. Therefore, each meeting should last from 45 minutes to an hour and focus on items such as the following: (1) managerial and organizational problems, (2) information sharing, (3) interpersonal issues, (4) obstacles to improvement, (5) training in manage-

ment skills, (6) individual needs, (7) feedback on job performance, and (8) personal concerns or problems.

The meeting always leads toward action items to be accomplished before the next meeting, some by the subordinate and others by the manager. Both parties prepare for the meeting, and both bring items to be discussed. It is not a formal appraisal session called by the manager, but a development and improvement session in which both the manager and subordinate have a stake. It is a chance for subordinates to have personal time with the manager to work out issues and report information; consequently, it helps eliminate unscheduled interruptions and long, inefficient group meetings. At each subsequent meeting, action items are reviewed from previous meetings, so that continuous improvement is encouraged. Table 4 summarizes the characteristics of the personal management interview program.

Boss's research found that a variety of benefits resulted in teams that instituted this program. It not only increased their effectiveness, but improved individual

1. The interview is regular and private.

2. The major intent of the meeting is continuous improvement in personal, interpersonal, and organizational performance, so the meeting is action oriented.

3. Both the manager and the subordinate prepare agenda items for the meeting. It is a meeting for both of them, not just for the manager.

4. Sufficient time is allowed for the interaction, usually about an hour.

5. Supportive communication is used so that joint problem solving and continuous improvement result (in both task accomplishment and interpersonal relationships).

6. The first agenda item is a follow-up on the action items generated by the previous meeting.

7. Major agenda items for the meeting might include:
   • Managerial and organizational problems
   • Organizational values and vision
   • Information sharing
   • Interpersonal issues
   • Obstacles to improvement
   • Training in management skills
   • Individual needs
   • Feedback on job performance
   • Personal concerns and problems

8. Praise and encouragement are intermingled with problem solving.

9. A review of action items generated by the meeting occurs at the end of the interview.

Table 4 Characteristics of a Personal Management Interview Program

accountability, department meeting efficiency, and communication flows. Managers actually found more discretionary time available because the program reduced interruptions and unscheduled meetings. Furthermore, participants defined it as a success experience in itself. When correction or negative feedback had to be communicated, and when coaching or counseling was called for (which is typical of almost every manager-subordinate relationship at some point), supportive communication helped strengthen the interpersonal relationship at the same time that problems were solved and performance improved. In summary, setting aside time for formal, structured interaction between managers and their subordinates in which supportive communication played a part produced markedly improved bottom-line results in those organizations that implemented the program.

Summary

The most important barriers to effective communication in organizations are interpersonal. Much technological progress has been made in the last two decades in improving the accuracy of message delivery in organizations, but communication problems still persist between managers and their subordinates and peers. A major reason for these problems is that the communication does not support a positive interpersonal relationship. Instead, it frequently engenders distrust, hostility, defensiveness, and feelings of incompetence and low self-esteem.

Such dysfunctional communication is seldom associated with situations in which compliments are given, congratulations are made, a bonus is awarded, or other positive interactions occur. Most people have little trouble communicating effectively in such situations. However, potentially harmful communication patterns are most likely to emerge when one is giving feedback on poor performance, saying "no" to a proposal or request, resolving a difference of opinion between two subordinates, correcting problem behaviors, receiving criticism from others, or facing other negative interactions. These situations also arise frequently in the context of coaching and counseling subordinates. Handling these situations in a way that fosters interpersonal growth and a strengthening of relationships is one mark of an effective manager.

In this chapter, we have pointed out that effective communicators adhere to the principles of supportive communication, thus ensuring greater clarity and understanding of messages while making other persons feel accepted, valued, and supported. Of course, it is possible to become overly concerned with technique in trying to incorporate these principles and thereby defeat the goal of being supportive. One can become artificial, or incongruent, by focusing on technique alone, rather than on honest, caring communication. But if the principles are practiced and consciously implemented in everyday interactions, they can be important tools for improving your communication competence.

Behavioral Guidelines

The following behavioral guidelines will help you practice supportive communication:

1. Differentiate between coaching situations, which require giving advice and direction to help foster behavior change, and counseling situations, in which understanding and problem recognition are the desired outcomes.

2. Use problem-oriented statements rather than person-oriented statements, that is, behavioral referents or characteristics of events, not attributes of the person.

3. Communicate congruently by acknowledging your true feelings without acting them out in destructive ways.

4. Use descriptive, not evaluative, statements. Describe objectively what occurred; describe your reactions to events and their objective consequences; and suggest acceptable alternatives.

5. Use validating statements that acknowledge the other person's importance and uniqueness; communicate an investment in the relationship by demonstrating your respect and flexibility; foster two-way interchanges; and identify areas of agreement or positive characteristics before pointing out areas of disagreement or negative characteristics.

6. Use specific rather than global (either-or, black-or-white) statements, and focus on things that can be controlled.

7. Use conjunctive statements that flow smoothly from what was said previously; ensure equal speaking opportunities for all; don't cause long pauses; don't completely control the topic; and acknowledge what was said before.

8. Own your statements, and encourage the other person to do likewise. Use personal words ("I") rather than impersonal words ("management").

9. Demonstrate supportive listening: Use a variety of responses to others' statements, depending on whether you are coaching or counseling someone else, but with a bias toward reflecting responses.

10. Implement a personal management interview program characterized by supportive communication, in order to coach, counsel, and foster personal development among subordinates.

Skill Analysis

Cases Involving Coaching and Counseling

Find Somebody Else

Ron Davis, the relatively new general manager of the machine tooling group at Parker Manufacturing, was visiting one of the plants. He scheduled a meeting with Mike Leonard, a plant manager who reported to him.

RON: Mike, I've scheduled this meeting with you because I've been reviewing performance data, and I wanted to give you some feedback. I know we haven't talked face-to-face before, but I think it's time we review how you're doing. I'm afraid that some of things I have to say are not very favorable.

MIKE: Well, since you're the new boss, I guess I'll have to listen. I've had meetings like this before with new people who come in my plant and think they know what's going on.

RON: Look, Mike, I want this to be a two-way interchange. I'm not here to read a verdict to you, and I'm not here to tell you how to do your job. There are just some areas for improvement I want to review.

MIKE: OK, sure, I've heard that before. But you called the meeting. Go ahead and lower the boom.

RON: Well, Mike, I don't think this is lowering the boom. But there are several things you need to hear. One is what I noticed during the plant tour. I think you're too chummy with some of your female personnel. You know, one of them might take offense and level a sexual harassment suit against you.

MIKE: Oh, come on. You haven't been around this plant before, and you don't know the informal, friendly relationships we have. The office staff and the women on the floor are flattered by a little attention now and then.

RON: That may be so, but you need to be more careful. You may not be sensitive to what's really going on with them. But that raises another thing I noticed—the appearance of your shop. You know how important it is in Parker to have a neat and clean shop. As I walked through this morning, I noticed that it wasn't as orderly and neat as I would like to see it. Having things in disarray reflects poorly on you, Mike.

MIKE: I'll stack my plant up against any in Parker for neatness. You may have seen a few tools out of place because someone was just using them, but we take a lot of pride in our neatness. I don't see how you can say that things are in disarray. You've got no experience around here, so who are you to judge?

RON: Well, I'm glad you're sensitive to the neatness issue. I just think you need to pay attention to it, that's all. But regarding neatness, I notice that you don't dress like a plant manager. I think you're creating a substandard impression by not wearing a tie, for example. Casualness in dress can be used as an excuse for workers to come to work in really grubby attire. That may not be safe.

MIKE: Look, I don't agree with making a big separation between the managers and the employees. By dressing like people out on the shop floor, I think we eliminate a lot of barriers. Besides, I don't have the money to buy clothes that might get oil on them every day. That seems pretty picky to me.

RON: I don't want to seem picky, Mike. But I do feel strongly about the issues I've mentioned. There are some other things, though, that need to get corrected. One is the appearance of the reports you send into division headquarters. There are often mistakes, misspellings, and, I suspect, some wrong numbers. I wonder if you are paying attention to these reports. You seem to be reviewing them superficially.

MIKE: If there is one thing we have too much of, it's reports. I could spend three-quarters of my time filling our report forms and generating data for some bean counter in headquarters. We have reports coming out our ears. Why don't you give us a chance to get our work done and eliminate all this paperwork?

RON: You know as well as I do, Mike, that we need to carefully monitor our productivity, quality, and costs. You just need to get more serious about taking care of that part of your responsibility.

MIKE: OK. I'm not going to fight about that. It's a losing battle for me. No one at headquarters will ever decrease their demand for reports. But, listen, Ron, I also have one question for you.

RON: OK. What's that?

MIKE: Why don't you go find somebody else to pick on? I need to get back to work.

Discussion Questions

1. What principles of supportive communication and supportive listening are violated in this case?

2. How could the interaction have been changed to produce a better outcome?

3. Categorize each of the statements by naming the rule of supportive communication that is either illustrated or violated.

4. What should Ron do in his follow-up meeting with Mike?

Rejected Plans

The following dialogue occurred between two employees in a large firm. The conversation illustrates several characteristics of supportive communication.

ELLEN: How did your meeting go with Mr. Peterson yesterday?

BOB: Well, uh, it went . . . aaah . . . it was no big deal.

ELLEN: It looks as if you're pretty upset about it.

BOB: Yeah, I am. It was a totally frustrating experience. I, uh, well, let's just say I would like to forget the whole thing.

ELLEN: Things must not have gone as well as you had hoped they would.

BOB: I'll say! That guy was impossible. I thought the plans I submitted were very clear and well thought out. Then he rejected the entire package.

ELLEN: You mean he didn't accept any of them?

BOB: You got it.

ELLEN: I've seen your work before, Bob. You've always done a first-rate job. It's hard for me to figure out why your plans were rejected by Peterson. What did he say about them?

BOB: He said they were unrealistic and too difficult to implement, and . . .

ELLEN: Really?

BOB: Yeah, and when he said that I felt he was attacking me personally. But, on the other hand, I was also angry because I thought my plans were very good, and, you know, I paid close attention to every detail in those plans.

ELLEN: I'm certain that you did.

BOB: It just really ticks me off.

ELLEN: I'll bet it does. I would be upset, too.

BOB: Peterson must have something against me.

ELLEN: After all the effort you put into those plans, you still couldn't figure out whether Peterson was rejecting you or your plans, right?

BOB: Yeah. Right. How could you tell?

ELLEN: I can really understand your confusion and uncertainty when you felt Peterson's actions were unreasonable.

BOB: I just don't understand why he did what he did.

ELLEN: Sure. If he said your plans were unrealistic, what does that mean? I mean, how can you deal with a rationale like that? It's just too general—meaningless, even. Did he mention anything specific? Did you ask him to point out some problems or explain the reasons for his rejection more clearly?

BOB: Good point, but, uh, you know . . . I was so disappointed at the rejection that I was kinda like in outer space. You know what I mean?

ELLEN: Yeah. It's an incapacitating experience. You have so much invested personally that you try to divest as fast as you can to save what little self-respect is left.

BOB: That's it all right. I just wanted to get out of there before I said something I would be sorry for.

ELLEN: Yet, in the back of your mind, you probably figured that Peterson wouldn't risk the company's future just because he didn't like you personally. But then, well . . . the plans were good! It's hard to deal with that contradiction on the spot, isn't it?

BOB: Exactly. I knew I should have pushed him for more information, but, uh, I just stood there like a dummy. But what can you do about it now? It's spilled milk.

ELLEN: I don't think it's a total loss, Bob. I mean, from what you have told me—what he said and what you said—I don't think that a conclusion can be reached. Maybe he doesn't understand the plans, or maybe it was just his off day. Who knows? It could be a lot of things. What would you think about pinning Peterson down by asking for his objections, point by point? Do you think it would help to talk to him again?

BOB: Well, I would sure know a lot more than I know now. As it is, I wouldn't know where to begin revising or modifying the plans. And you're right, I really don't know what Peterson thinks about me or my work. Sometimes I just react and interpret with little or no evidence.

ELLEN: Maybe, uh . . . maybe another meeting would be a good thing, then.

BOB: Well, I guess I should get off my duff and schedule an appointment with him for next week. I am curious to find out what the problem is, with the plans, or me. (Pause) Thanks, Ellen, for helping me work through this thing.

Discussion Questions

1. Categorize each statement in the case according to the supportive communication characteristic or type of response it represents. For example, the first statement by Bob obviously is not very congruent, but the second one is much more so.

2. Which statements in the conversation were most helpful? Which do you think would produce defensiveness or close off the conversation?

3. What are the potential disadvantages of giving outright advice for solving Bob's problem? Why doesn't Ellen just tell Bob what he ought to do? Is it incongruent to ask Bob what he thinks is the best solution?

Skill Practice

Exercises for Diagnosing Communication Problems and Fostering Understanding

United Chemical Company

The role of manager encompasses not only one-on-one coaching and counseling with an employee but also frequently entails helping other people understand coaching and counseling principles for themselves. Sometimes it means refereeing interactions and, by example, helping other people learn about correct principles of supportive communication. This is part of the task in this exercise. In a group setting, coaching and counseling become more difficult because multiple messages, driven by multiple motives, interact. Skilled supportive communicators, however, help each group member feel supported and understood in the interaction, even though the solution to an issue may not always be the one he or she would have preferred.

Assignment

In this exercise you should apply the principles of supportive communication you have read about in the chapter. First, you will need to form groups of four people each. Next, read the case and assign the following roles in your group: Max, Sue, Jack, and an observer. Assume that a meeting is being held with Max, Sue, and Jack immediately after the end of the incidents in the following case. Play the roles you have been assigned and try to resolve the problems. The observer should provide feedback to the three players at the end of the exercise. An Observer's Form to assist in providing feedback is in Appendix I.

The Case

The United Chemical Company is a large producer and distributor of commodity chemicals, with five production plants in the United States. The main plant in Baytown, Texas, is not only a production plant but also the company's research and engineering center.

The process design group consists of eight male engineers and their supervisor, Max Kane. The group has worked together steadily for a number of years, and good relationships have developed among all the members. When the workload began to increase, Max hired a new design engineer, Sue Davis, a recent master's degree graduate from one of the foremost engineering schools in the country. Sue was assigned to a project that would expand the capacity of one of the existing plant facilities. Three other design engineers were assigned to the project along with Sue: Jack Keller (age 38, 15 years with the company), Sam Sims (age 40, 10 years with the company), and Lance Madison (age 32, 8 years with the company).

As a new employee, Sue was very enthusiastic about the opportunity to work at United. She liked her work very much because it was challenging and it offered her a chance to apply much of the knowledge she had gained in her university studies. On the job, Sue kept mostly to herself and her design work. Her relations with her fellow project members were friendly, but she did not go out of her way to have informal conversations with them during or after working hours.

Sue was a diligent employee who took her work seriously. On occasions when a difficult problem arose, she would stay after hours in order to come up with a solution. Because of her persistence, coupled with her more current education, Sue usually completed her portion of the various project stages several days ahead of her colleagues. This was somewhat irritating to her because on these occasions she had to go to Max to ask for additional work to keep her busy until her coworkers caught up to her. Initially, she had offered to help Jack, Sam, and Lance with their assignments, but each time she was abruptly turned down.

About five months after Sue had joined the design group, Jack asked to see Max about a problem the group was having. The conversation between Max and Jack went as follows:

MAX: Jack, I understand you want to discuss a problem with me.

JACK: Yes, Max, I don't want to waste your time, but some of the other design engineers want me to discuss Sue with you. She is irritating everyone with her know-it-all, pompous attitude. She's just not the kind of person we want to work with.

MAX: I can't understand that, Jack. She's an excellent worker, and her design work is always well done and usually flawless. She's doing everything the company wants her to do.

JACK: The company never asked her to disrupt the morale of the group or to tell us how to do our work. The animosity in our group could eventually result in lower-quality work for the whole unit.

MAX: I'll tell you what I'll do. Sue has a meeting with me next week to discuss her six-month performance. I'll keep your thoughts in mind, but I can't promise an improvement in what you and the others believe is a pompous attitude.

JACK: Immediate improvement in her behavior is not the problem; it's her coaching others when she has no right to. She publicly shows others what to do. You'd think she was lecturing an advance class in design with all her high-powered, useless equations and formulas. She'd better back off soon, or some of us will quit or transfer.

During the next week, Max thought carefully about his meeting with Jack. He knew that Jack was the informal leader of the design engineers and generally spoke for the other group members. On Thursday of the following week, Max called Sue into his office for her mid-year review. One portion of the conversation went as follows:

MAX: There is one other aspect I'd like to discuss with you about your performance. As I just related to you, your technical performance has been excellent; however, there are some questions about your relationships with the other workers.

SUE: I don't understand. What questions are you talking about?

MAX: Well, to be specific, certain members of the design group have complained about your apparent "know-it-all-attitude" and the manner in which you try to tell them how to do their job. You're going to have to be patient with them and not publicly call them out about their performance. This is a good group of engineers, and their work over the years has been more than acceptable. I don't want any problems that will cause the group to produce less effectively.

SUE: Let me make a few comments. First of all, I have never publicly criticized their performance to them or to you. Initially, when I finished ahead of them, I offered to help them with their work but was bluntly told to mind my own business. I took the hint and concentrated only on my part of the work. What you don't understand is that after five months of working in this group I have come to the conclusion that what is going on is a rip-off of the company. The other engineers are goldbricking; they're setting a work pace much slower than they're capable of. They're more interested in the music from Sam's radio, the local football team, and the bar they're going to go to for TGIF. I'm sorry, but this is just not the way I was raised or trained. And finally, they've never looked on me as a qualified engineer, but as a woman who has broken their professional barrier.

Source: Szilagyi & Wallace, 1983, pp. 204–205.

Byron vs. Thomas

Effective one-on-one coaching and counseling are skills that are required in many settings in life, not just in management. It is hard to imagine a parent, roommate, Little League coach, room mother, or good friend who would not benefit from training in supportive communication. Because there are so many aspects of supportive communication, however, it is sometimes difficult to remember all of them. That is why practice, with observation and feedback, is so important. These attributes of supportive communication can become a natural part of your interaction approach as you conscientiously practice and receive feedback from a colleague.

Assignment

In the following exercise, one individual should take the role of Hal Byron, and another should take the role of Judy Thomas. To make the role-play realistic, do not read each other's role descriptions. When you have finished reading, role-play a meeting between Hal Byron and Judy Thomas. A third person should serve as the observer. An Observer's Form to assist in providing feedback is in Appendix I.

Hal Byron, Department Head

You are Hal Byron, head of the operations group—the "back room"—in a large bank corporation. This is your second year on the job, and you have moved up rather quickly in the bank. You enjoy working for this firm, which has a reputation for being one of the finest in the region. One reason is that outside opportunities for management development and training are funded by the bank. In addition, each employee is given an opportunity for a personal management interview each month, and these sessions are usually both productive and developmental.

One of the department members, Judy Thomas, has been in this department for 19 years, 15 of them in the same job. She is reasonably good at what she does, and she is always punctual and efficient. She tends to get to work earlier than most employees in order to peruse the *American Banker* and *U.S.A. Today.* You can almost set your watch by the time Judy visits the rest room during the day and by the time she makes her phone call to her daughter every afternoon.

Your feeling about Judy is that although she is a good worker, she lacks imagination and initiative. This has been indicated by her lack of merit increases over the last five years and by the fact that she has had the same job for 15 years. She's content to do just what is assigned, nothing more. Your predecessor must have given hints to Judy that she might be in line for a promotion, however, because Judy has raised this with you more than once. Because she has been in her job so long, she is at the top of her pay range, and without a promotion, she cannot receive a salary adjustment above the basic cost-of-living increase.

The one thing Judy does beyond the basic minimum job requirements is to help train young people who come into the department. She is very patient and methodical with them, and she seems to take pride in helping them learn the ropes. She has not been hesitant to point out this contribution to you. Unfortunately, this activity does not qualify Judy for a promotion, nor could she be transferred into the training and development department. Once you suggested that she take a few courses at the local college, paid for by the bank, but she matter-of-factly stated that she was too old to go to school. You surmise that she might be intimidated because she doesn't have a college degree.

As much as you would like to promote Judy, there just doesn't seem to be any way to do that in good conscience. You have tried putting additional work under her control, but she seems to be slowing down in her productivity rather than speeding up. The work needs to get done, and expanding her role just puts you behind schedule.

This interview coming up is probably the time to level with Judy about her performance and her potential. You certainly don't want to lose her as an employee, but there is not going to be a change in job assignment for a long time unless she changes her performance dramatically.

Judy Thomas, Department Member

You are a member of the operations group in a large bank corporation. You have been with the bank now for 19 years, 15 of them in the same job. You enjoy the company because of its friendly climate and because of its prestigious image in the region. It's nice to be known as an employee of this firm. However, lately have become more dissatisfied as you've seen person after person come into the bank and get promoted ahead of you. Your own boss, Hal Byron, is almost 20 years your junior. Another woman who joined the bank the same time you did is now a senior vice president. You can't understand why you've been neglected. You are efficient and accurate in your work, you have a near-perfect attendance record, and you consider yourself to be a good employee. You have gone out of your way on many occasions to help train and orient young people who are just joining the bank. Several of them have written letters later telling you how important your help was in getting them promoted. A lot of good that does you!

The only thing you can figure out is that there is a bias against you because you haven't graduated from college. On the other hand, others have moved up without a diploma. You haven't taken advantage of any college courses paid for by the bank, but after a long day at work, you're not inclined to go to class for another three hours. Besides, you only see your family in the evenings, and you don't want to take time away from them. It doesn't take a college degree to do your job, anyway.

Your monthly personal management interview is coming up with your department head, Hal Byron, and you've decided the time has come to get a few answers. Several things need explaining. Not only haven't you been promoted, but you haven't even received a merit increase for five years. You're not getting any credit for the extra contributions you make with new employees, nor for your steady, reliable work. Could anyone blame you for being a little bitter?

Skill Application

Activities for Communicating Supportively

Suggested Assignments

1. Tape-record an interview with someone such as a coworker, friend, or spouse. Focus on the issues or challenges faced right now by that person. Try to serve as a coach or counselor. Categorize your statements in the interview on the basis of the supportive communication principles in the chapter. (The Rejected Plans case provides an example of such an interview.)

2. Teach someone you know the concepts of supportive communication and supportive listening. Provide your own explanations and illustrations so the person understands what you are talking about. Describe your experience in your journal.

3. Think of an interpersonal problem you share with someone, such as a roommate, parent, friend, or instructor. Discuss the problem with that person, using supportive communication. Write up the experience in as much detail as possible. Concentrate on the extent to which you and the other person used the eight principles of supportive communication. Record and describe areas in which you need to improve.

4. Write two mini-case studies. One should recount an effective coaching or counseling situation. The other should recount an ineffective coaching or counseling situation. The cases should be based on a real event, either from your own personal experience or from the experience of someone you know well. Use all the principles of supportive communication and listening in your cases.

Application Plan and Evaluation

The intent of this exercise is to help you apply this cluster of skills in a real-life, out-of-class setting. Now that you have become familiar with the behavioral guidelines that form the basis of effective skill performance, you will improve most by trying out those guidelines in an everyday context. Unlike a classroom activity, in which feedback is immediate and others can assist you with their evaluations, this skill application activity is one you must accomplish and evaluate on your own. There are two parts to this activity. Part 1 helps prepare you to apply the skill. Part 2 helps you evaluate and improve on your experience. Be sure to write down answers to each item. Don't short-circuit the process by skipping steps.

Part 1. Planning

1. Write down the two or three aspects of this skill that are most important to you. These may be areas of weakness, areas you most want to improve, or areas that are most salient to a problem you face right now. Identify the specific aspects of this skill that you want to apply.

2. Now identify the setting or the situation in which you will apply this skill. Establish a plan for performance by actually writing down a description of the situation. Who else will be involved? When will you do it? Where will it be done?

    Circumstances:

    Who else?

    When?

    Where?

3. Identify the specific behaviors you will engage in to apply this skill. Operationalize your skill performance.

4. What are the indicators of successful performance? How will you know you have been effective? What will indicate you have performed competently?

Part 2. Evaluation

5. After you have completed your implementation, record the results. What happened? How successful were you? What was the effect on others?

6. How can you improve? What modifications can you make next time? What will you do differently in a similar situation in the future?

7. Looking back on your whole skill practice and application experience, what have you learned? What has been surprising? In what ways might this experience help you in the long term?

Building Effective Teams

skill development

Skill Assessment

Diagnostic Surveys for Building Effective Teams

Team Development Behaviors

Step 1: Before you read the material in this chapter, please respond to the following statements by writing a number from the rating scale below in the left-hand column (Preassessment). Your answers should reflect your attitudes and behavior as they are now, not as you would like them to be. Be honest. This instrument is designed to help you discover your level of competency in building effective teams so you can tailor your learning to your specific needs. When you have completed the survey, use the scoring key in Appendix I to identify the skill areas discussed in this chapter that are most important for you to master.

Step 2: After you have completed the reading and the exercises in this chapter and, ideally, as many as you can of the Skill Application assignments at the end of this chapter, cover up your first set of answers. Then respond to the same statements again, this time in the right-hand column (Postassessment). When you have completed the survey, use the scoring key in Appendix I to measure your progress. If your score remains low in specific skill areas, use the behavioral guidelines at the end of the Skill Learning section to guide further practice.

Rating Scale

1	Strongly disagree	4	Slightly agree
2	Disagree	5	Agree
3	Slightly disagree	6	Strongly agree

Assessment

Pre- Post- *When attempting to build and lead an effective team:*

1. I am knowledgeable about the different stages of development that teams can go through in their life cycles.

2. I make certain that all team members are introduced to one another when a team first forms.

3. I provide directions, answer team members' questions, and clarify goals, expectations, and procedures when the team first comes together.

4. I help team members establish a foundation of trust among one another and between themselves and me.

5. I ensure that standards of excellence—not mediocrity or mere acceptability—characterize the team's work.

6. I provide a great deal of feedback to team members regarding their performance.

7. I encourage team members to balance individual autonomy with interdependence among themselves.

_____ 4 _____ 8. I help team members become at least as committed to the success of the team as to their own personal success.

_____ 4 _____ 9. I help members learn to play roles that assist the team in accomplishing its tasks as well as building strong interpersonal relationships.

_____ 4 _____ 10. I articulate a clear, exciting, value-laden vision of what the team can achieve.

_____ 4 _____ 11. I help team members become committed to the team vision.

_____ 4 _____ 12. I encourage a win/win philosophy in the team: that is, when one member wins, every member wins.

_____ 4 _____ 13. I help the team avoid groupthink, or making the group's cohesion and survival more important than accomplishing its goal.

_____ 4 _____ 14. I use process management procedures to help the group become more efficient and more productive, and to prevent errors.

_____ 4 _____ 15. I encourage team members to represent the team's vision, goals, and accomplishments to outsiders.

_____ 4 _____ 16. I diagnose and capitalize on the team's core competencies.

_____ 4 _____ 17. I encourage the team to achieve dramatic breakthrough innovations as well as small continuous improvements.

_____ 4 _____ 18. I help the team work toward preventing mistakes, not just correcting them after-the-fact.

_____ 4 _____ 19. I manage difficult team members effectively through supportive communication, collaborative conflict management, and empowerment.

Diagnosing the Need for Team Building

Teamwork has been found to dramatically affect organizational performance. Some managers have credited teams with helping them to achieve incredible results. On the other hand, teams don't work all the time in all organizations. Therefore, managers must decide when teams should be organized. To determine the extent to which teams should be built in your organization, complete the instrument below.

Think of an organization in which you participate (or will participate) that produces a product or service. Answer these questions with that organization in mind. Write a number from a scale of 1 to 5 in the blank at the left; 1 indicates that there is little evidence; 5 indicates there is a lot of evidence.

_____ 1. Production or output has declined or is lower than desired.

_____ 2. Complaints, grievances, or low morale are present or increasing.

_____ 3. Conflicts or hostility between members is present or increasing.

_____ 4. Some people are confused about assignments, or their relationships with other people are unclear.

_____ 5. Lack of clear goals and lack of commitment to goals exist.

_____ 6. Apathy or lack of interest and involvement by members is in evidence.

_____	7.	Insufficient innovation, risk taking, imagination, or initiative exists.
_____	8.	Ineffective and inefficient meetings are common.
_____	9.	Working relationships across levels and units are unsatisfactory.
_____	10.	Lack of coordination among functions is apparent.
_____	11.	Poor communication exists; people are afraid to speak up; listening isn't occurring; and information isn't being shared.
_____	12.	Lack of trust exists among members and between members and senior leaders.
_____	13.	Decisions are made that some members don't understand, or with which they don't agree.
_____	14.	People feel that good work is not rewarded or that rewards are unfairly administered.
_____	15.	People are not encouraged to work together for the good of the organization.
_____	16.	Customers and suppliers are not part of organizational decision making.
_____	17.	People work too slowly and there is too much redundancy in the work being done.
_____	18.	Issues and challenges that require the input of more than one person are being faced.
_____	19.	People must coordinate their activities in order for the work to be accomplished.
_____	20.	Difficult challenges that no single person can resolve or diagnose are being faced.

Source: Adapted from Dyer, 1987.

■ Skill Learning

Developing Teams and Teamwork

Near the home of one of the authors of this book, scores of Canada geese spend the winter. They fly over the house to the nature pond nearby almost every morning. What is distinctive about these flights is that the geese always fly in a V pattern. The reason for this pattern is that the flapping wings of the geese in front create an up-draft for the geese that follow. This V pattern increases the range of the geese collectively by 71 percent compared to flying alone. On long flights, after the lead goose has flown at the front of the V for awhile, it drops back to take a place in the V where the flying is easier. Another goose then takes over the lead

position, where the flying is most strenuous. If a goose begins to fly out of formation, it is not long before it returns to the V because of the resistance it experiences when not supported by the other geese's wing flapping.

Another noticeable feature of these geese is the loud honking that occurs when they fly. Canada geese never fly quietly. One can always tell when they are in the air because of the noise. The reason for the honking is not random, however. It occurs among geese in the rear of the formation in order to encourage the lead goose. The leader doesn't honk—just those who are supporting and urging on the leader.

If a goose is shot, becomes ill, or falls out of formation, two geese break ranks and follow the wounded or ill goose to the ground. There they remain, nurturing their companion, until it is either well enough to return to the flock or dies.

This remarkable phenomenon serves as an apt metaphor for our chapter on teamwork. The lessons garnered from the flying V formation help highlight important attributes of effective teams and skillful teamwork. For example:

▶ Effective teams have interdependent members. Like geese, the productivity and efficiency of an entire unit is determined by the coordinated, interactive efforts of all its members.

▶ Effective teams help members be more efficient working together than alone. Like geese, effective teams outperform even the best individual's performance.

▶ Effective teams function so well that they create their own magnetism. Like geese, team members desire to affiliate with a team because of the advantages they receive from membership.

▶ Effective teams do not always have the same leader. As with geese, leadership responsibility often rotates and is shared broadly in skillfully led teams.

▶ In effective teams, members care for and nurture one another. No member is devalued or unappreciated. All are treated as an integral part of the team.

▶ In effective teams, members cheer for and bolster the leader, and vice versa. Mutual encouragement is given and received by each member.

▶ In effective teams, there is a high level of trust among members. Members are interested in others' success as well as their own.

Because any metaphor can be carried to extremes, we don't wish to overemphasize the similarities between Canada geese and work teams. But these seven points, which are the focus of this chapter, are among the important attributes of teams. Learning how to foster effective team processes, team roles, team leadership, and positive relationships among team members are among the most important team-building skills discussed in this chapter. Our intent is to help you improve your skill in managing teams, both as a leader and as a team member.

The Advantages of Teams

Whether one is a manager, a subordinate, a student, or a homemaker, it is almost impossible to avoid being a member of a team. Some form of teams and teamwork permeate our everyday lives. What we discuss in this chapter, therefore, is applicable to team activity in many settings outside the workplace. However, our focus here is limited primarily to teams and teamwork in employing organizations rather than in homes, classrooms, or in the world of sports.

According to the *Wall Street Journal,* the first work team ever formed in an organization was established in Filene's department store in Boston in 1898. This innovation was slow to catch on, however, because the Industrial Revolution emphasized work processes and production techniques predicated on individualized tasks and specialized roles. Mass production focused on a "one-person/one-job" philosophy. However, a 1993 survey of 1,293 U.S. organizations by the American Society for Quality Control (ASQC) and the Gallup Organization found that over 80 percent of respondents reported some form of work-team activity, mainly problem-solving teams. Typically, two or more teams were found per company, but almost all teams were of recent origin, the median lifespan being only five years. Two-thirds of full-time employees indicated that they participate in teams, and 84 percent participate in more than one team (ASQC, 1993). Teams and teamwork, in other words, have begun to permeate modern organizational life.

One reason this is the case is that increasing amounts of data show improvements in productivity, quality, and morale when teams are utilized. For example, a noted management consultant, Tom Peters (1987, p. 306) asserts:

> Are there any limits to the use of teams? Can we find places or circumstances where a team structure doesn't make sense? Answer: No, as far as I can determine. That's unequivocal, and meant to be. Some situations may seem to lend themselves more to team-based management than others. Nonetheless, I observe that the power of the team is so great that it is often wise to violate apparent common sense and force a team structure on almost anything.

Many companies have attributed their improvements in performance directly to the institution of teams in the workplace (Wellins et al., 1991). For example, by using teams:

- Shenandoah Life Insurance Company in Roanoke, Virginia, saved $200,000 annually because of reduced staffing needs, while increasing its volume 33 percent.

- Westinghouse Furniture Systems increased productivity 74 percent in three years.

- AAL increased productivity by 20 percent, cut personnel by 10 percent, and handled 10 percent more transactions.

- Federal Express cut service errors by 13 percent.

- Carrier reduced unit turnaround time from two weeks to two days.

- Volvo's Kalamar facility reduced defects by 90 percent.

- General Electric's Salisbury, North Carolina, plant increased productivity by 250 percent compared to other GE plants producing the same product.

- Corning cellular ceramics plant decreased defect rates from 1,800 parts per million to 9 parts per million.

- AT&T's Richmond operator service increased service quality by 12 percent.

- Dana Corporation's Minneapolis valve plant trimmed customer lead time from six months to six weeks.

- General Mills plants are 40 percent more productive than plants operating without teams.

Other more scientific and systematic studies of the impact of teams have found equally impressive results. Literally thousands of studies have been conducted on groups and teams and their impact on various performance outcomes. One of the first and most well-known studies ever conducted on teams was undertaken by Coch and French (1948) in the Harwood Company, a manufacturer of men's shirts, shorts, and pajamas. Faced with the necessity of responding to competitors' lower prices, Harwood decided to speed up the line and make other process changes. Workers had responded badly, however, to previous changes in the production process, and they resisted the threat of further changes. To im-

plement these planned changes, Harwood management used three different types of strategies.

One group of employees received an explanation of the new standards to be imposed, the proposed changes in the production process to be implemented, and why the changes were needed. A question-answer period followed the explanation. A second group of employees was presented the problem, asked to discuss it and reach agreement on solutions, and then elect representatives to generate the new standards and procedures. In a third group, every member was asked to discuss and become involved in establishing and implementing the new standards and procedures. All members participated fully as a team.

The results of this comparison were dramatic. Despite having their jobs simplified, members of the first group showed almost no improvement in productivity; hostility toward management escalated; and, within 40 days, 17 percent of the employees had left the company. Members of the second group regained their previous levels of productivity within 14 days and improved slightly thereafter. Morale remained high and no employee left the company. Members of the third group, on the other hand, who fully participated as a team, regained earlier productivity levels by the second day and improved 14 percent over that level within the month. Morale remained high, and no one left the company.

Other classic studies of coal miners, pet food manufacturers, and auto workers revealed similar advantages of teams (e.g., Trist, 1969; Walton, 1965). More recently, one of the most comprehensive surveys ever conducted on employee involvement in teams was carried out among the Fortune 1000 companies by Lawler, Mohrman, and Ledford (1992). They found that employee involvement in teams had a strong positive relationship with several dimensions of organizational and worker effectiveness. Table 1 shows the percent of organizations reporting improvement and positive impact as a result of team involvement. In general, Lawler and his colleagues found that among firms that were actively using teams, both organizational and individual effectiveness were above average and improving in virtually all categories of performance. In firms without teams or in which teams were infrequently used, effectiveness was average or low in all categories.

In studies of self-directed teams, Near and Weckler (1990) found that individuals in self-directed teams scored significantly higher than individuals in traditional work structures on innovation, information sharing, employee involvement, and task significance.

PERFORMANCE CRITERIA	PERCENT INDICATING IMPROVEMENT
Changed management style to more participatory	78
Improved organizational processes and procedures	75
Improved management decision making	69
Increased employee trust in management	66
Improved implementation of technology	60
Elimination of layers of management supervision	50
Improved safety and health	48
Improved union-management relations	47
PERFORMANCE CRITERIA	PERCENT INDICATING POSITIVE IMPACT
Quality of products and services	70
Customer service	67
Worker satisfaction	66
Employee quality of work life	63
Productivity	61
Competitiveness	50
Profitability	45
Absenteeism	23
Turnover	22

Table 1 Impact of Involvement in Teams on Organizations and Workers (*N* = 439 of the *Fortune* 1000 firms)
Source: Lawler et al. (1992).

Macy et al. (1990) reported that the use of self-directed teams correlated highly with increases in organizational effectiveness, heightened productivity, and reduced defects. Wellins et al. (1991) reported that two-thirds of companies that implemented self-directed work teams could run their companies with fewer managers, and in 95 percent of the cases, a reduced number of managers was reported to be beneficial to company performance. The results of other well-known studies have produced similar outcomes (Ancona & Caldwell, 1992; Hackman, 1990; Gladstein, 1984).

Many of the reasons for these positive outcomes of teams have been known for years. Maier (1967), for example, in a classic description of the conditions under which teams are more effective than individuals acting alone, and vice versa, pointed out that teams:

▶ Produce a greater number of ideas and pieces of information than individuals acting alone, so decision making and problem solving are more informed and are of higher quality.

▶ Improve understanding and acceptance among individuals involved in problem solving and decision making due to team members' participation in the process.

▶ Have higher motivation and performance levels than individuals acting alone because of the effects of "social facilitation": that is, people are more energized and active when they are around other people.

▶ Offset personal biases and blind spots that inhibit effective problem analysis and implementation but that are not noticed by single individuals.

▶ Are more likely to engage in a "risky shift"—that is, to entertain risky alternatives and to take innovative action—than individuals acting alone.

In addition, teams are usually more fun. Consider, for example, the two advertisements that appeared next to one another in a metropolitan newspaper, both seeking to fill the same type of position. They are reproduced in Figure 1. While neither advertisement is negative or inappropriate, they are substantially different. Which job would you rather take? Which firm would you rather work for? The team-focused job seems more desirable, doesn't it?

On the other hand, teams are not a panacea for everything that ails organizations, nor do they represent a magic potion that managers can use to accomplish their objectives. Just getting people together and calling them a team by no means makes them a team. A leading expert on teams, Richard Hackman (1993), pointed out that mistakes are common in team building and team management. Rewarding and recognizing individuals instead of the team, not maintaining stability of membership over time, not providing teams with autonomy, not fostering interdependence among team members, using the team to make all decisions instead of having individuals make decisions when appropriate, failing to orient all team members, having too many members on the team, not providing appropriate structure for the team, and not providing the team with needed resources are all common mistakes Hackman found in his studies of teams. Moreover, a team is not always an appropriate mechanism for dealing with a challenge facing an organization. For example, simple, routine, or highly formalized work is not well-suited for teams. Verespei (1990) observed:

All too often corporate chieftains read the success stories and ordain their companies to adopt work teams—NOW. Work teams don't always work and may even be the wrong solution to the situation in question.

Figure 1 A Team-Oriented and a Traditional Advertisement for a Position

Teams, in other words, can be very powerful tools for managers in producing organizational success, but they are by no means a "sure thing." The Assessment instrument, Diagnosing the Need for Team Building, helps identify the extent to which teams will help an organization improve its performance. Teams can take too long to make decisions; they may drive out effective action with groupthink; and they can create confusion and frustration for their members. All of us have been irritated by being members of an inefficient team, a team dominated by one member, or having to take responsibility for the output of a team that compromised on excellence in order to get agreement from everyone. "A camel," it is said, "is a horse designed by a team."

Teams can be incredibly effective as they develop certain attributes of high performance. It is well-established, for example, that teams perform better than even the most competent individuals performing alone when certain attributes are present. An examination of high-performing teams reveals at least 16 attributes that distinguish them from teams that perform less well (Petrock, 1991). Consider, for example, a World Cup soccer team, an NBA basketball team, a world-class string quartet, or a jazz orchestra. The attributes listed below are among the most crucial for ensuring high performance. Helping you learn how to establish these attributes is an important purpose of this chapter.

Clear goals. Sports and music performance are motivating to team members because the goals are clear and are constantly emphasized.

Goals that are known by all. Every team member can give the same answer to the question: "What are we trying to accomplish?"

Goals achieved in small steps. Large goals are achieved in small steps, such as innings, downs, holes, frames, sections, bars, and sets—each with subobjectives.

Standards of excellence. All performance is measured against a standard of excellence, and mediocrity is never acceptable.

Feedback of results. All team members get immediate feedback on how they are doing and how the team is doing.

Skills and knowledge used. All team members have an opportunity to use all their skills and abilities when they participate.

Continuous training. Because constant improvement is expected, all team members are being trained continuously, on and off the playing field or stage.

Equipment and facilities. Adequate resources are provided for the team to succeed at its job.

Autonomy. Team members can exercise self-initiative and can make their own decisions on how they will perform.

Performance-based rewards. Rewards are based on accomplishments—not title, effort, or politics.

Competition. The risk of losing is always possible, and competition occurs not only against an opponent but against personal past performance.

Praise and recognition. Praise is greatest among team members themselves but comes from many sources and is continuous.

Team commitment. Team members are committed to the success of one other and to the team, so that when one fails, all feel a sense of failure.

Plans and tactics. Every team member is aware of the strategy to be used to accomplish the team's objective, and no competition is entered without advance planning.

Rules and penalties. Rules and penalties are known in advance by everyone, and they are fair, consistent, and immediate.

Performance measures. Many aspects of performance are measured: for example, batting averages, hits in scoring position, singles, doubles, triples, home runs, on-base percentages, runs-batted-in, power ratings, percent hits versus left- and right-handed pitchers are all measured for baseball hitters; pitch, tone quality, flow, mistakes, dynamics, precision, blend, sight-reading are all measured for quartets.

Team failure is common, so how can success in teams be assured? How can managers ensure the effectiveness of the teams in which they are involved? What should one learn to become a skillful team leader and team member? Because of the rapid growth of teams, as well as the potential positive impact teams can have on organizations' success, it is clear that understanding teams and teamwork is a prerequisite for any effective manager in modern organizations. We now turn, therefore, to the key management skills of team building and teamwork.

Stages of Team Development

In effective teams, team members' behavior is interdependent, and personal goals are subservient to the accomplishment of the team goal. A commitment to, and desire for team membership is present. Even though individuals may be formally designated as a team, if they act so as to bring exclusive credit to themselves, to accomplish their own objectives instead of the team's objective, or to maintain independence from others, they are not truly a team, regardless of their name. A key challenge, then, is to determine how to build the elements of a team into an independent group of individuals who have no prior commitment to one another or to a common task.

To effectively build, lead, or participate in a team one must understand the stages of development that teams follow as they form and carry out their functions. Effective managers are skillful at helping teams be successful as they progress from early stages of development—when a team is still struggling to become a coherent entity—to a more mature stage of development—when the team has become a highly effective, smoothly functioning organization. This chapter focuses on helping you improve your skill in diagnosing and leading each phase of team development.

Evidence of a predictable pattern of team development has been available since the early part of this century. Beginning with Dewey's (1933) emphasis on five (cognitive) stages of learning and Freud's (1921) analysis of children's (affective) responses to authority figures, research has proliferated on the cognitive and affective changes that occur in groups and teams over time. In fact, several thousand studies of groups and teams have appeared in just the last decade. Researchers have studied a wide variety of types of groups and teams with varying compositions and attributes. Problem-solving teams, quality circles, therapy groups, task forces, interpersonal growth groups, student project teams, and many other types have been studied extensively. Studies have ranged from teams meeting for just one session to teams with working lives extending over several years. Membership in teams has varied widely, ranging from children to aged people, top executives to line workers, students to instructors, volunteers to prison inmates, professional athletes to playground children, and so on. The analyses have focused on dynamics such as team-member roles, unconscious cognitive processes, group dynamics, problem-solving strategies, communication patterns, leadership actions, interpersonal needs, decision-making quality, innovativeness, and productivity.

Despite the variety in composition, purpose, and longevity across teams being investigated, the stages of group and team development emerging from these studies have been strikingly similar. For a review and summary of a dozen or so team-stage development models, see Cameron and Whetten (1981), Cameron and Whetten (1984), and Quinn and Cameron (1983). Teams tend to develop through four separate stages. These stages were first labeled by Tuckman (1965) as *forming, conforming, storming,* and *performing.* Because of their rhyme and parsimony, these labels are still widely used today. Table 2 summarizes the four main stages of team development. (The ordering of stages 2 and 3 are reversed from Tuckman's original model as a result of research conducted by Quinn & Cameron, 1988; Cameron & Whetten, 1981; and Greiner, 1972.)

In order for teams to be effective and for team members to benefit most from team membership, teams must progress through the first three stages of development to achieve Stage 4. In each separate stage, particular challenges and issues predominate, and it is by successfully managing these issues and overcoming the challenges that a team matures and becomes more effective. Skillful managers, whether serving as team leaders or team members, help the team progress to the next stage of development. Table 3 summarizes these challenges and issues.

To explain each stage and identify ways in which skilled managers assist teams in moving forward toward increasingly high performance and effectiveness, we discuss the dominant *team member questions, interpersonal relationships, task issues,* and *effective leader behaviors* that characterize each stage. Being able to diagnose the stage of a team's development and adopt appropriate leader behaviors is a skill that separates the most effective managers from those who are less effective.

The Development of a Team

To illustrate the development of a real team over these four stages, we will look at what turned out to be one of the highest-performing teams in history: the one formed to plan and carry out logistical support for soldiers in the Persian Gulf War (Pagonis, 1993). This team was organized in 1990 as a result of President Bush's announcement that the United States would

STAGE	EXPLANATION
Forming	The team is faced with the need to become acquainted with its members, its purpose, and its boundaries. Relationships must be formed and trust established. Clarity of direction is needed from team leaders.
Conforming	The team is faced with creating cohesion and unity, differentiating roles, identifying expectations for members, and enhancing commitment. Providing supportive feedback and fostering commitment to a vision are needed from team leaders.
Storming	The team is faced with disagreements, counterdependence, and the need to manage conflict. Challenges include violations of team norms and expectations and overcoming groupthink. Focusing on process improvement, recognizing team achievement, and fostering win/win relationships are needed from team leaders.
Performing	The team is faced with the need for continuous improvement, innovation, speed, and capitalizing on core competencies. Sponsoring team members' new ideas, orchestrating their implementation, and fostering extraordinary performance are needed from the team leaders.

Table 2   Four Stages of Team Development

STAGE	CATEGORY	CHARACTERISTICS
Forming	Team Member Questions	• Who are these other people? • What is going to happen? • What is expected of me? • Where are we headed and why? • Who is the leader? • What are our goals? • How do I fit in? • How much work will this involve?
	Interpersonal Relationships	• Silence • Self-consciousness • Dependence • Superficiality • Reactivity • Uncertainty
	Task Issues	• Orient members. • Become comfortable with team membership. • Establish trust. • Establish relationships with the leaders. • Establish clarity of purpose. • Deal with feelings of dependence.
	Effective Leader Behaviors	• Make introductions. • Answer questions. • Establish a foundation of trust. • Model expected behaviors. • Clarify goals, procedures, rules, and expectations.

Table 3   Typical Attributes of the Four Stages of Team Development

STAGE	CATEGORY	CHARACTERISTICS
Conforming	Team Member Questions	• What are the norms and expectations? • How much should I conform? • What role can I perform? • Will I be supported? • Where are we headed? • How much should I invest and commit?
	Interpersonal Relationships	• Cooperativeness • Ignoring disagreements • Conformity to standards and expectations • Obedience to leader directions • Heightened interpersonal attraction • Commitment to a team vision
	Task Issues	• Maintain unity and cohesion. • Differentiate and clarify roles. • Determine levels of personal investment. • Clarify the future. • Decide on levels of commitment to the team's future.
	Effective Leader Behaviors	• Facilitate role differentiation among team members. • Show support to team members. • Provide feedback. • Articulate a vision of the future for the team. • Help generate commitment to the vision.
Storming	Team Member Questions	• How will we handle disagreements? • How will we communicate negative information? • Can the team be changed? • How can we make decisions amidst disagreement? • Do we really need this leader? • Do I want to maintain my membership in the team?
	Interpersonal Relationships	• Polarization of team members • Coalitions or cliques being formed • Competition among team members • Disagreement with the leader • Challenging others' points of view • Violating team norms
	Task Issues	• Manage conflict. • Legitimize productive expressions of individuality. • Overcome groupthink. • Examine key work processes of the team. • Turn counterdependence into interdependence.
	Effective Leader Behaviors	• Identify a common enemy and reinforce the vision. • Generate commitment among team members. • Turn students into teachers. • Be an effective mediator. • Provide individual and team recognition. • Foster win/win thinking.

Table 3 *(continued)*

STAGE	CATEGORY	CHARACTERISTICS
Performing	Team Member Questions	• How can we continuously improve? • How can we foster innovativeness and creativity? • How can we build on our core competence? • What improvements can be made to our processes? • How can we maintain a high level of energy and commitment to the team?
	Interpersonal Relationships	• High mutual trust • Unconditional commitment to the team • Multifaceted relationships among team members • Mutual training and development • Entrepreneurship • Self-sufficiency
	Task Issues	• Capitalize on core competence. • Foster continuous improvement. • Anticipate needs of customers and respond in advance of requests. • Enhance speed and timeliness. • Encourage creative problem solving.
	Effective Leader Behaviors	• Foster innovation and continuous improvement simultaneously. • Advance the quality culture of the team. • Provide regular, ongoing feedback on team performance. • Play sponsor and orchestrator roles for team members. • Help the team avoid reverting back to earlier stages.

Table 3 *(continued)*

send troops to Saudi Arabia in order to confront Iraqi aggression in Kuwait.

The tasks of this team were daunting. It was charged with transporting over half a million people and their personal belongings to the other side of the world, on short notice. But transporting the people was only part of the challenge. Supporting them once they arrived, moving them into position for a surprise attack, supporting their battle plans, and then getting them and their equipment back home were even greater challenges. Over 122 million meals had to be planned, moved, and served—approximately the number eaten by all the residents of Wyoming and Vermont in three months. Fuel (1.3 billion gallons) had to be pumped—about the same amount used in Montana, North Dakota, and Idaho in a year—in order to support sol-diers driving 52 million miles. Tanks, planes, ammunition, carpenters, cashiers, morticians, social workers, doctors, and a host of support personnel had to be transported, coordinated, fed, and housed. More than 500 new traffic signs had to be constructed and installed in order to help individuals speaking several different languages navigate the relatively featureless terrain of Saudi Arabia. Five hundred tons of mail had to be sorted and processed each day. Over 70,000 contracts with suppliers had to be negotiated and executed. All green-colored equipment—over 12,000 tracked vehicles and 117,000 wheeled vehicles—had to be repainted desert brown and then repainted green when shipped home. Soldiers had to be trained to fit in with an unfamiliar culture that was intolerant of typical soldier-relaxation activity. Supplies had to be distributed at a moment's notice to several different locations, some of them behind enemy lines, in the heat of battle. Traffic control was monumental, as evidenced by one key checkpoint near the front where 18 vehicles per minute passed, seven days a week, 24 hours a day, for six weeks. Over 60,000 enemy prisoners of war had to be transported, cared for, and detained. Because the war ended far sooner than anyone predicted, most of the equipment, ammunition, and supplies had to be brought back home—but only after thorough scrubbing to remove microorganisms or pests and shrinkwrapping. Since large, bulk containers had been broken up into smaller units during the war, it took twice as long to gather and ship materials out of Saudi Arabia as it did to ship them in. In short, this team was faced with a set of tasks that had never before been accomplished on that scale and in a time frame that would have been laughable if it weren't factual. The team assigned to accomplish these tasks had to be assembled and guided from the very first stage through the final stage of team development.

The various stages of this team's development can be found in the 1993 book *Moving Mountains*, written by General Pagonis, leader of the logistics support team. Pagonis was awarded a third star during Desert Storm for providing outstanding logistical support. He helped plan and execute the famous "end run" that took Saddam Hussein's army completely by surprise. Most observers now agree that it was the success of the logistics team that really won the Persian Gulf War for the United States.

To better understand how General Pagonis' logistics team could reach such a high level of effectiveness—a level where enormously complicated activities were coordinated flawlessly and precisely without a single leader standing up front barking out directions—it is necessary to understand the aspects of each of the four stages of team development. Each stage is explained in some detail below, with the required management and leadership behaviors given special attention.

The Forming Stage

Team member questions, interpersonal relationships, and task issues. Most performers know that at the beginning of a concert, the audience is "cold." Because people are not initially very responsive, major performers use a warm-up act to get the audience "in-tune" or to "become one" with the performer. Similarly, when team members first come together, they are much like an audience at the outset of a concert. They are not a team, but an aggregation of individuals sharing a common setting. Something must happen for them to feel that they are a cohesive unit. Recall an instance in which you met with a group of people for the first time. It may have been at the outset of a semester in school, in a committee or task force meeting, in a church or professional group, or on an intramural sports team. When you first came together with other potential team members, you probably did not feel integrated into a cohesive unit. In fact, you likely had several *questions* on your mind such as:

▶ Who are these other people?

▶ What is going to happen?

▶ What is expected of me?

▶ Where are we headed and why?

▶ Who is the leader?

▶ What are our goals?

▶ How do I fit in?

▶ How much work will this involve?

The questions uppermost in the minds of participants in a new team have to do with establishing a sense of security and direction, getting oriented, and becoming comfortable with the new situation. Sometimes, new team members can articulate these questions, while at other times they are little more than general feelings of discomfort or disconnectedness. Uncertainty and ambiguity tend to predominate as individuals seek some type of understanding and structure. Because there is no shared history with the team, there is no unity among members. Thus, the typical *interpersonal relationships* that predominate in this stage are:

▶ Silence

▶ Self-consciousness

▶ Dependence

▶ Superficiality

▶ Reactivity

▶ Uncertainty

Even though some individuals may enter a team situation with great enthusiasm and anticipation, they are usually hesitant to demonstrate their emotions to others until they begin to feel at ease. Moreover, without knowing the rules and boundaries, it feels risky to speak out or to even ask questions. Seldom are new members willing to actively query a leader when a team first meets together, even though uncertainty prevails. When the leader asks questions of team members, rarely does someone jump at the chance to answer them. When answers are given, they are likely to be brief. Little interaction occurs among team members themselves, most communication is targeted at the team leader or person in charge, and each individual is generally thinking more of himself or herself than of the team. Interactions tend to be formal and guarded. Congruent behaviors are masked in the interest of self-protection.

Individuals cannot begin to feel like a team until they become familiar with the rules and boundaries of their setting. They don't know whom to trust, who will take initiative, what constitutes normal behavior, or what kinds of interactions are appropriate. They are not yet a real team but only a collection of individuals. Therefore, the task of the team in this stage is less focused on producing an output than on developing the team itself. Helping team members become comfortable with one another takes precedence over task accomplishment. A team faces the following kinds of *task issues* in its first stage of development:

▶ Orienting members

▶ Becoming comfortable with team membership

▶ Establishing trust

▶ Establishing relationships with the leader

▶ Establishing clarity of purpose

▶ Dealing with feelings of dependence

Effective leader behaviors. Teams can remain in the first stage for an extended period, and many do when no clear direction is provided about what the team is to accomplish, what the rules are, or what each member's responsibilities entail. Some teams never move past this stage of development but remain a loose aggregation of individuals without the magnetism or commitment that characterize high-performing teams. The lifespan of such a team is likely to be short. Unless

a skillful person takes time to deal with the issues and anxieties of team members, it will become progressively harder for the team to develop beyond this stage. Such teams eventually dissolve. On the other hand, this stage can be relatively brief if a leader of the team takes the following actions:

▶ Makes introductions

▶ Answers questions

▶ Establishes a foundation of trust

▶ Models expected behaviors

▶ Clarifies goals, procedures, rules, and expectations

In the initial stage of his own team's development, General Pagonis tackled this challenge head on. He began with the process of recruiting his team members.

Over the years I have developed a very distinctive leadership style. Gus Pagonis's command style, like everyone else's, is unique. This meant that I had choices to make. Would I rather have the world's best port operation officer, if he was someone who didn't already know my style? Or would I rather have the world's second best port operation officer who knew my style intimately and was comfortable with it? The answer was obvious; we couldn't waste time fighting our own systems. Equally important, we couldn't afford the time that would be wasted as a new person tried to impress me, or get on my good side. We needed an instant body of leaders, strengthened by a united front. We needed to know that we could depend on one another unconditionally. We needed the confidence that the mission, and not personal advancement, would always be paramount in the mind of each participant (p. 78).

In the initial stage of team development, Pagonis needed to bring other team members up to speed on their mission.

[The team] got down to work with a redoubled sense of urgency. They were soon fully familiar with the plan that had been roughed out by [the highest commanding officers] and me. . . . We quickly got to a joint understanding of what I took to be our role in the theater. . . . Our session . . . was very successful, mainly because from the outset we had a well-defined structure for invention. We worked toward several clearly expressed goals, and there was an imposed time limit to keep us on track. And finally, our various experiences were complementary. We needed each other and we knew it (pp. 82–83).

Skillful team leaders act more like directors than facilitators in this first stage. This is not a time for team leaders to rely on free and open discussion and consensus decision making to accomplish an outcome. Direction, clarity, and structure are needed instead. The first task is to ensure that all team members know one another and that their questions are answered (even unasked questions which are on the minds of team members). Because relatively little participation may occur during this stage, the temptation is for team leaders to rush ahead or to short-circuit introductions and instructions. Skillful team leaders leave time for questions, however, and they urge team members to reveal their uncertainties. Guidelines, boundaries, and expectations are clarified so that team members understand how they fit in, how much will be required of them, and how much trust they can have in the team.

In the case of the Persian Gulf logistics team, the first critical task undertaken by General Pagonis was to make certain that objectives, rules and regulations, time frames, and resources were clearly laid out. Each member of the team received maximum information in order for each to become comfortable with his or her team membership: "They were soon fully familiar with the plan that had been roughed out, . . . a joint understanding of what I took to be our role in the theater, . . . a well-defined structure for invention, . . . clearly expressed goals, and . . . an imposed time limit to keep us on track."

In the chapter on Empowering and Delegating, we discussed five dimensions upon which trust is built: reliability, fairness, caring, openness, and competence. Team leaders must model these attributes in their own behavior in order to establish this foundation of trust. This means being consistent and dependable in actions and congruent in communication. It means being equitable and fair and showing personal concern for all team members. It means sharing information openly, honestly, and clearly, while exhibiting sensitivity to the needs of all team members. Finally, it means helping team members become aware of the competence and resources available to them.

As stated by General Pagonis (p. 88): "Keeping your [team members] abreast of your actions, as well as the

rationale behind those actions, puts everybody on an equal information footing. I believe that information is power, but only if it is shared."

In sum, one of the crucial responsibilities of a team leader is to help clarify for all team members the structure of the team, without which a team will have a difficult time progressing past the forming stage of development. When the team leader successfully provides the necessary clarity and direction, however, the team can progress to the second stage.

The Conforming Stage

Team member questions, interpersonal relationships, and task issues. Once a team has resolved the issues of the forming stage, those issues are replaced by others that lead the team into a new stage of development. When a team begins to function as a unit and team members become comfortable in their setting, team members experience pressure to conform to the emerging norms. For example, recall a time when you became a member of an ongoing team. Chances are that you almost immediately felt pressure to conform. That is because team members become inclined to behave consistently with other team members' expectations. The more team members interact with one another, the more they develop common behaviors and perspectives. This conformity may affect the amount of work done by the team, styles of communicating, approaches to problem solving, and even dress.

Team members also begin to identify a unique role for themselves in this stage. They try to find their own place in the group. In the case of General Pagonis's logistics team, the roles of "firefighter," "fixer," and "cheerleader" began to emerge, even though these roles were not prescribed as part of the formal responsibilities.

The basic problem was that we were trying to set up a logistical structure for reception in the middle of deployment. According to doctrine and common sense, you set up the structure first, and only then do you begin deployment. But the reality of the military situation didn't allow us this luxury. Truth be told, we spent less of our time as logisticians, and more of our time as managers, fixers, firefighters, father confessors, and cheerleaders. There was simply nobody else around to play any of these roles (p. 87).

The major focus of team members, then, shifts from overcoming uncertainty and increasing clarity in the forming stage to becoming unified and identifying roles that can be played by each member in the conforming stage. Typical *questions* in team members' minds during this stage include:

▶ What are the norms and expectations?

▶ How much should I conform?

▶ What role can I perform?

▶ Will I be supported?

▶ Where are we headed?

▶ How much should I invest and commit?

During the conforming stage, team members become contented with team membership and begin to value the team's goals more than their own personal goals. Individual needs begin to be met through the team's accomplishments. The team, rather than the leader or a single person, takes responsibility for solving problems, confronting and correcting mistakes, and ensuring success. Agreement and willingness to go along characterize the climate of the team, since members are willing to put aside personal biases for the good of the group. Individuals experience feelings of loyalty to the team, and the *interpersonal relationships* that most characterize team members include:

▶ Cooperativeness

▶ Ignoring disagreements

▶ Conformity to standards and expectations

▶ Obedience to leader directions

▶ Heightened interpersonal attraction

▶ Commitment to a team vision

In this stage, however, tension arises between forces pushing the team toward cohesion and forces pushing the team toward differentiation. At the same time strong bonds of team unity are being formed, individuals try to differentiate themselves from one another and adopt unique roles in the team. They seek to become complementary to one another rather than duplicative. The presence of differentiated roles in the team may actually foster team cohesion and unity, as illustrated by Pagonis's logistics team, in which members were selected specifically to achieve complementarity. But the potential tension gives rise to the following *task*

issues that must be addressed in this stage of development:

▶ Maintaining unity and cohesion

▶ Differentiating and clarifying roles

▶ Determining levels of personal investment

▶ Clarifying the future

▶ Deciding on levels of commitment to the team's future

In identifying which roles to perform in order to contribute the most to the success of the team, members have two main categories of roles from which to choose: **task-facilitating roles** and **relationship-building roles**. It is difficult for team members to emphasize both types of roles equally, and most people tend to contribute in one area more than the other. That is, some team members tend to be more task focused whereas others tend to be more relationship focused. Task-facilitating roles are those that help the team accomplish its outcome objectives—for example, to produce a product or service, solve a problem, or generate a new idea. Among the common task-facilitating roles are:

Direction giving. Identifying ways to proceed or alternatives to pursue and clarifying goals and objectives.

Information seeking. Asking questions, analyzing knowledge gaps, requesting opinions, beliefs, and perspectives.

Information giving. Providing data, offering facts and judgments, and highlighting conclusions.

Elaborating. Building on the ideas expressed by others; providing examples and illustrations.

Coordinating. Pulling ideas together, and helping others examine one another's suggestions and comments; helping members work together.

Monitoring. Developing measures of success and helping to maintain accountability for results.

Process analyzing. Analyzing processes and procedures used by the team in order to improve efficiency and timeliness.

Reality testing. Exploring whether ideas presented are practical or workable.

Enforcing. Keeping the team focused on the task at hand and driving out all side issues.

Summarizing. Combining ideas and summing up points made in the team; helping members understand the conclusions that have been reached.

Relationship-building roles are those that emphasize the interpersonal aspects of the team. They focus on assisting team members to feel good about one another, to enjoy the team's work, and to maintain a tension-free climate. Among the common relationship-building roles are:

Supporting. Praising the ideas of others and pointing out others' contributions.

Harmonizing. Mediating differences between others, and finding a common ground in disputes and conflicting points of view.

Tension relieving. Using jokes and humor to reduce tension and put others at ease.

Confronting. Challenging unproductive or disruptive behaviors; helping to ensure proper behavior in the team.

Energizing. Motivating others toward greater effort and accomplishment; exuding enthusiasm.

Developing. Assisting others to learn, grow, and achieve; orienting and coaching members of the team.

Facilitating. Helping build solidarity among team members and helping interactions to be smooth.

Processing. Reflecting group feelings and helping to smooth out the team's functioning.

Without both types of roles being played, a team does not advance past the second stage of development. Some members must ensure that the team accomplishes its tasks, while others must ensure that members remain bonded together interpersonally. These are usually not the same individuals. Each team member begins to play different roles, with some roles becoming more dominant than others. The key is to have a balance between task-oriented roles and relationship-building roles displayed in the team. The downfall of many teams is that they become unidimensional—for example, they emphasize task accomplishment exclusively—and do not give equal attention to both types of roles.

The next time you are in a team setting, try keeping track of the behaviors displayed by each team member. See if you can identify the "task masters" and the "relationship builders." Which roles do you most naturally play yourself? The advantage of being able to recognize different roles is that team development cannot progress unless many of these roles are present and effectively performed. Knowing which roles are needed and being able to play multiple roles helps perpetuate team effectiveness.

Of course, each role can also have a downside if performed ineffectively or in inappropriate circumstances. For example, elaborating may be disruptive if the team is trying to reach a quick decision; tension relieving may be annoying if the team is trying to be serious; enforcing may create resistance when the team is already experiencing high levels of pressure; facilitating may mask real differences of opinion and tension among team members. However, even more likely is the presence of other unproductive roles that team members play. These roles inhibit the team or its members from achieving what they could have achieved, and they destroy morale and cohesion. They are called **blocking roles.** We point out a few of them here because, as you analyze the teams to which you belong, you may recognize these roles being performed and be able to confront them. Among common blocking roles are:

Overanalyzing. Splitting hairs and examining every detail excessively.

Overgeneralizing. Blowing something out of proportion and drawing unfounded conclusions.

Fault-finding. Unwilling to see the merits of others' ideas or behaviors.

Premature decision making. Making decisions before goals are stated, information is shared, alternatives are discussed, or problems are defined.

Presenting opinions as facts. Failing to examine the legitimacy of proposals and labeling personal opinions as truth.

Rejecting. Rejecting ideas based on the person who stated them rather than on their merits.

Pulling rank. Using status, expertise, or title to get ideas accepted rather than discussing and examining their value.

Dominating. Excessive talking, interrupting, or cutting others off.

Stalling. Not allowing the group to reach a decision or finalize a task by sidetracking the discussion, being unwilling to agree, repeating old arguments, and so on.

Remaining passive. Not being willing to engage in the team's task. Staying on the fringe or refusing to interact with other team members. Expecting others to do the team's work.

Resisting. Blocking all attempts to change, to improve, or to make progress. Being disagreeable and negative about virtually all suggestions from other team members.

Effective leader behaviors.   Each of the above-mentioned blocking roles has the potential to inhibit a team from efficiently and successfully accomplishing its task by crushing morale, destroying consensus, creating conflict, and making ill-informed decisions. Effective team leaders work with team members to avoid blocking roles while at the same time ensuring that task-facilitating and relationship-building roles are adequately performed by team members. Maintaining a balance of task and relationship role emphasis and ensuring that roles being performed are not disruptive or destructive is an important responsibility of the team leader. In addition, the following leader behaviors are required in this stage of the team's development:

▶ Facilitate role differentiation among team members

▶ Show support to team members

▶ Provide feedback

▶ Articulate a vision of the future for the team

▶ Help generate commitment to the vision

Helping a team develop cohesion relies at least partly on providing feedback to team members. This means giving them information about how they are doing as individuals as well as how the team is doing as a unit. In providing feedback to others, team leaders and team members should use the following guidelines:

Focus feedback on behavior rather than persons. Individuals can control and change their behavior. They cannot change their personalities or physical characteristics.

Focus feedback on observations rather than inferences and on descriptions rather than judgments. Facts and objective evidence is more trustworthy and acceptable than opinions and conjectures.

Focus feedback on behavior related to a specific situation, preferably to the "here-and-now," rather than on abstract or past behavior. It will merely frustrate people if they cannot pinpoint a specific incident or be-havior to which you are referring. Similarly, people cannot change something that has already happened and is "water under the bridge."

Focus feedback on sharing ideas and information rather than giving advice. Explore alternatives together. Unless requested, avoid giving directive feedback and demands; instead, help recipients identify changes and improvements themselves.

Focus feedback on the amount of information that the person receiving it can use, rather than on the amount you might like to give. Information overload causes people to stop listening. Not enough information leads to frustration and misunderstanding.

Focus feedback on the value it may have to the receiver, not on the emotional release it provides for you. Feedback should be for the good of the recipient, not merely for you to let off steam.

Focus feedback on time and place so that personal data can be shared at appropriate times. The more specific feedback is, or the more it can be anchored in a specific context, the more helpful it can be.

In addition to providing feedback to help team members become a cohesive unit, the most important thing a team leader can do is to articulate a vision of the future for the team. Peter Senge (1991) asserted that every effective, high-performing team and organization has a clear, inspirational vision. General Pagonis's agreement with this proposition is illustrated by his statement: "Every successful venture grows out of a vision. . . . It's the vision that motivates, embraces, and sets limits, all at once" (p. 171). In one of the best studies published on high-performing teams, Katzenbach and Smith (1993) stated:

> The best teams invest a tremendous amount of time and effort exploring, shaping, and agreeing on a [vision] that belongs to them collectively and individually. . . . With enough time and sincere attention, one or more broad, meaningful aspirations invariably arise that motivate teams to provide a fundamental reason for their extra effort (p. 50).

All teams have specific goals and objectives to achieve, but a vision is something different. It helps illuminate the core values and principles that will guide the team in the future. It gives a sense of direction. It provides a glimpse of possibilities, not just probabilities. It evokes deeper meaning and deeper commitment than task or goal statements. It is intended to help team members think differently about themselves and their future. It serves as a glue to bind the team together. Finally, it does all of this by way of three characteristics:

Left-brained and right-brained.   An effective vision statement contains objective targets, goals, and action plans (left-brain components) as well as metaphors, colorful language, and emotion (right-brain components). It captures the head (left-brain) as well as the heart and imagination (right-brain) of team members. The most motivating vision statements—for example, Martin Luther King's "I Have a Dream" speech, Winston Churchill's "Never Give Up" speech, John F. Kennedy's "Ask Not What Your Country Can Do for You" speech, Henry V's "Saint Crispin's Day" speech—contain both left-brained elements (specific objectives) and right-brained elements (emotional imagery). Leaders articulate the vision using stories and metaphors as well as targets and goals.

Interesting.   Murray Davis (1971) pointed out that what people judge to be interesting and energizing has little to do with truth or legitimacy. Rather, what's interesting is information that contradicts weakly held assumptions and challenges the status quo. If a vision is consistent with what is already believed or known (e.g., "We will accomplish our work"), people tend to dismiss it as common sense. They don't remember it, and it doesn't motivate them. If a vision is contradictory to strongly held assumptions, or if it blatantly challenges core values of team members (e.g., "Every team member will become rich"), it is labeled ridiculous, silly, or blasphemous. A vision that helps create a new way to view the future, on the other hand, that challenges the current state of things, is viewed as interesting and energizing. For example, "We will land on the moon in 10 years" was just contradictory enough, just outlandish enough, just enough of a stretch to be interesting. It not only made people think, it provided something new to think about. The vision of effective leaders stretches perspectives and contradicts status quo or easily attained targets.

Passion and principles.   Effective visions are grounded in core values that team members believe in and about which they feel passionate. Even if a team's

task objective were to vanish, for example, members might still desire to affiliate with the team because of the core principles associated with its vision. Therefore, the principles in the vision must be personal. A vision focused on "increasing productivity" is less magnetic than a vision based on "personal growth." "Achieving profitability" is less magnetic than "building a better world." Furthermore, such principles are best phrased using superlatives. Notice the difference in how you feel about the following comparisons: "exceptional performance" versus "good performance"; "passionately involved" versus "committed"; "explosive growth" versus "substantial growth"; "awesome products" versus "useful products." Visions based on the former phrases engender more enthusiasm and passion than those based on the latter phrases.

Consider as an example of such language the 1987 vision statement of John Scully, former CEO of Apple Computer Company:

> We are all part of a journey to create an extraordinary corporation. The things we intend to do in the years ahead have never been done before. . . . One person, one computer is still our dream. . . . We have a passion for changing the world. We want to make personal computers a way of life in work, education, and the home. Apple people are paradigm shifters. . . . We want to be the catalyst for discovering new ways for people to do things. . . . Apple's way starts with a passion to create awesome products with a lot of distinctive value built in. . . . We have chosen directions for Apple that will lead us to wonderful ideas we haven't as yet dreamed.

Once a vision of the future has been articulated, it is important that leaders ensure that team members commit to it. Although a vision may exist, if team members do not accept the vision as their own, it is worthless and may, in fact, tear apart rather than solidify a team. Team leaders can foster commitment to their vision and, hence, to team cohesion in three principal ways.

Public commitment.   When people state their commitments in public, they are motivated to behave consistently with those public declarations (Salancik, 1977). The internal need for congruence enhances the probability that public statements will be followed by consistent actions. For example, during World War II, good cuts of meat were in short supply. Lewin (1951) found a significant difference between the commitment level of shoppers who promised aloud to buy more plentiful but less desirable cuts of meat (e.g., liver, kidneys, brains) compared to those who promised to do so in private. In another study, students in a college class were required to set goals for how much they would read and what kinds of scores they would get on exams. Only half the students were allowed to state these goals publicly to the rest of the class. By mid-semester, the students who stated their goals publicly averaged 86 percent improvement compared to 14 percent improvement for the other students. These findings reinforce the fact that effective team leaders provide opportunities for team members to restate the vision themselves in a public setting. When they do so—that is, when team members are given the opportunity to explain the vision to others—their own commitment increases.

Consensus through participation.   Having the opportunity to be involved in formulating plans to accomplish the vision also engenders commitment to it. Effective team leaders therefore foster commitment by involving team members in reaching consensus about various aspects of the vision. For example, in a classic study of how former opponents of a vision came to be supporters, Selznick (1949) studied the resistance of local farmers to the Tennessee Valley Authority's (TVA) plans to build a dam. To elicit farmers' commitment to the project, the TVA made local farmers members of the board that would plan and supervise the construction project. When farmers began to make public statements explaining the TVA project, they became committed to it (Selznick, 1949).

One way to enhance the participation and agreement of all team members is to use a technique such as the Nominal Group Technique (NGT) (Delbecq, Van de Ven, & Gustafson, 1975). This technique ensures that everyone on the team is heard and that consensus is reached. The technique consists of six steps:

1. Team members are presented with a challenge or issue—for example, how to accomplish the vision.

2. Individual team members silently and independently write down their ideas. This is the nominal (noninteracting) phase.

3. Each team member (one at a time, in round-robin fashion) presents an idea to the group. No discussion of ideas occurs. All ideas are recorded for the team to see.

4. After all individuals have presented their ideas, a discussion of the merits of the ideas occurs. Ideas are merged, eliminated, expanded, and modified.

5. Team members privately vote on their preferred ideas. This might be done by having each team member select the top two or three ideas, divide 10 points among alternatives, rank-ordering alternatives, or other decision-making alternatives.

6. A revised list of the best ideas is presented to team members for discussion. If a consensus emerges, the team is finished. If not, the procedure returns to Step 2 and continues through more rounds until the best ideas are identified and agreement is reached.

The point is to help all team members participate and express their own personal opinions while still building team consensus.

Frequent communication.   Commitment is enhanced if the vision is communicated frequently. If leaders stop communicating the vision or if they change themes in their interactions with the team, members tend to think that the vision isn't important anymore. Unless leaders continually and consistently articulate, rehearse, and reinforce the vision, it loses its power, and commitment erodes. Leaders must also serve as models of the principles in the vision. No question should exist in the minds of those who interact with team leaders as to what the vision is. One leader who exemplifies this principle is Jan Carlzon, former CEO of Scandinavian Airlines (SAS), a highly touted team leader and executive. Carlzon states:

Good leaders spend more time communicating than anything else. From my first day at SAS I've made communicating, particularly with our employees, a top priority. In fact, during the first year I spent exactly half my working hours out in the field talking to SAS people. The word going around was that any time three employees gathered, Jan Carlzon would probably show up and begin talking with them. . . . When we began reorganizing SAS, our critics scoffed at our efforts as mere promotional gimmicks. They claimed we had become too marketing oriented, but in fact we hadn't increased our marketing budget one cent. Rather, we were spending our money more effectively on messages that were easily understood (Carlzon, 1987, pp. 88, 92).

In summary, skillful managers in the conforming stage of development help build cohesion and unity, help team members engage in productive but differentiated roles, and help create commitment to a motivating vision. When they do so, the team can then move on to the next stage of development.

The Storming Stage

Team member questions, interpersonal relationships, and task issues.   Invariably, the differentiation that begins to occur in the conforming stage leads to conflict and counterdependence in the team. Playing different roles causes team members to develop different perspectives. Virtually every team goes through a stage where team members question the legitimacy of the team's direction, the leader, the roles of other team members, the opinions or decisions being espoused, and the task objectives. This is a natural phase of development in the team because, up to now, the team has largely been characterized by harmony and consensus. Individual differences have been suppressed for the good of the team. However, such a condition will not last forever without team members becoming uncomfortable that they are losing their individual identity, subjugating their feelings, or stifling their differing perspectives. The team, in other words, has never learned how to cope with conflict, differences, and disruptions. It has merely repressed them. Its long-term success, however, will depend on how well it manages this storming stage of development. The team can disintegrate if this stage is not managed well. Typical questions that arise in team members' minds during this stage are:

- How can we make decisions amidst disagreement?
- How will we handle dissension?
- How will we communicate negative information?
- Can the team be changed?
- Do we really need this leader?
- Do I want to maintain my membership in the team?

An old Middle Eastern proverb states: "All sunshine makes a desert." Similarly, team growth implies that some struggles must occur, some discomfort must be experienced, and some obstacles must be overcome for the team to prosper. The team must learn to deal with adversity—especially that produced by its own members. If team members are more interested in keeping peace than in solving problems and accomplishing tasks, the team will never become effective, and its long-term viability will be threatened. No one wants to remain in a team that will not allow for individuality and uniqueness and that wants to maintain harmony more than it wants to accomplish its goals. Consequently, harmony is sometimes sacrificed as the team attacks problems and accomplishes objectives.

Moreover, as team members become more comfortable in their membership and roles as a result of passing through the forming and conforming stages, they begin to participate more openly and more frequently. This increased participation always uncovers differences in perspective. Such expressions of individuality and difference often create conflict. The team therefore experiences a stormy phase of development that, if managed well, can help it be even more effective than if no conflict had been encountered.

Team members in this third stage of development do not cease to care about one another, and they remain committed to the team and its success. But they do begin to take sides on issues, to find that they are more compatible with some team members than with others, and to agree with some points of view rather than with others. This differentiation in roles and perspectives creates interpersonal relationships characterized by:

- Polarization of team members
- Coalitions or cliques being formed
- Competition among team members
- Disagreement with the leader
- Challenging others' points of view
- Violating team norms

The storming stage does not necessarily imply that the team becomes chaotic, self-destructive, or mean-spirited. Rather, the same results occur as when teenagers begin to separate from their parents, when junior managers or interns in companies begin to break away from their mentors, and when pupils begin to challenge their teachers. Separation anxiety, competition, and even resentment may arise, mainly because the old pattern of relationships has changed. The unquestioned authority of the leader is challenged and no longer inviolate. Independence and interdependence replace dependence. Disagreements are common. Therefore, effective conflict management strategies take on added importance as team members are required sometimes to adopt an **initiator role,** sometimes a **responder role,** and sometimes a **mediator role** in addressing inevitable conflicts. Team members must sometimes confront others and express disagreement (initiator), sometimes defend their own point of view against others who disagree with or confront them (responder), and sometimes help referee or mediate a disagreement among other team members (mediator). See the chapter on Managing Conflict for guidelines in performing those three roles.

It is also common in the storming stage for team members to test and challenge the boundaries and norms of the team. This might include small aberrations such as coming late, holding side conversations in team meetings, or interrupting the team's work. It might also encompass more significant challenges, such as trying to oust the team leader, generating new rules to replace the original ones, or building a coalition to alter the team's goals and objectives significantly. During Desert Storm, for example, a relatively rigid military command hierarchy—along with the urgency of the mission to be performed—inhibited large deviations from established norms and rules, but small aberrations occurred constantly. For example, logistics team members painted personal logos on some tanks and trucks, insider code names were given to people and locations as a bit of sarcasm, and challenges to top brass mandates became more common in briefing rooms.

The testing of norms and boundaries is sometimes merely an expression of a need for individuality, while in other instances it is a product of strong feelings that the team can be improved. The main task issues to be addressed by the team in this stage include:

- Managing conflict
- Legitimizing productive expressions of individuality
- Overcoming groupthink
- Examining key work processes of the team

- Turning counterdependence into interdependence

Conflict, coalition formation, and counterdependence create conditions that may lead to the norms and values of the team being questioned. Rather than being stifled, resisted, or shut off, however, effective teams encourage members to turn those challenges into constructive suggestions for improvement. General Pagonis's philosophy about the way to manage differences was to encourage their expression:

The key is to be open to different experiences and perspectives. If you can't tolerate different kinds of people, you're not likely to learn from different kinds of perspectives. Effective leaders encourage contrary opinions, an important source of vitality. This is especially true in the military where good ideas come in an incredible variety of packages (Pagonis, 1993, p. 24).

The team must be careful during this stage to restate and reinforce the overall vision for the team, and not to confuse it with more specific, short-term goals or processes. Abandoning the core vision will not help the team progress beyond this stage of development; instead, the team will become mired in debates about key values. Coalitions must be reminded of the common vision and principles that bond the overall team, even though different subgroups may take different positions on issues.

General Pagonis ensured that this was the case in his team.

[Our] strength was flexibility, both as individuals and as a group. Organizations must be flexible enough to adjust and conform when their environments change. But the flexibility can degenerate into chaos in the absence of well-established goals. . . . Once everyone in the organization understands the goals of the organization, then each person sets out several objectives by which to attain those goals within his or her own sphere of activity. . . . When it works, cooperation and collegiality are enhanced, and in-fighting and suboptimization are minimized (p. 83).

It is important for team members to feel that they can legitimately express their personal uniqueness and idiosyncrasies, so long as they are not destructive to the overall team. It is clear from research on teams that they are more effective if membership is heterogeneous than if all team members act, believe, and see things the same way (Murnigham, 1981). Maintaining flexibility in the team implies that tolerance for individuality is acceptable and that changes and improvements are promoted. Note the approach taken by General Pagonis:

> I never tell a subordinate how to carry out a specific goal. Dictating terms to a subordinate undermines innovation, decreases the subordinate's willingness to take responsibility for his or her actions, increases the potential for suboptimization of resources, and increases the chances that the command will be dysfunctional if circumstances change dramatically. Our first month in the theater only underscored my sense that our [team] would have to be incredibly elastic (Pagonis, 1993, p. 119).

Expressing individuality does not mean, of course, that commitment to the overall team's success need be abandoned. In fact, it is important during this stage to reinforce constantly the need for team members to focus on the welfare of the overall group and the achievement of the vision. One of the best ways for this to happen is for the team to make certain that a **win/win philosophy** permeates the team's activities. As discussed in the chapters on Managing Conflict and Communicating Supportively, a win/win philosophy means that team members try to ensure that everyone benefits from their actions. All changes, challenges, or suggestions are pursued for the good of the team, not for self-aggrandizement at the expense of the team. Team members should understand that they are better off only if all team members are better off. Losing and causing others to lose (e.g., not getting rewarded, not accomplishing the objective, not feeling good about oneself) is not acceptable. For example, Pagonis's statement that each of his team members "needed to know that we could depend on one another unconditionally . . . that the mission, and not personal advancement, would always be paramount in the mind of each participant" illustrates the manner in which uniqueness, individuality, and differences are ideally managed.

The advantage of storming: overcoming groupthink. One of the potential problems with a win/win philosophy in a team, however, is that it can lead to the emergence of a phenomenon called **groupthink** (Janis, 1972). Groupthink occurs when the cohesiveness and inertia developed in a group or team drives out good decision making or problem solving. The preservation of the team takes precedence over accurate decisions or high-quality task accomplishment. Not enough conflict occurs.

Irv Janis (1972) conducted research in which he chronicled several high-performing teams that in one instance performed in a stellar fashion, but performed disastrously in another instance. His classic example was the cabinet of President John F. Kennedy. This team worked through what is often considered one of the best sets of decisions ever made in handling the Cuban Missile Crisis, in which the former Soviet Union was inhibited from placing warhead missiles in Cuba by means of a high-stakes confrontation by Kennedy and his cabinet. But this was also the same team that made the disastrous decisions related to the Bay of Pigs fiasco, in which a planned overthrow of Fidel Castro's government in Cuba became a logistical nightmare, a confluence of indecision, and an embarrassing defeat for the same formerly high-functioning team.

What was the difference? Why did the same team do so well in one circumstance and so poorly in another? The answer is groupthink. Groupthink typically occurs when the following attributes arise in teams.

Illusion of invulnerability. Members feel assured that the team's past success will continue. ("Because of our track record, we cannot fail.")

Shared stereotypes. Members dismiss disconfirming information by discrediting its source. ("These people just don't understand these things.")

Rationalization. Members rationalize away threats to an emerging consensus. ("The reason they don't agree with us is . . .")

Illusion of morality. Members believe that they, as moral individuals, are not likely to make wrong decisions. ("This team would never knowingly make a bad decision or do anything immoral.")

Self-censorship. Members keep silent about misgivings and try to minimize doubts. ("I must be wrong if others think that way.")

Direct pressure. Sanctions are imposed on members who explore deviant viewpoints. ("If you don't agree, why don't you leave the team?")

Mind-guarding. Members protect the team from being exposed to disturbing ideas. ("Don't listen to them. We need to keep the rabble rousers at bay.")

Illusion of unanimity. Members conclude that the team has reached a consensus because the most vocal members are in agreement. ("If Dave and Melissa agree, there must be a consensus.")

The problem with groupthink is that it leads teams to commit more errors than normal. As an example, consider the following commonly observed scenario. Not wanting to make a serious judgment error, a leader convenes a meeting of his or her team. In the process of discussing an issue, the leader expresses a preference for one option. Other team members, wanting to appear supportive, present arguments justifying the decision. One or two members tentatively suggest alternatives, but they are strongly overruled by the majority. The decision is carried out with even-greater conviction than normal because everyone is in agreement, but the consequences are disastrous. How did this happen? While the leader brought the team together to avoid making a bad decision, the presence of groupthink actually made a bad decision more likely. Without the social support provided by the team, the leader may have been more cautious in implementing a personally preferred but uncertain decision.

To avoid groupthink, each team should make certain that the following characteristics are present:

Critical evaluators. At least one team member should be assigned to perform the role of critic or evaluator of the team's decisions.

Open discussion. The team leader should not express an opinion at the outset of the team meeting but should encourage open discussion of differing perspectives by team members.

Subgroups. Multiple subgroups in the team may be formed to develop independent proposals.

Outside experts. Invite outside experts to listen to the rationale for the team's decision and critique it.

Devil's advocate. Assign at least one team member to play devil's advocate during the discussion if it

seems that too much homogeneity exists in the team's discussion.

Second-chance meetings. Sleep on the team's decision and revisit it afresh the next day. The expression of team members' second thoughts should be encouraged.

Process management. Another highly effective activity to avoid groupthink, enhance the team's task accomplishment, and manage the storming stage of development is for team members to examine carefully the team's processes. **Team processes** are those methods of interacting and doing work that have emerged over the first two stages of development. Such an examination is important because the norms and team processes that the team developed in the forming and conforming stages may become the source of team member dissatisfaction as well as of groupthink. Alternative ways to approach problems and accomplish tasks may be preferred by some members, but no opportunity has existed in previous stages to try them out without creating conflict. Feelings of opposition or counterdependence may therefore begin to arise among team members. This counterdependence can be transformed into interdependence by using **process management** techniques.

Process management was developed as part of the Total Quality Management (TQM) and the reengineering movements. It involves the assessment, analysis, and improvement of sets of activities in which teams engage. A **process** is a sequential set of activities designed to lead to a specific outcome. For example, unloading a ship, transporting ammunition to the front, or feeding troops are among the processes that had to be managed by General Pagonis's team. The importance of process management during the storming stage of development is that it focuses and coordinates team members in a task sequence that minimizes the negative effects of conflict, disruption, and difference. Even though individuals are differentiated, well-managed processes minimize discord by coordinating efforts and capitalizing on team members' unique contributions. Good process management doesn't ignore individuality; it optimizes it. Moreover, it helps position the team to move into the final stage of development. Consider General Pagonis's approach:

I arranged to take a day or two away from headquarters with a group of key people from the command [the team]. We use this brief respite from our everyday activities to take a long look at what our organization is doing. These sessions . . . gave us a chance to work as a group, in a focused way. . . . From Day One, I held large, open classes where we discussed scenarios and potential solutions. I would pose a question to the group: "O.K., you have a ship that docked at Ad Dammam this morning. It's ready to be unloaded, and the onboard crane breaks. What's our response?" Collectively, the group would work toward one of several solutions. . . .These group sessions served several useful purposes at once. Obviously, they brought potential challenges into the open so we could better prepare for them. . . . Equally important, they promoted collaborative discussion across ranks and disciplines (pp. 101, 177).

Process management consists of three main activities: (1) process assessment, (2) process analysis, and (3) process improvement. The objective of the first step, **process assessment**, is to identify the sequence of tasks, activities, and individuals involved in delivering an output. This is done by listing, in sequential order, each identifiable activity performed from the beginning of a process to its completion. Table 4 shows a simplified list of the activities involved in replenishing items used by soldiers at a particular location during Desert Storm. Of course, this single process must be linked closely with other processes such as transporting the supplies to the site (upstream of this process) and distributing the supplies after they have been stored to soldiers in the field (downstream of this process). In other words, a network of processes exists for each team. But all processes cannot be assessed simultaneously. Instead, process assessment articulates specifically what actions and what people are involved in a single, identifiable process.

A "map" of the process is then constructed showing inputs, outputs, and hand-offs between different individuals in the team. A **process map** shows each of the activities in relationship to one another. Different types of symbols indicate decision points, activities, indirect links, and so forth. Reviewing details of map symbols and mapping techniques is beyond the scope of this chapter, however, and interested readers may want to read Morris & Brandon (1993) for a more de-

tailed explanation of process mapping. It doesn't take an expert to generate a useful process map, however, and it can be very helpful in coordinating and improving team members' performance. An effective way to develop a process map is to have each team member identify what he or she does, the person(s) with whom he or she interacts and coordinates, and what information is shared. A simple and effective method for constructing a process map is outlined below, and Figure 2 provides an illustration of a process map for the steps listed in Table 4.

Member jobs. Each team member writes down his or her specific job on a Post-It note. These notes are placed on a wall in the sequence in which they occur in the process. These job descriptions serve as the major categories of activities.

Activities. Each specific activity and hand-off within each job category is written separately on a Post-It

The steps involved in replenishing supplies at a military outpost during the Persian Gulf War may include the ones that follow. These same steps are also applicable to most businesses that procure and distribute supplies.

1. Forecast use for each item based on past use.
2. Identify unusual circumstances that will affect future use.
3. Calculate how many of each item to order.
4. Complete a written order form.
5. Determine when to place an order.
6. Submit the order for needed items.
7. Receive ordered items.
8. Confirm received items were ordered.
9. Check off items received from the receipt list.
10. Reconcile order list with receipt list.
11. Contact individuals to transport items received to storage.
12. Move items received to the storage area.
13. Log in items to be stored.
14. Store items in a way that allows for easy access.

Table 4   Process Analysis: A Simplified Process for Replenishing Supplies for Soldiers

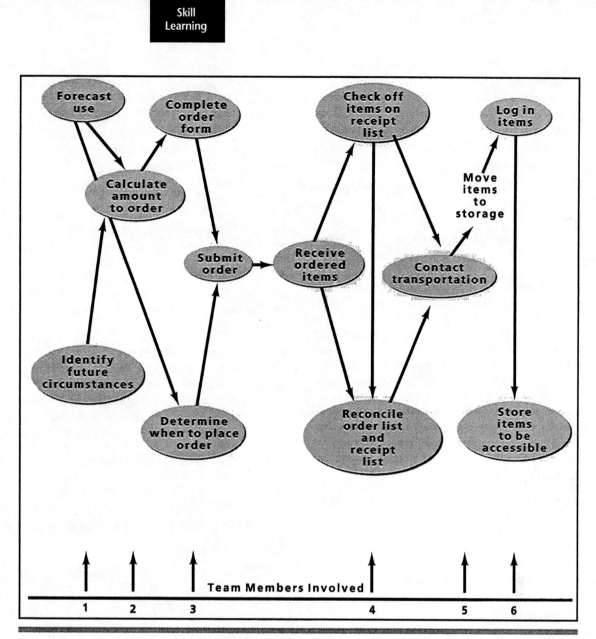

Figure 2 A Simplified Process Map: Replenishing Supplies

note by each team member. These notes are stuck on the wall in the order in which they occur.

Criteria. Measures or indicators of success are attached to each activity. The question is addressed, "How would I know if this activity was highly effective?"

Communication. The information given to and required from someone else is recorded on a Post-It note. These notes are placed next to the activities for which the information is needed.

Differentiation. Different color notes may be used to differentiate information exchanges, activities, and criteria.

Mapping. Construct a map of the task and communication sequence by drawing boxes around each separate activity. Link it with an arrow to other activities from which it receives something or to which it gives something. Do the same for information exchanges. Generate a linear map that shows how the process begins, what happens as it unfolds, and how it concludes. Note who is involved in each separate boxed item.

The second step in process management is **process analysis.** The purpose of this step is to identify a better way to perform a particular process. It involves analyzing the current process and then identifying a target for how much the process can be improved. The question to be asked is, "How much time can be saved, waste reduced, or mistakes avoided by improving the current process?" Ideas for improvements may come from observing others perform the same process (benchmarking), from team members' past experience, from finding small improvements (small wins) that can be made, from customers' recommendations and feedback, or from a radical redesign of the entire sequence of activities (reengineering). Using the ideas for improvement gathered from this variety of sources, an "ideal" process map is drawn. A comparison is then made between the current "as is" process map and the "should be" map. Guidelines for comparing current and ideal process maps include:

▶ Look for *disconnects*—connections that should be present but are not.

▶ Look for *redundancies*—activities that are performed more than once.

▶ Look for *delays* and *waiting time.*

▶ Look for indicators of *poor performance*—errors, mistakes, and defects.

▶ Look for ways to accomplish the process that are *cheaper* or use fewer resources.

▶ Look for ways to *prevent mistakes* before they occur.

The third step in process management is **process improvement,** in which the process itself is changed so as to foster advancement. This means trying out new ways of accomplishing the same outcome, changing the outcome so that it is improved, or providing more value and benefit to those involved. Proposed improvements in the process should generally be tried out in a practice room, a bullpen, or in a pilot test, because it is difficult to revamp an entire process without evidence that proposed changes will make it better. Changes that promise to speed up or improve the process, that alter the outcome of the process, or that promise to enhance payback for team members usually need to be tried out in advance of wholesale restructuring.

The point of using process management techniques in this stage of team development is to help team members focus their different perspectives and felt need for independence into team-improvement activities. By concentrating on the required interdependence that the team must experience to accomplish its tasks, conflict and disunity are constructively managed. Effective team performance is enhanced, and the team becomes prepared for the next stage of development.

Effective leader behaviors. Whereas all team members must be involved in process management and in reinforcing the vision of the team, the leader has special responsibility to ensure that these two things occur. In addition to those two key factors, other leader behaviors that are most effective in this stage are:

▶ Identify a common enemy to increase feelings of cohesion.

▶ Reinforce the vision.

▶ Generate commitment among team members.

▶ Turn students into teachers.

▶ Provide individual and team recognition.

▶ Foster win/win thinking.

When survival is at stake, internal conflict and individual differences in a team are set aside in favor of the needs of the larger team. For example, Franklin D. Roosevelt was accused of allowing the bombing of Pearl Harbor in 1941 in order to mobilize the American people to stop debating among themselves and enter the war. Saddam Hussein targeted the United States as the "evil empire" in order to remain in power despite widespread hunger, hardship, and repression in Iraq. The loss of U.S. markets to foreign companies in the 1980s mobilized corporate research and development efforts to increase quality and productivity as never before. The National Institute of Education's National Commission on Excellence in Education (1983) chose to report its findings on declining educational excellence as an open letter to the public in order to emphasize the threat to American society and to mobilize public support for change. The report began with the statement:

> If an unfriendly foreign power had attempted to impose on America the mediocre educational performance that exists today, we might well have viewed it as an act of war. As it stands, we have allowed this to happen to ourselves (p. 5).

Effective team leaders can overcome resistance and conflict by identifying factors outside the organization that threaten its welfare. If threats originating inside the organization are pointed out, conflict and rigidity are reinforced. Members tend to blame one another, find scapegoats, and try to reduce their discomfort (see Cameron, Kim, & Whetten, 1987). On the other hand, when threats are external, cooperation increases and individuals mobilize to overcome resistance. Managing the storming stage, therefore, involves raising the consciousness of people inside the organization to the presence of external threats.

Another way to manage storming behavior is to enhance the commitment of team members by *turning students into teachers.* In order to increase the commitment of newly hired engineers, one division within Dow Corning Corporation requires its engineers to spend time recruiting new employees on college campuses. Every other year, engineers are sent to college campuses to attract the best graduating students for positions at Dow Corning. However, recruiting occurs not just in engineering schools but in business schools, law schools, math and chemistry departments, and so on. Those trained to recruit students stay home, and the engineers are assigned to do that task.

Why would Dow Corning do such a thing? Why leave the experts home and send engineers to do a job for which they have not been trained? One reason for this strategy is that it helps increase the commitment of the newly hired engineers. To recruit college students, the engineers must publicly praise Dow Corning, restate the corporate vision, and point out its merits. After making such public pronouncements, individuals become committed to what they have espoused. In other words, new engineers are traditionally treated as students in the company, being recipients of the corporate vision and values. By becoming teachers of others outside the company, however, engineers convert themselves. Since a core competence of Dow Corning is chemical engineering, the intent is to increase the commitment of this crucial group by turning them into teachers of others.

Figure 3 illustrates a similar system used by Xerox Corporation in order to institutionalize a major change in the company's culture. Resistance to change, conflict, and differences in perspective were all effectively managed by forming teams across the company, labeled "family groups." Each family group engaged in four activities to generate commitment and implement the change:

Learn. Principles were taught and discussed.

Apply. Action plans were formed and an improvement agenda was implemented.

Teach. The principles and successful experiences were taught to others.

Inspect. The performance and action plans of others were measured and monitored.

Teams were exposed to the desired information four times: when they learned it, when they applied it, when they taught it, and when they inspected it. More importantly, team members' commitment to both the information and the team was ensured because of their involvement in each of these four steps.

Throughout this and other stages of team development, the team leader also needs to ensure that rewards and recognition are provided to the team, not just to individuals. A common mistake in teams is for individuals to be singled out for praise or awards instead of the team. "Employee of the month," "top salesperson," and "high scorer" are all awards that can destroy team cohesion and perpetuate team member competition and divisiveness. Team members are motivated to work for individual recognition instead of the good of the team. Consequently, team leaders need to ensure that the team itself is recognized and rewarded for achievement, not just individuals. This might be done, for example, with team-recognition ceremonies, T-shirts or trophies for all team members, or team pictures published in the newspaper. The point is to build commitment and unity in the team in order to counteract the tendency of the team to become fragmented during the storming stage. By so doing, the team is made ready to enter the fourth stage of development: performing.

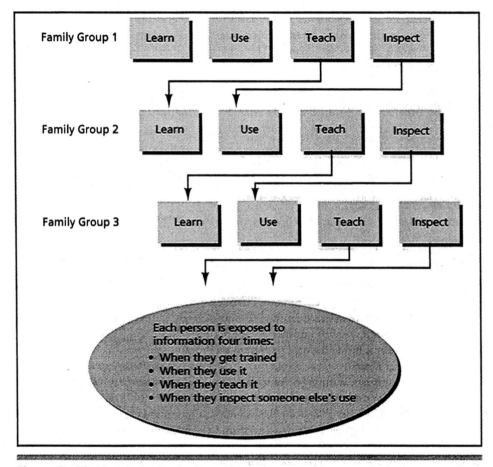

Figure 3 The Xerox Dissemination Process

The Performing Stage

Team member questions, interpersonal relationships, and task issues. When a team reaches the performing stage of development, it is able to function as a highly effective and efficient unit. Because it has worked through the issues embedded in each of the previous stages of development, the team is able to work at a high level of performance. The team has overcome issues of lack of trust, uncertainty, unclear expectations, nonparticipativeness, dependence, and self-centeredness typical of the first, or forming stage of development. It has clarified a vision, team member roles, the degree of personal commitment to the team, and the leader's direction typical of the conforming stage. It has overcome tendencies toward counterdependence, conflict, polarization, and disharmony typical of the storming stage. It now has the potential to develop the attributes of a high-performing team.

As illustrated by General Pagonis's team, the consequence of working through these various stages of development and reaching the stage of high performance was a well-oiled, robust team that pulled off one of the greatest logistical feats in military history.

> I meet with skepticism, even disbelief, when I tell people that I didn't issue a single order during the ground war. This is only slightly a stretch of the truth. Yes, people sought and got guidance. But the people in my command knew exactly what they were supposed to do in almost every conceivable circumstance. They had been trained and encouraged to think on their feet. I felt they could even deal with the inconceivable (p. 148).

A listing of attributes of high-performance teams is provided in Table 5, based on the research of Katzenbach and Smith (1993) and Hackman (1990).

- **Performance outcomes**

  High-performing teams *do* things. They *produce* something; they don't just discuss it. Without accomplishment, teams dissolve and become ineffective over time.

- **Specific, shared purpose and vision**

  The more specific the purpose, the more commitment, trust, and coordination can occur. Individuals don't work for themselves; they work for one another in pursuit of the shared purpose. The shared purpose can also be the same as a motivating vision of what the team should achieve.

- **Mutual, internal accountability**

  The sense of internal accountability is far greater than any accountability imposed by a boss or outsider. Self-evaluation and accountability characterize a high-performing team.

- **Blurring of formal distinctions**

  Team members do whatever is needed to contribute to the task, regardless of previous positions or titles. Team membership and team roles are more predominant than outside status.

- **Coordinated, shared work roles**

  Individuals always work in coordination with others on the team. The desired output is a single group product, not a set of individual products.

- **Inefficiency leading to efficiency**

  Because teams allow for lots of participation and sharing, mutual influence about purpose, and blurring of roles, they may initially be inefficient. As the team develops, because they come to know one another so well and can anticipate each other's moves, they become much more efficient than single people working alone.

- **Extraordinarily high quality**

  Teams produce outcomes above and beyond current standards of performance. They surprise and delight their various constituencies with quality levels not expected and never before obtained. An intolerance of mediocrity exists, so standards of performance are very high.

- **Creative continuous improvement**

  Large-scale innovations as well as never-ending small improvements characterize the team's processes and activities. Dissatisfaction with the status quo leads to a constant flow of new ideas, experimentation, and a quest for progress.

- **High credibility and trust**

  Team members trust one another implicitly, defend members who are not present, and form interdependent relationships with one another. Personal integrity and honesty characterize team activities and team member interactions.

- **Clarity of core competence**

  The unique talents and strategic advantages of the team and its members are clear. The ways in which these competencies can be utilized to further the team's objectives are well understood. Extraneous activities and deflections from the team's core mission are given low priority.

Table 5   Some Attributes of High-Performing Teams
Source: Katzenbach and Smith (1993); Petrock (1991); Hackman (1990).

These attributes are those that produce the benefits enumerated earlier in the chapter (e.g., productivity improvements, quality achievements, speed, and cost reductions). By and large, teams produce dramatic successes in organizations only if they reach the performing stage of development.

The team in the performing stage is not, of course, free of issues. Rather, team members still face a set of *questions* that tend to predominate in this stage:

▶ How can we continuously improve?

▶ How can we foster innovativeness and creativity?

- How can we build on our core competence?

- What further improvements can be made to our processes?

- How can we maintain a high level of energy and contribution to the team?

Team members' questions in this stage change from being static to being dynamic. They shift in focus from building the team and accomplishing objectives to fostering change and improvement. Continuous improvement replaces accomplishment as a key objective. Up to this point, the team has been trying to manage and resolve issues that lead to three key results in the team: (1) accomplishing tasks or objectives, (2) coordinating and integrating team members' roles, and (3) assuring the personal well-being of all team members. A process was necessary to ensure the collective responsibility and involvement of all team members in the team's tasks and goals. By successfully managing the issues that dominate the first three stages of development, however, the team does not need to continue to focus exclusively on making itself a competent unit. Instead, it can now turn to achieving a level of performance above the ordinary. This leads *interpersonal relationships* to be characterized by:

- High mutual trust

- Unconditional commitment to the team

- Multifaceted relationships among team members

- Mutual training and development

- Entrepreneurship

- Self-sufficiency

Team members in this stage are confident that they have an important role to play in the team and that they are competent enough to perform it and contribute to the team's success. They are self-sufficient. On the other hand, they are also closely connected to other members of the team in terms of their commitment and personal concern for them. This does not mean that all high-performing team members are close personal friends. Rather, they exhibit a sense of mutual responsibility and concern for one another as they carry out their work. Their relationships are not limited merely to accomplishing a task together but also extend to ensuring that each team member is learning, developing, and improving. Coaching and assisting one another is common. In General Pagonis's high-performing team, for

example, team members were continuously briefing one another and helping other team members become more competent. One example is the way Pagonis kept one of his key team members informed even though this team member wasn't invited to some key meetings:

Very early on I had gotten in the habit of sneaking John Carr into these briefing sessions with CINC [General Schwarzkopf and others] by having Carr flip my slides in and out of the overhead projector. That way, he stayed as smart and as current about the CINC's plans as I did (p. 131).

In addition to multifaceted relationships and unconditional commitment to one another, team members also take responsibility individually for continuously improving the team and its processes. Unlike the storming stage, however, this improvement is not based on counterdependence or needs to display individuality. Rather, it is based on a genuine commitment to seeing the team perform better than it is currently performing. Therefore, experimentation, trial-and-error learning, freewheeling discussions of new possibilities, and personal responsibility by everyone for upgrading performance is typical. The major *task issues* in this stage include:

- Capitalizing on core competence

- Fostering continuous improvement

- Anticipating needs of stakeholders and responding in advance of requests

- Enhancing speed and timeliness

- Encouraging creative problem solving

In this stage of development, the team becomes more aware of its **core competence** (see Prahalad & Hammel, 1990). Over time, teams develop particular areas of expertise or proficiency. Team members' styles, individual skills, patterns of interaction, and the team's vision help produce certain areas of specialty that the team develops as its own. It might be playing defense for a basketball team, solving complicated problems in a NASA team, or producing new ideas in an R&D team. In the case of General Pagonis' logistics team, it was, among other things, the team's ability to communicate clearly even minute details of the operation to all team members, to coordinate a myriad of activities concurrently, and to plan simultaneously for a large number of contingencies. It was these areas of core competence that explain Pagonis' remarkable claim that, once the ground war began, he did not issue a single order. The logistics support simply unfolded like clockwork.

Team core competence refers not only to an aggregation of individual team member skills but also includes knowledge, styles, communication patterns, and ways of behaving that come to characterize a team. They are unique features that are difficult to duplicate and give the team a special strength. By knowing its own core competence, a team can capitalize on these strengths and focus its energies on activities in which it can excel.

In addition to clarifying core competence, the performing stage is also characterized by a focus on the pursuit of both **continuous improvement** and **innovation.** Continuous improvement refers to small, incremental changes team members initiate. Continuous improvement can be represented by a hundred 1 percent changes. Innovation, on the other hand, represents large, visible, discontinuous changes. Innovations are breakthroughs that can be represented by a single 100 percent change. Traditionally, people in Eastern cultures have been thought to be continuous-improvement oriented; people in Western cultures have been thought to be innovation-oriented (Imai, 1986, p. 32):

> We find that the West has been stronger on the innovation side and Japan stronger on the Kaizen [the Japanese word for continuous improvement] side. These differences in emphasis are also reflected in the different social and cultural heritages, such as the Western educational system's stress on individual initiative and creativity as against the Japanese educational system's emphasis on harmony and collectivism.

Table 6 summarizes the differences between a continuous-improvement approach and an innovation approach to team development. Contrary to Imai's claim, high-performing teams in this stage of development emphasize both types of improvement: small and continuous as well as large and dramatic. A discussion of how to

ELEMENT	KAIZEN	INNOVATION
Effect	Long-term, long-lasting, undramatic	Short-term, dramatic
Procedure	Small steps	Large steps
Time frame	Continuous, incremental	Intermittent, nonincremental
Change	Gradual, constant, predictable	Abrupt, unpredictable
Involvement	Everyone	A few champions
Approach	Collectivism, group effort, systems approach	Rugged individualism, individual ideas and effort
Mode	Maintenance and improvement	Scrap and rebuild
Spark	Conventional know-how and state of the art	Technological breakthroughs, new inventions, new theories
Requirements	Little up-front investment, large effort to maintain it	Large up-front investment, little effort to maintain it
Orientation	People	Technology
Evaluation	Process, efforts, systems	Profits, outcomes
Training	Generalist	Specialist
Goal	Adaptability	Creativity
Information	Widely shared, open communication	Not widely shared, proprietary

Table 6 Characteristics of Innovation and Continuous Improvement (Kaizen)
Source: Imai, pp. 24, 32 (1986).

foster creative breakthroughs and innovation is contained in the chapter on Solving Problems Creatively. The implementation of a continuous-improvement approach, on the other hand, mostly depends on team members' orientation or the culture developed in the team. To illustrate this point, we will share a conversation one of the authors had with a Japanese executive who indicated that, as far as he was concerned, the United States had "lost the war." When asked what he meant, the executive clarified his statement by saying it was the economic war that had been lost. The United States was still ahead in economic productivity and size, he said, but Japan was catching up fast. And when Japan overtook the United States, the war would be over. He was challenged to justify this conclusion, and his rationale is noteworthy. He said:

> When you in the West receive a new product or technology, you assume that is the best it will ever be. Durability is at the highest level, no defects are present, and no repairs are needed. On the other hand, when we in the East receive a new product or technology, we assume that is the worst it will ever be, because we haven't had a chance to improve it yet. From now on, it gets better.

This statement illustrates the culture that is needed in high-performing teams, to develop a continuous-improvement approach coupled with an innovation approach to team performance. Addressing this challenge, along with others noted below, are part of the major tasks of the team leader.

Effective leader behaviors.　Teams functioning in the performing stage do not require strong, directive leadership in the traditional sense. They become more and more like a self-managing team, able to manage their own processes, training, rewards, and membership. On the other hand, an important role for a leader does exist that relates more to the cultural or cognitive aspects of the team than to its task performance or relationship building. Prescriptions for effective leader behaviors in this stage include:

- Foster innovation and continuous improvement simultaneously.
- Advance the quality culture of the team.
- Provide regular, ongoing feedback on team performance.

- Play sponsor and orchestrator roles for team members.
- Help the team avoid reverting back to earlier stages.

After having moved through the first three stages of development in the Persian Gulf, General Pagonis's logistics team moved into a stage characterized by innovation and continuous improvement. On one occasion, for example, Pagonis directed two team members to generate a solution to the problem of how to provide combat troops the same kinds of meals that support people and civilians were enjoying.

> Imagine that you've been at some remote and desolate desert site for weeks, or even months, consuming dehydrated or vacuum-packed military rations. One day, unannounced, an odd-looking vehicle with the word "Wolfmobile" painted on it comes driving into your camp. The side panels open up, and a smiling crew inside offers to cook you a hamburger to order. "Side of fries? How about a Coke?" Morale shot up everywhere the Wolfmobiles pulled in—a little bit of home in the desert (p. 129).

This incident illustrates the major task of the leader during this high-performance stage of development. It is to help team members expand their focus from merely accomplishing their work and maintaining good interpersonal relationships to seeking to upgrade and elevate the team's performance.

One way to do that is to help the team's approach to quality become more advanced. Table 7 summarizes three different phases of quality culture in which teams and organizations can operate. Few reach the third, most advanced level of quality culture, but if they are to be most successful, teams should do so. High-performing teams strive for this third phase. We briefly explain each of these phases and show how they relate to this stage of team development (see Cameron, 1992; Cameron & Barnett, 1998).

Error detection.　Most teams and organizations operate in the first phase of quality culture: error detection. In producing a product or service, they try to avoid mistakes and reduce waste (e.g., minimize rework, repair, scrap). They produce an outcome and then check to make certain that the work was done correctly. In other words, they "inspect-in" quality. In

ERROR DETECTION	ERROR PREVENTION	CREATIVE QUALITY AND CONTINUOUS IMPROVEMENT
Regarding Products	**Regarding Products**	**Regarding Products**
• Inspect and detect errors	• Prevent errors	• Improve and escalate on current standards of performance
• Reduce waste, cost of failure, and rework	• Expect zero defects	• Create new alternatives
• Correct mistakes	• Design and produce it right the first time	• Concentrate on things-gone-right
• Focus on the *output*	• Focus on *processes* and root causes	• Focus on the improving *suppliers* and *customers* as well as *processes*
Regarding Customers	**Regarding Customers**	**Regarding Customers**
• Avoid what may annoy customers	• Satisfy and exceed customer expectations	• Surprise and delight customers
• Respond to complaints quickly and accurately	• Help customers avoid future problems	• Engage in extra-mile restitution
• Reduce dissatisfaction	• Obtain customer preferences in advance, and follow up	• Anticipate customer expectations
• Focus on customer *needs* and requirements	• Focus on customer *preferences*	• *Create customer preferences*

Table 7 Phases of Quality Culture Development
Source: Cameron (1992).

their relationships with customers, they try to avoid annoying or dissatisfying them by responding to complaints in a timely and accurate manner. They focus on what customers need or require, and they ask customers after the product or service has been delivered how satisfied they are with it. By and large, this is a reactive or defensive approach to quality. It assures that the team meets basic requirements, but errors are identified after-the-fact.

Error prevention. In the second phase of quality—error prevention—the team shifts its emphasis toward avoiding mistakes by producing a product or service right the first time. Errors are prevented by focusing on how the task is accomplished (i.e., the process) and by holding all team members, not just inspectors or checkers, accountable for quality. Finding out why mistakes occurred is more important than finding individual errors. In relationships with customers, the emphasis moves from mere customer requirements to preferences and expectations. The team strives to exceed expectations and to help customers reach a high level of satisfaction with the product or service, not just nonannoyance. One way this happens is by training customers before a product or service is delivered to know what to expect and to share their preferences and

expectations before the product or service is produced. That way, customization can occur.

Innovation with continuous improvement. The third phase of quality—innovation coupled with continuous improvement—focuses on improvement rather than preventing errors. The team's standard changes from hitting a target to improving performance. Its objective is to achieve levels of quality in the product or service that are not only unexpected but unrequested. Problems are solved for customers and benefits provided that they don't expect anyone to deliver. New standards are actually created for customers because the team surprises and delights them. It is this third phase of quality culture that characterizes the world's best companies and its highest-performing teams.

The role of the leader in the performing stage of development is to help the team achieve this way of approaching the quality of its work. Team members are encouraged to: (1) strive continuously to improve their own and the team's work processes; (2) deliver extra-mile restitution to customers when mistakes do occur; (3) anticipate requests and respond in advance of receiving them; and (4) help solve problems for customers, and for other team members, that they don't expect anyone to solve for them. Research is clear that the highest levels of commitment and loyalty from customers and from team members, as well as organizational effectiveness, result from such an approach (Cameron, 1992, 1994; Cameron & Barnett, 1998).

Figure 4 illustrates these three phases of quality in the form of a graph. The vertical axis on the graph represents *satisfaction*, and it ranges from high satisfaction ("love it") on the top to low satisfaction ("hate it") on the bottom. The horizontal axis represents *performance* and ranges from low performance ("awful") on the left to high performance ("great") on the right. To understand the figure, consider the experience of purchasing an automobile. If we were to ask you what features are of most interest to you when purchasing a new car, you might list gas mileage, having four doors, roominess, a responsive engine, and good handling. If the auto dealer showed you a car that exactly met your expectations, we would position you at the intersection of the two axes

at point A, that is, in the middle of the satisfaction axis and in the middle of the performance axis. However, if you discovered that the car performed much better than you expected—say, gas mileage was better and the engine was more powerful—satisfaction would also increase to point B in the figure. If, however, the car got terrible gas mileage and rattled and leaked, that is, performed lower than expected, satisfaction would also decrease to point C on the graph. Connecting points A, B, and C results in a **performance curve.** These are the features that the team tries to improve continuously, to drive satisfaction up by finding ways to push performance to the right side of the axis. These features are identifiable and easily recognized.

If, when you got into your new car, however, you discovered that although the features you requested were satisfactory, the car had no carpet and no shock absorbers, you would no doubt be dissatisfied. But, we

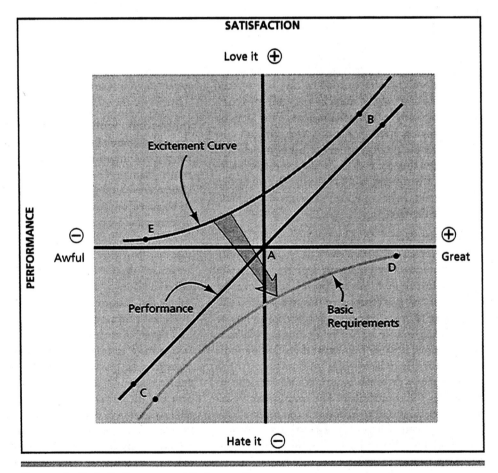

Figure 4   Basic, Performance, and Excitement Factors

suspect, we could ask you for a comprehensive list of features you are looking for in a car and you would probably never list carpet and shock absorbers. That is because you assume that these items are basic features of all new cars. If such basic features are missing, people are dissatisfied. However, no one cares much about whether the shock absorbers are painted red or black, cost $5 or $35, or whether there are one or two on each tire, so long as the ride is smooth. This illustrates the fact that a **basic curve** also exists in the figure. If certain basic features are absent, people are upset (point C). But the presence of additional basic features does not lead to a rise in satisfaction (point D). Having more of a basic feature simply does not add value.

Now assume that when you got into the car, the seat automatically adjusted itself to fit your height and leg length, the mirrors automatically adjusted themselves, and the seat became heated almost immediately on cold winter days. You were given something that you didn't expect—a delightful surprise. Satisfaction would go up to point B. On the other hand, if no such features were present in the car, satisfaction would not decrease, because these features weren't expected in the first place (point E). Connecting points B and E creates an **excitement curve** that shows what happens when innovation and breakthroughs occur. Loyalty and commitment are products of receiving features on the excitement curve.

The point of this figure is simple. Every team must perform its basic work competently and accomplish its basic, required tasks (the basic curve). It should also continuously improve its task accomplishment and strive to generate higher performance and satisfaction with its products or services (the performance curve). However, it can become a high-performance team by producing innovations, delightful surprises, and breakthroughs in task accomplishment and service delivery (the excitement curve). An important task of the team leader in this stage of development is to help the team accomplish all three kinds of activities.

As in previous stages of development, another important task of the team leader is to provide constant feedback to the team on its performance and make certain that adequate information is circulated among team members. Praise and pats on the back cannot be too frequent, but they should not be targeted primarily at individuals. The team as a unit needs to be recognized and kept informed. A common prescription of high-performing team leaders, in fact, is "communicate, communicate, communicate." Most team lead-

ers suggest that this is the key to their success (see Katzenbach & Smith, 1993). Communicating praise and feedback should occur at regularly scheduled intervals (consistency) and should be frequent.

In addition, as discussed in the chapters on Solving Problems Creatively and Empowering and Delegating, good team leaders also play sponsoring and orchestrator roles. This means that they help sponsor the ideas and activities of other team members by obtaining resources, removing obstacles, and providing encouragement to them. They help sponsor others' success. Sponsoring team members means encouraging them, recognizing them, and facilitating their development. Good team leaders also play orchestrator roles by seeing to it that team activities are coordinated, suggestions are fit into the team's plans for the future, and that the innovative suggestions of team members are integrated and harmonized together. Team leaders don't have to be the sources of all good ideas or change efforts. In fact, sponsoring and orchestrating the ideas and actions of their team members makes the entire team, including themselves, more effective.

We have pointed out thus far that teams progress through four different stages of development. The fourth, or final, stage is the one achieved by high-performing teams and the one toward which all teams should aspire. The issues that must be resolved along the way, however, and the changes that team leaders must make to push the team along to the next stage of development are significant. Leaders of effective teams do not become such by accident. They are able to diagnose which stage a team is in and to identify the main issues facing the team. They can therefore answer team members' questions, facilitate effective interpersonal relationships in the team, resolve task issues, and display effective leadership behaviors.

Handling Difficult Team Members

Despite the best efforts of a team leader or the conductor of a meeting, some participants do not always behave in ways that help the team be successful. Some people may be more interested in self-aggrandizement than in team success. They may criticize other team members or try to dominate the meeting agenda. Sometimes, they don't pull their own weight and don't take responsibility. This latter tendency toward "social loafing" is especially common. It has been observed that when three people pull together on a rope, they achieve only two and a half times the power of individuals acting alone. In fact, the larger the group, the less effort put forth by any single individual member (Latane, Williams, & Harkins, 1979). This is because of four factors:

Equity of effort. "No one else is working up to his potential, so why should I?"

Loss of accountability. "I'm an insignificant part of this large group, so no one will notice or care what I do."

Sharing of rewards. "Why should I work harder than others when we will all get the same reward?"

Coordination loss. "The more people involved, the more I have to wait for others, talk to others, and coordinate my work with others, so I'm less efficient."

How do effective team leaders cope with disruptive, difficult, or loafing team members? When students are writing a report together during a semester, how do they assure that all team members will take equal responsibility for the report? How do business task forces ensure that when team members enter a meeting, they will not use it as a forum to impress the boss? If everyone on the team gets the same reward, what is to keep some members from getting a reward that they didn't earn? Table 8 identifies 11 disruptive behaviors that are common in teams, along with suggested responses. The general rule is to avoid embarrassing or intimidating team members, regardless of their disruptive behavior. The way difficult team members are handled not only sets the tone for the kind of discussion that will ensue but also helps determine what kind of feelings will characterize team members. It sets the tone and the culture of the team. In these situations, instead of attacking and being defensive, use supportive communication, collaborative conflict management, and techniques of empowerment (as discussed in the chapters on Communicating Supportively, Managing Conflict, and Empowering and Delegating). Discuss concerns in an open, direct, problem-oriented, and supportive manner.

TYPE	BEHAVIOR	SUGGESTED RESPONSE
Hostile	"It'll never work." "That's a typical engineering viewpoint."	"How do others here feel about this?" "You may be right, but let's review the facts and evidence." "It seems we have a different perspective on the details, but we agree on the principles."
Know-It-All	"I have worked on this project more than anyone else in this room . . ." "I have a Ph.D. in Economics, and . . ."	"Let's review the facts." (Avoid theory or speculation.) "Another noted authority on this subject has said . . ."
Loudmouth	Constantly blurts out ideas or questions. Tries to dominate the meeting.	Interrupt: "Can you summarize your main point/question for us?" "I appreciate your comments, but we should also hear from others." "Interesting point. Help us understand how it relates to our subject."
Interrupter	Starts talking before others are finished.	"Wait a minute, Jim, let's let Jane finish what she was saying."
Interpreter	"What John is really trying to say is . . ." "John would respond to that question by saying . . ."	"Let's let John speak for himself. Go ahead, John, finish what you were saying." "John, how would you respond?" "John, do you think Jim correctly understood what you said?"

Table 8 Suggestions for Handling Difficult Team Members
Source: Adapted from Peoples, 1988, pp. 147–155.

TYPE	BEHAVIOR	SUGGESTED RESPONSE
Gossiper	"Isn't there a regulation that you can't . . ." "I thought I heard the V.P. of Finance say . . ."	"Can anyone here verify this?" (Assuming no response.) "Let's not take the time of the group until we can verify the accuracy of this information."
Whisperer	Irritating side conversation going on between two people.	Hints: 1. Walk up close to the guilty parties and make eye contact. 2. Stop talking and establish dead silence. 3. Politely ask the whisperers to wait until the meeting is over to finish their conversation.
Silent Distractor	Reads newspapers, rolls their eyes, shakes their heads, fidgets.	Hints: Ask them questions to determine their level of interest, support, and expertise. Try to build an alliance by drawing them into the discussion. If that doesn't work, discuss your concerns with them during a break.
Busy-Body	Ducks in and out of the meeting repeatedly, taking messages, dealing with crises.	Hints: Preventive measures include: scheduling the presentation away from the office, checking with common offenders before the meeting to ask if the planned time is OK for minimum interruptions.
Latecomer	Comes late and interrupts the meeting.	Hints: Announce an odd time (8:46) for the meeting to emphasize the necessity for promptness. Make it inconvenient for latecomers to find a seat, and stop talking until they do. Establish a "latecomer's kitty" for refreshments.
Early Leaver	Announces, with regrets, that they must leave for another important activity.	Hints: Before starting, announce the ending time and ask if anyone has a scheduling conflict.

Table 8 *(continued)*

Summary

Because almost everyone is a member of at least one team at work or in nonwork activities, because teams are becoming increasingly prevalent in the workplace, and because teams have been shown to be powerful tools to improve the performance of individuals and organizations, it is important to become proficient in leading and participating in teams. But merely putting people together with an assigned task does not make them into a team. Because teams develop through different stages—each with its own unique challenges and issues—it takes skill to help a team become a high-performing unit. Different behaviors are required in each of the four stages of team development. We have described the different attributes of each of these stages and have provided guidelines for managing the issues that characterize them.

Behavioral Guidelines

1. Determine the stage in which your team is operating by identifying the major questions, interpersonal relationships, and task issues that characterize the team. Use Table 2 for a comprehensive listing. Adopt the appropriate leadership behaviors that correspond to that stage of development.

2. Become familiar with the attributes of high-performing teams and make certain that these attributes characterize your team. In particular, ensure that goals are clear, known by everyone, and achieved in small steps; that standards of excellence, rather than mere acceptability, are applied; that feedback on results is provided; that team members can use all their skills and knowledge, and that they are continuously trained; that adequate equipment and facilities, performance measures, and rules and penalties are available; that performance-based rewards and praise and recognition are prevalent; that team members have autonomy; that plans and tactics to beat a specific competitor are in place; and that team members have a sense of commitment to the team.

3A. When a team is in the forming stage of development:

▶ Make certain that all team members are introduced to one another.

▶ Answer team members' questions, even those that they don't ask aloud.

▶ Work to establish a foundation of trust and openness between yourself and the team members, and among the team members themselves.

▶ Model the behaviors that you expect from all team members, such as honesty, openness, friendliness, and so on.

▶ Clarify the goals, procedures, and expectations of the team.

3B. When a team is in the conforming stage of development:

▶ Facilitate role differentiation among team members by helping them learn to perform various task-facilitating and relationship-building roles.

▶ Show support to team members by complimenting and recognizing them.

▶ Provide feedback to individuals on the team and to the team as a unit. Feedback may be positive or negative, but make certain that it focuses on behavior rather than people, on observations rather than inferences, on the here-and-now situation rather than the past, on sharing information rather than giving advice, on the amount of information that can be useful to the team members rather than the amount you might like to give, on the value it will have to team members rather than just letting off steam, and on a specific time and place.

▶ Articulate a vision of the future for the team that is both left-brain and right-brain oriented, interesting to team members, and that expresses passion regarding core principles.

▶ Help generate commitment to the vision by encouraging team members to express public approval of the vision, participate in articulating and implementing it, and communicating it frequently.

3C. When a team is in the storming stage of development:

▶ Adopt a mediator role when conflict is encountered.

▶ Encourage a win/win philosophy in the team: If a single team member wins, everyone wins.

▶ Reemphasize the vision for the team and its core principles in order to maintain a strong team bond.

▶ Avoid groupthink by encouraging open discussion, having at least one team member critically evaluate the team's decisions, forming subgroups in the team, formally designating a devil's advocate in the team, having important decisions reviewed by an outside expert, and holding second-chance meetings to review the team's decisions.

▶ Encourage the team to assess, analyze, and improve its processes by identifying the sequence of steps used to accomplish each task, mapping those steps, and identifying ways to improve the process by making it faster, more efficient, and of higher quality.

▶ To enhance team cohesion and commitment, identify a common enemy or external adversary for the team.

▶ Turn students into teachers by having team members represent team values and goals to outsiders.

▶ In addition to providing recognition to individuals in the team, make certain that rewards and recognition are given to the team as a unit.

3D. When a team is in the performing stage of development:

▶ Capitalize on the core competence of the team by articulating clearly what that competence is and building upon those strengths.

▶ Foster both innovation, or dramatic breakthrough changes, and continuous improvement, or small incremental changes, among all team members.

▶ Advance the quality culture of the team by moving from an error-detection approach through error-prevention to creative quality. Work toward "excitement" in the team's outputs and services.

▶ Provide regular, ongoing feedback on team performance.

▶ Play sponsor and orchestrator roles for team members so that their ideas and changes are integrated with those of others and receive adequate support.

▶ Help the team avoid reverting back to earlier stages of development by continuing to emphasize the attributes of high-performance teams.

4. Handle difficult team members not by embarrassing or intimidating them, but by helping them to become more productive contributors to the team's effort through supportive communication, conflict management, and empowerment.

Skill Analysis

Cases Involving Building Effective Teams

The *Tallahassee Democrat*'s ELITE Team

Katzenbach and Smith (1993, pp. 67–72), as part of their extensive research on teams, observed the formation of a team at the *Tallahassee Democrat,* the only major newspaper left in Tallahassee, Florida. Here is their description of how the team, which called itself "ELITE Team," performed over time. All incidents and names are factual. As you read the description, look for evidence of team development stages.

Fred Mott, general manager of the *Democrat,* recognized [the declining profitability and distribution of most major metropolitan newspapers] earlier than many of his counterparts. In part, Mott took his lead from Jim Batten, who made "customer obsession" the central theme of his corporate renewal effort shortly after he became Knight-Ridder's CEO. But the local marketplace also shaped Mott's thinking. The Democrat was Tallahassee's only newspaper and made money in spite of its customer service record. Mott believed, however, that further growth could never happen unless the paper learned to serve customers in ways "far superior to anything else in the marketplace." The ELITE

Team story actually began with the formation of another team made up of Mott and his direct reports. The management group knew they could not hope to build a "customer obsession" across the mile-high barriers isolating production from circulation from advertising without first changing themselves. It had become all too common, they admitted, for them to engage in "power struggles and finger pointing."

Using regularly scheduled Monday morning meetings, Mott's group began to "get to know each other's strengths and weaknesses, bare their souls, and build a level of trust." Most important, they did so by focusing on real work they could do together. For example, early on they agreed to create a budget for the paper as a team instead of singly as function heads.

Over time, the change in behavior at the top began to be noticed. One of the women who later joined the ELITE Team, for example, observed that the sight of senior management holding their "Monday morning come-to-Jesus" meetings really made a difference to her and others. "I saw all this going on and I thought, 'What are they so happy about?'"

Eventually, as the team at the top got stronger and more confident, they forged a higher aspiration: to build customer focus and break down the barriers across the broad base of the paper. . . .

A year after setting up the new [team], however, Mott was both frustrated and impatient. Neither the Advertising Customer Service department, a series of customer surveys, additional resources thrown against the problem in the interim, nor any number of top management exhortations had made any difference. Ad errors persisted, and sales reps still complained of insufficient time with customers. In fact, the new unit had turned into another organizational barrier.

Customer surveys showed that too many advertisers still found the *Democrat* unresponsive to their needs and too concerned with internal procedures and deadlines. People at the paper also had evidence beyond surveys. In one instance, for example, a sloppily prepared ad arrived through a fax machine looking like a "rat had run across the page." Yet the ad passed through the hands of seven employees and probably would have found its way into print if it had not been literally unreadable! As someone commented, "It was not anyone's job to make sure it was right. If they felt it was simply their job to type or paste it up, they just passed it along." This particular fax, affectionately know as the "rat tracks fax," came to symbolize the essential challenge at the *Democrat*. . . .

At the time, Mott was reading about Motorola's quality programs and the goal of zero defects. He decided to heed Dunlap's advice by creating a special team of workers charged with eliminating all errors in advertisements. Mott now admits he was skeptical that frontline people could become as cohesive a team as he and his direct reports. So he made Dunlap, his trusted confidante, the leader of the team that took on the name ELITE for "ELIminate The Errors."

A year later, Mott was a born-again believer in teams. Under ELITE's leadership, advertising accuracy, never before tracked at the paper, had risen sharply and stayed above 99 percent. Lost revenues from errors, previously as high as $10,000 a month, had dropped to near zero. Ad sales reps had complete confidence in the Advertising Customer Service department's capacity and desire to treat each ad as though the *Democrat*'s existence were at stake. And surveys showed a huge positive swing in advertiser satisfaction. Mott considered all of this nothing less than a minor miracle.

The impact of ELITE, however, went beyond numbers. It completely redesigned the process by which the *Democrat* sells, creates, produces, and bills for advertisements. More important yet, it stimulated and nurtured the customer obsession and cross-functional cooperation required to make the new process work. In effect, this team of mostly frontline workers transformed an entire organization with respect to customer service.

ELITE had a lot going for it from the beginning. Mott gave the group a clear performance goal (eliminate errors) and a strong mix of skills (12 of the best people from all parts of the paper). He committed himself to follow through by promising, at the first meeting, that "whatever solution you come up with will be implemented." In addition, Jim Batten's customer obsession movement helped energize the task force.

But it took more than a good sendoff and an overarching corporate theme to make ELITE into a high-performance team. In this case, the personal commitments began to grow, unexpectedly, over the early months as the team grappled with its challenge. At first, the group spent more time pointing fingers at one another than coming to grips with advertising errors. Only when one of them produced the famous "rat tracks fax" and told the story behind it did the group start to admit that everyone—not everyone else—was at fault. Then, recalls one member, "We had some pretty hard discussions. And there were tears in those meetings."

The emotional response galvanized the group to the task at hand and to one another. And the closer it got, the more focused it became on the challenge. ELITE decided to look carefully at the entire process by which an ad was sold, created, printed, and billed. When it did, the team discovered patterns in the errors, most of which could be attributed to time pressures, bad communication, and poor attitude. . . .

Commitment to one another drove ELITE to expand its aspirations continually. Having started with the charge to eliminate errors, ELITE moved on to break down functional barriers, then to redesigning the entire advertising process, then to refining new standards and measures for customer service, and, finally, to spreading its own brand of "customer obsession" across the entire *Democrat*. . . . Inspired by ELITE, for example, one production crew started coming to work at 4 a.m., to ease time pressures later in the day. . . .

To this day, the spirit of ELITE lives on at the *Democrat*. "There is no beginning and no end," says Dunlap. "Every day we experience something we learn from." ELITE's spirit made everyone a winner—the customers, the employees, management, and even Knight-Ridder's corporate leaders. CEO Jim Batten was so impressed that he agreed to pay for managers from other Knight-Ridder papers to visit the *Democrat* to learn from ELITE's experience. And, of course, the 12 people who committed themselves to one another and their paper had an impact and an experience none of them will ever forget.

Discussion Questions

1. What were the stages of development of the ELITE Team? Identify specific examples of each of the four stages of development as you progress through the case.

2. How do you explain the team's reaching a high-performance condition? What were the major predictive factors?

3. Why didn't Mott's top management team reach a high level of performance? Why was an ELITE team needed? What was his team lacking?

4. Make recommendations about what Mott should do now to capitalize on the ELITE Team experience. If you were to become a consultant to the *Tallahassee Democrat*, what advice would you give Mott about how he can capitalize on team building?

The Cash Register Incident

A store owner had just turned off the lights in the store when a man appeared and demanded money. The owner opened a cash register. The contents of the cash register were scooped up, and the man sped away. A member of the police force was notified promptly.

This exercise is accomplished in two steps, the first by yourself and the second in a team with four or five other people.

Step 1: Assume that you observed the incident described in the paragraph above. Later, a reporter asks you questions about what you observed in order to write an article for the local newspaper. Answer the questions from the reporter by yourself. Do not talk with anyone else about your answers.

Answer

Y	yes
N	no
DK	don't know

Step 2: The reporter wants to interview your entire team together. As a team, discuss the answers to each question and reach a consensus decision—that is, one with which everyone on the team agrees. Do not vote or engage in horse-trading. The reporter wants to know what you all agree upon.

Statements about the Incident

"Now, as a reporter, I'm interested in what happened here. Can you tell me just what occurred? I'd like to see if you can confirm or deny the following statements that I've picked up by talking to some other people."

Statement

Alone   Team

_____ _____ 1. Did a man appear after the owner turned off his store lights?

_____ _____ 2. Was the robber a man?

_____ _____ 3. Is it true that the man did not demand money?

_____ _____ 4. The man who opened the cash register was the owner, right?

_____ _____ 5. Did the store owner scoop up the contents of the cash register?

_____ _____ 6. OK, so someone opened the cash register, right?

_____ _____ 7. Let me get this straight, after the man who demanded the money scooped up the contents of the cash register, he ran away?

_____ _____ 8. The contents of the cash register contained money, but you don't know how much?

_____ _____ 9. Did the robber demand money of the owner?

_____ _____ 10. OK, by way of summary, the incident concerns a series of events in which only three persons are involved: the owner of the store, a man who demanded money, and a member of the police force?

_____ _____ 11. Let me be sure I understand. The following events occurred: Someone demanded money, the cash register was opened, its contents were scooped up, and a man dashed out of the store?

When you have finished your team decision making and mock interview with the reporter, the instructor will provide correct answers. Calculate how many answers you got right as an individual, then calculate how many right answers your team achieved.

Discussion Questions

1. How many individuals did better than the team as a whole? Why?

2. How could your team discussion have been improved?

3. What roles did different members of the team play? Who was most helpful? Who was least helpful?

Team Diagnosis and Leadership Exercise

Consider a team in which you are now a member. If you belong to a team in a college class, select that one. Or you may select a team at your employment, in your church or community, or you may even diagnose your family. Use the following questions to help you determine the stage of development in which your team is operating. Then design a strategy for effectively leading this team to the next higher stage of development or, if in Stage 4, to a high level of performance. Share that strategy with others in class in a small group setting, and add at least one good idea from someone else's strategy to your own design.

Use the following scale in your rating of your team right now.

Rating Scale

1   Not typical at all of my team   3   Somewhat typical of my team

2   Not very typical of my team   4   Very typical of my team

Stage 1

_____ 1. Not everyone is clear about the objectives and goals of the team.

_____ 2. Not everyone is personally acquainted with everyone else in the team.

_____ 3. Only a few team members actively participate.

_____ 4. Interactions among team members are very safe or somewhat superficial.

_____ 5. Trust among all team members has not yet been established.

_____ 6. Many team members seem to need direction from the leader in order to participate.

Stage 2

_____ 7. All team members know and agree with the objectives and goals of the team.

_____ 8. Team members all know one another.

_____ 9. Team members are very cooperative and actively participate in the activities of the team.

_____ 10. Interactions among team members are friendly, personal, and nonsuperficial.

_____ 11. A comfortable level of trust has been established among team members.

_____ 12. Some team members play different roles from others; for example, some push for task accomplishment, others focus on relationships, others help clarify issues, and so on.

Stage 3

_____ 13. Disagreements and differing points of view are openly expressed by team members.

_____ 14. Competition exists among some team members.

_____ 15. Some team members do not follow the rules or the team norms.

_____ 16. Subgroups or coalitions exist within the team.

_____ 17. Discussion issues seem to get polarized—either-or, black-or-white—when examined by the team with some members on one side and others on the other side.

_____ 18. The authority or competence of the team leader is being questioned or challenged.

Stage 4

_____ 19. Team members focus a lot of energy on cooperating actively to improve the team's performance.

_____ 20. Team members feel free to try out new ideas, experiment, share something crazy, or do novel things.

_____ 21. The standards of excellence and expectations for team performance by team members themselves are very high.

_____ 22. Not all team members always agree, but each is given respect and value, and disagreements are resolved productively.

_____ 23. An unconditional commitment exists to the team and its success, so self-aggrandizement is at a minimum.

_____ 24. The team is very fast in making decisions or producing output but maintains very high quality standards.

Scoring

Add up the scores for the items in each stage of team development. Generally, one stage stands out clearly as having the highest scores. If more than one stage receives high scores, it will be necessary for the team leader to manage more than one set of developmental issues. However, because team stages develop sequentially, this is a rare occurrence.

Total of Stage 1 items

Total of Stage 2 items

Total of Stage 3 items

Total of Stage 4 items

Leadership Strategy

1. Identify at least two or three strategies that you can implement to enhance team performance, overcome the obstacles to improvement, and foster higher levels of team effectiveness. Use the guidelines in Table 3 in this chapter for thought-starters, but do not limit

yourself to just those suggested in the table. Stretch yourself to identify an appropriate leadership strategy for improving your team at the stage in which it is performing. Especially focus on what the team should *start doing, stop doing,* and *continue doing.*

Strategies

2. Now identify who will be involved, when you will begin to apply your strategy, and how you will execute the intervention (i.e., the process you will use to implement it).

Who

When

How

3. Share this plan with a small group, receive feedback and suggestions on it, and add at least one new idea from another group member's plan that you had not thought of yourself.

New Idea

Skill Practice

Jimmy Lincoln

Jimmy has a grim background. He is the third child in an inner-city minority family of seven. He has not seen his parents for several years. He recalls that his father used to come home drunk and beat up family members; everyone ran when he came staggering home.

His mother, according to Jimmy, wasn't much better. She was irritable and unhappy, and she always predicted that Jimmy would come to no good end. Yet she worked, when her health allowed, to keep the family in food and clothing. She frequently decried the fact that she was not able to be the kind of mother she would like to be.

Jimmy quit school in the seventh grade. He had great difficulty conforming to the school routine: misbehaving often, playing truant frequently, and getting into fights with schoolmates. On several occasions, he was picked up by the police and, along with members of his group, questioned during investigations into cases of both petty and grand larceny. The police regarded him as a "high-potential troublemaker."

The juvenile officer of the court saw in Jimmy some good qualities that no one else seemed to sense. This man, Mr. O'Brien, took it on himself to act as a father figure to Jimmy. He had several long conversations with Jimmy, during which he managed to penetrate to some degree Jimmy's defensive shell. He represented to Jimmy the first semblance of personal, caring influence in his life. Through Mr. O'Brien's efforts, Jimmy returned to school and obtained a high school diploma. Afterwards, Mr. O'Brien helped him obtain his first job.

Now, at age 22, Jimmy is a stockroom clerk at Costello Pharmaceutical Laboratory. On the whole, his performance has been acceptable, but there have been glaring exceptions. One involved a clear act of insubordination, though the issue was fairly unimportant. On another occasion, Jimmy was accused by a co-worker, on circumstantial grounds, of destroying some expensive equipment. Though the investigation is still open, it appears that the destruction was accidental. He also seems to have lost an extremely important requisition (although he claims never to have seen it). In addition, Jimmy's laid-back attitude and wisecracking ways tend to irritate his co-workers.

It is also important to note that Jimmy is not an attractive young man. He is rather weak and sickly, his appearance is disheveled, and he shows unmistakable signs of long years of social deprivation. Researchers in the lab have commented that his appearance doesn't fit in with the company's image. Others have wondered aloud (half jokingly, half seriously) whether he is counting drugs or taking drugs.

Jimmy's supervisor is fairly new to management and is not sure how to handle this situation. He sees merit in giving Jimmy the benefit of the doubt and helping him out, but he frankly wonders if it is worth the hassle. Seeking advice, the *supervisor* organizes a committee of individuals close to the situation. These include the *crew chief* (who has expressed frustration about the effects of Jimmy's performance and reputation on the morale of the work group), a *seasoned manager* (who has a reputation for being even-handed), a *union representative* (who tends to view most acts of employee discipline as an infringement on employee rights), a *member of the personnel department* (who is concerned about following proper company procedures), and a *member of the company's affirmative action office* (who is concerned that managers at Costello do not fully understand the handicap workers like Jimmy bring with them to the workplace and hence the need to give them special assistance and direction).

Assignment

There are six roles described in this exercise. After reading the case, fill out the "personal preference" part of the worksheet in Appendix I. Do this from the perspective of your assigned role.

When the worksheet has been completed, the supervisor should act as chair of the committee and begin the discussion. The group's assignment is to reach consensus on the rank-ordered options from this list. Group members should stay in character during the discussion. For example, they should not compare their lists and use a statistical process to generate their rank-order. Observers should be assigned to give the group feedback on their performance, using the Meeting Evaluation Worksheet and the Role Evaluation Worksheet.

Worksheet
Identify which of the alternatives you prefer in responding to Jimmy Lincoln. Be prepared to explain and to defend your choices.

Personal Preference	Group Decision	
_____	_____	1. Give Jimmy a warning that at the next sign of trouble a formal reprimand will be placed in his file.
_____	_____	2. Do nothing, as it is unclear that Jimmy has done anything seriously wrong. Back off and give him a chance to prove himself.

_____ _____ 3. Create strict controls (do's and don'ts) for Jimmy with immediate discipline for any misbehavior.

_____ _____ 4. Give Jimmy a great deal of warmth and personal attention (overlooking his annoying mannerisms) so he will feel accepted.

_____ _____ 5. Fire him. It's not worth the time and effort spent for such a low-level position.

_____ _____ 6. Treat Jimmy the same as everyone else, but provide an orderly routine so he can develop proper work habits.

_____ _____ 7. Call Jimmy in and logically discuss the problem with him and ask what you can do to help.

_____ _____ 8. Do nothing now, but watch him so you can reward him the next time he does something good.

Process Assessment

Using the examples in Table 4 and Figure 2 as examples, generate a formal process assessment, analysis, and improvement strategy for one of the following processes. Do this activity in your team, and use the following steps:

1. Identify all the activities involved in the process. Organize them into a sequential flow.

2. Map the activities to show how they are connected to one another, who is involved in the activities, what coordination occurs, and what communication lines are operative.

3. Now generate an ideal process map. That is, generate the same process where time, waste, and errors could be cut in half. Design from scratch a "perfect" process.

4. Based on the ideal map, refine the process map you generated in Step 2 and show the improvements you can make in it.

5. Make a presentation of your process assessment, analysis, and improvement strategy to the larger class. They should critique it in terms of its realism, the accuracy of the assessment and the map, and the amount of improvement you identified.

Potential Processes to Analyze

Select a process in which you are involved that could be improved through process assessment, analysis, and improvement procedures. If none comes readily to mind, you may select one of the following:

1. The process used for course registration in your college.

2. The process used to serve a meal at the college cafeteria.

3. The process used to evaluate students and teachers in your college or training facility.

4. The process used to repair and service your car.

5. The process used to rent an automobile at an airport.

6. The process involved in obtaining a college degree.

7. The process used to restock food on supermarket shelves.

Skill Application

Activities for Building Effective Teams

Suggested Assignments

1. Teach someone else how to determine which stage of development a team is in and what leader behaviors are most effective in each separate stage.

2. Analyze the characteristics of a team in which you are a member. Determine in what ways its functioning could be improved. Based on the attributes of high-performance teams discussed earlier, identify what could be done to improve its performance.

3. Conduct a role analysis of a real team meeting that is trying to make a decision, solve a problem, or examine an issue. Who performed what roles? Which team members were most helpful? Which team members were least helpful? Provide feedback to the team on what roles you saw being played, what roles were missing, and what improvements could have made the team more effective.

4. Write out a formal vision statement for a team you are leading. Make certain that the vision possesses the attributes of effective, energizing vision statements discussed in the chapter. Identify specifically what you can do to get team members to commit to that vision.

5. Use the Nominal Group Technique in a team meeting to reach a consensus decision. Follow precisely the steps outlined in the text.

6. Select a team assigned to perform a task or produce an outcome. Do a formal process assessment and analysis by listing the activities involved in the process and constructing a process map. Then generate ways to improve the process by eliminating redundancies, cutting out time, or finding ways to prevent mistakes.

7. For a team in which you participate, identify the basic services that it must deliver, the performance services that it should deliver, and the excitement services that it could deliver to its customers if it were not only to satisfy, but also surprise and delight them.

Application Plan and Evaluation

The intent of this exercise is to help you apply this cluster of skills in a real-life, out-of-class setting. Now that you have become familiar with the behavioral guidelines that form the basis of effective skill performance, you will improve most by trying out those guidelines in an everyday context. Unlike a classroom activity, in which feedback is immediate and others can assist you with their evaluations, this skill application activity is one you must accomplish and evaluate on your own. There are two parts to this activity. Part 1 helps prepare you to apply the skill. Part 2 helps you evaluate and improve on your experience. Be sure to write down answers to each item. Don't short-circuit the process by skipping steps.

Part 1. Planning

1. Write down the two or three aspects of this skill that are most important to you. These may be areas of weakness, areas you most want to improve, or areas that are most salient to a problem you face right now. Identify the specific aspects of this skill that you want to apply.

2. Now identify the setting or the situation in which you will apply this skill. Establish a plan for performance by actually writing down a description of the situation. Who else will be involved? When will you do it? Where will it be done?

   Circumstances:

   Who else?

   When?

   Where?

3. Identify the specific behaviors you will engage in to apply this skill. Operationalize your skill performance.

4. What are the indicators of successful performance? How will you know you have been effective? What will indicate you have performed competently?

Part 2. Evaluation

5. After you have completed your implementation, record the results. What happened? How successful were you? What was the effect on others?

6. How can you improve? What modifications can you make next time? What will you do differently in a similar situation in the future?

7. Looking back on your whole skill practice and application experience, what have you learned? What has been surprising? In what ways might this experience help you in the long term?

Making Oral and Written Presentations

skill development

■ Skill Learning

Making Oral and Written
  Presentations
Essential Elements of Effective
  Presentations
Summary and Behavioral
  Guidelines

⬡ Skill Practice

Speaking as a Leader
Quality Circles at Battle
  Creek Foods

■ Skill Learning

Making Oral and Written Presentations

Taylor Billingsley was hired as a sales representative in the Apex Communications Corporation in 1972. With training and hard work, she advanced through the levels of the corporation, finally landing the position of senior vice-president in charge of personnel. Though she had anticipated that this position would require some adjustments, she was surprised at the kinds of changes she faced during her first few weeks on the job. Taylor had a lot of ideas about how to make the personnel division work more efficiently, but she realized almost immediately that she had to convince others to adopt them. In addition, she had to establish her own credibility—to make her employees and interested outsiders understand and appreciate her personal commitments and management style.

In the first few days on the job, Taylor had several opportunities to communicate her philosophy and expectations during a number of meetings with the departments in her division. Some of these meetings were formal, such as when she first accepted the position; others were more informal, including lunch meetings with the division heads. Immediately following the anouncement of her appointment, she also wrote a memo to her division heads and their employees outlining some of her ideas for moving the department forward. In separate memos she addressed the personnel development and financial benefits departments, introducing a new project and encouraging them to move ahead full speed to develop a new policy on research teams.

Then Taylor began a round of visits with people who worked in her division. She talked individually with several workers and responded to the questions posed by informal groups. She was asked to write up her evaluation of morale among workers in her division and forward it to the corporate chief executive officer. The latest financial reports released by the company's controller's office revealed that quarterly figures were down unexpectedly; it seemed that certain costs had risen dramatically. Taylor was concerned and adjusted a report she had written for a scheduled meeting with the region's top executives to reflect these new developments. Later, she spoke to an assembled employee group in the cafeteria in an effort to calm their fears about job cuts. At another facility located in a tough urban environment, the task proved more difficult. Workers were outspokenly critical of the company and challenged much of the information she presented. Following these meetings, Taylor was the featured dinner speaker at a regional Chamber of Commerce meeting.

Taylor Billingsley experienced the challenges of management in her new position. During her first two weeks, she addressed dozens of groups on a broad range of subjects; she wrote even more reports and memos. In most of this communication, Taylor was not simply presenting facts. Instead, she was conveying support, pointing a new direction, generating enthusiasm, communicating a sense of caring, building good will, and underscoring the value of teamwork. Some situations called for polite, ceremonial messages; others were confrontational. Some covered familiar material; others stretched her ability to find the right words to convey her ideas. At the end of her first two weeks, Taylor began to appreciate the importance of communication skills.

Managers have to master the basic elements of public communication and be flexible enough to adapt them to varying situations (Barrett, 1977; Mambert, 1976; Peoples, 1988; Sanford & Yeager, 1963; Wilcox, 1967). Like Taylor Billingsley, you may find yourself addressing many different audiences through speeches and in writing. Like Taylor Billingsley, you will probably discover very quickly that your effectiveness as a manager depends in large part upon your ability to communicate with your coworkers and customers. Unfortunately, these skills are often lacking in new managers. According to a recent survey of major business recruiters, the biggest deficiencies in today's college graduates were the lack of good oral communication and writing skills (Endicott Report, 1992). Considering that speaking and writing skills are central to good management and that they are also relatively weak in many new employees, we should turn our attention to how managers can develop these two critical skills. Let's focus first on the core ingredients of good communication and then examine the specific requirements of speaking and writing.

Essential Elements of Effective Presentations

How can one person meet all of the communication demands confronting a good manager? There are five basic steps to making effective presentations—we'll label them the Five Ss. These five Ss are sequential in the sense that each step builds upon the preceding steps. Good communication depends heavily on adequate forethought and preparation. As shown in Figure 1, the first three steps involve preparation, the fourth and fifth focus on the spoken or written presentation itself. Adequate preparation is the cornerstone of effective communication (Collins and Devanna, 1990; Wells, 1989; Gelles-Cole, 1985).

1. Formulate a **strategy** for the specific audience and occasion. This is the phase in which you develop your purposes in relationship to the audience and situation.

2. Develop a clear **structure.** This step translates your broad strategy into specific content.

3. **Support** your ideas with examples, illustrations, and other material adapted to your audience. This will reinforce your ideas.

4. Prepare your material to create a presentation **style** that will enhance your ideas. How you present your ideas is often as important as what you present.

5. **Supplement** your presentation with confident, informed responses to questions and challenges. Your performance in a spontaneous, free-flowing discussion or exchange of memos should be as impressive and informative as your prepared presentation.

We have maintained throughout this book that effective personal performance is a function of skill, knowledge, and practice. This is especially the case with communication. The key to gaining confidence in making oral and written presentations is preparation and practice. If you follow the basic five steps, you should be on your way to delivering effective messages. Specific guidelines for implementing these five steps will be presented in the following sections.

Formulate a Specific Strategy

Identify your purpose.   Before collecting information or writing notes, you should clarify your general purpose for speaking or writing. Are you trying to motivate, inform, persuade, demonstrate, or teach? Your general purpose is to inform if you are providing information, demonstrating a technique, or delivering a report. When your purpose is to inform, you are concerned with the transmission and retention of ideas and facts. On the other hand, if you are motivating workers for higher production, convincing others to adopt your ideas, or stimulating pride in the company, your general purpose is to persuade. Persuasion requires the use of motivational language, convincing argument, and audience adaptation. Your general purpose may affect how you structure your message and how you supplement your ideas as well as your style of presentation. That is why it is important to identify your general purpose first.

Your specific purpose should be easier to determine once you have identified your general purpose (see Figure 2). You can discover your specific purpose by asking, "What do I want my listeners to learn?" or "What behaviors or attitudes do I want my listeners to adopt?" You may answer, "I want my listeners or readers to learn the six steps in our new accounting procedure" or "I want them to spend more time with customers." Each of these is a specific purpose. It determines how you will tailor the remainder of your preparation to your audience and the demands of the situation.

Figure 1   The Five Ss Approach to an Effective Presentation

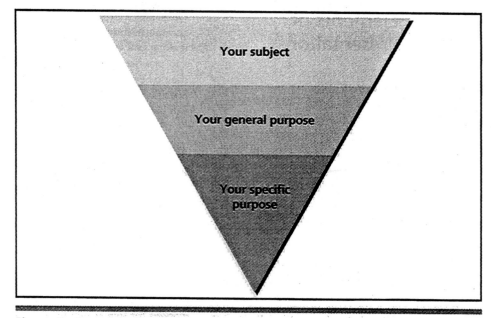

Figure 2 Determining Your Purpose

Tailor your message to your specific audience.
The success of your communication is partially dependent upon your audience's understanding and receptivity. The key to developing an audience-appropriate message is to understand their knowledge of the topic, attitude toward your message, and expectations of your presentation. If they already know what you are trying to teach them, they'll become bored and possibly hostile. Start with what they already know, then expand on it. If you are teaching a new accounting procedure, begin with the one your listeners currently use, then add the new steps. Remember that audiences retain more information if the material is associated with something they already know, rephrased and repeated, reinforced with visual aids, and limited to three to five new ideas. Motivated listeners retain more, so explain how they can use the information early in your message.

Your audience's attitudes toward your message are also critical to consider. Hostile receivers don't learn as readily as eager receivers. If your audience is hostile, start by setting realistic goals. If you try to do too much, you might trigger a boomerang effect in which your audience becomes even more hostile. Emphasize common ground by sharing similar values or parallel goals. For example, you might point out that increased profits are good for everyone in the company or that everyone has a stake in improving plant conditions.

For hostile or uncommitted listeners it is important to develop a two-sided message (see Table 1). Present both sides of the issue. Use strong arguments built on logic and extensive evidence (Sprague & Stuart, 1995). Choose neutral language as you develop your ideas.

For hostile listeners, it is also important to build your credibility. Show yourself to be calm, fair, reasonable, and well informed. Use humor directed at yourself to ease tension (Sprague & Stuart, 1995).

Meet the demands of the situation. Your receivers' expectations of your presentation are also important. The situation frequently determines expectations, such as the level of formality. Some situations clearly demand more formal presentations. If you are expected to address a board meeting, you should prepare carefully. On the other hand, if you are asked for your off-the-cuff comments, a prepared speech is not appropriate or practical. In this case, it is permissible to present more spontaneous remarks. Written communication also involves certain expectations. Invitations to a company picnic can be posted on bulletin boards, but invitations to a board of directors meeting are sent individually. Some situations are tricky. For example, television often appears informal, however you should carefully think out your comments. Banquets and ceremonies may encourage an informal, friendly atmos-

You should use a one-sided message when:

- your audience already favors your position.
- your audience is not well educated in general or on the topic.
- you require a public commitment from your audience.

You should use a two-sided message when:

- your audience initially disagrees with your position.
- your audience is well educated in general or on the topic.
- your audience will experience counter-persuasion on the topic.

Research suggests that the best way to present a two-sided message is to first give the arguments that support your position. Organize those arguments beginning with the weakest and ending with the strongest. Then, present the argument of your opposition. Organize the opposition arguments beginning with the strongest and ending with the weakest. In this way, you take advantage of your listeners' tendency to remember the most recent thing they hear: your strong argument and your opponent's weak argument.

Table 1 One-Sided Versus Two-Sided Messages
Source: Adapted from Michael Sproule, *Speechmaking: An Introduction to Rhetorical Competence* (Dubuque, IA: William C. Brown, 1991).

phere, but don't be fooled. These aren't the same settings as one-on-one or small group events.

The settings of business presentations can create a number of constraints that you must anticipate. (Remember that forethought and preparation are keys to effective communication.) Consider these common occurrences. A meeting schedule runs over so that your 20-minute presentation must be condensed to five minutes. Be prepared with a short version that highlights information that will serve your strategy. After presenting your committee's proposal for changing customer service procedures, which the committee has studied for three months, an influential nonmember distributes an outline of a competing proposal. Be prepared to answer specific criticisms of your proposal while maintaining a tone of cordial professionalism.

Language is also affected by the situation. More formal language choices and more correct sentence structure are demanded by formal situations. Slang, colloquialisms, contractions, and less-rigid grammar can add to the ease of informal settings. Determine your audience's expectations and adapt your language to them. Most experts agree that your language should be one step more intense than your audience's.

Develop a Clear Structure

Begin with a forecast. In general, an effective introduction does three things. First, it catches the listeners' attention and sets a tone for the message. Second, it provides your listeners with a reason for listening or reading. And, finally, it gives them a road map or quick sketch of the message. At a supervisor's meeting, you might start out your talk on a new plan for production changes this way: "Do you realize that we have not changed our basic production process in four years? In that time, seven new competitors have entered the market, and we've lost 9 percent of market share. But with three changes, we can get more production, which will generate 3 percent more profits and pay raises in the next fiscal year. First, we reorganize Bay 2; second, we install a track between the parts room and the assembly line; and, third, we set up a phone connection between the parts room and the assembly line. Let me spend a few minutes filling out the details of each change and explaining why these changes will save us money." This introduction gets your audience's attention because it portrays the immediacy of the problem and shows why your listeners have an important stake in what you have to say. By setting the larger context of increased competition, you intensify their reason for listening and counter possible resistance to change, which is common in organizations.

Choose an appropriate organizational pattern. Organization is critical because it affects comprehension of the message. Learners retain more when messages are organized. Organization also affects your credibility as a speaker or writer. A person who is organized is viewed more positively than one who is not. And, organization affects attitude change. Your receivers are more likely to be influenced by your viewpoint if it is organized. Finally, an organized message is more likely to be retained, and thus to influence the listener.

There are many patterns of organization to choose from (see Table 2). In general, you should order your thoughts using continua like time, direction, causal process, problem-solving sequence, complexity, space, or familiarity. A related technique is to organize your material as a series of answers to typical questions. Another common technique is called "sandwiching." This involves three steps. First, you emphasize the advantages of the plan. Second, you realistically assess the risks or concerns associated with it. Third, you reinforce the benefits by showing how they outweigh the costs, demonstrate how risks can be minimized with proposed safeguards, or show how resistance to change can be overcome.

As you plan your message consider your listeners' orientation. The main question to ask is "What does my audience already know or think?" Start from that point, then move closer to the desired knowledge or point of view.

Written and spoken communication vary in the amount of detailed information that can be conveyed in a single effort. Because a memo or report can be reread, the receiver doesn't have to remember all the information. However, speeches can't be reheard. It's more important to limit the amount of information presented orally. How many points can you make in a speech? Three main points are preferred by most speakers, but many listeners can remember up to five main points. Seven chunks of information is about the limit of a person's immediate short-term memory at any one time. Since people must remember what you have said if they are to act on it, dividing your speech into no more than five major chunks should make your ideas easier to remember (Miller, 1967). If your presentation is long, consider using visual aids, such as overhead transparencies or handouts, to reinforce the message.

Use transitions or signposts to signal your progress. It is important to give your audience a "road map" at the beginning of your message. Don't stop there but continue to help them follow you

STRATEGY	EXPLANATION
Chronological	Traces the order of events in a time sequence (such as past, present, and future or first step, second step, and third step).
Spatial	Arranges major points in terms of physical distance (such as north, central, and south) or direction from each other (such as internal and external).
Causal	Develops ideas from cause (such as diagnosing a disease from its causes) to effect or results to cause (such as from its symptoms to the disease).
Topical	Enumerates aspects of the topic (such as size, color, shape, or texture).
Monroe's Motivated Sequence	Follows a five-step process: 1. gaining attention 2. showing a need 3. presenting a solution 4. visualizing the results when the solution is implemented 5. calling for action to implement the solution
Familiarity-acceptance order	Begins with what the listener knows or believes and moves on to new ideas.
Inquiry order	Develops the topic in steps the same way you acquire the information or solve a problem.
Question-answer	Raises and answers a series of listeners' questions.
Problem-solution	First establishes that a problem exists then develops a plan to solve the problem.
Elimination order	Surveys all the available solutions and systematically eliminates each possibility until only one remains.

Table 2 Common Patterns of Organization

through it. To do this, signal when you're moving from one idea to another by summarizing the first idea, then forecasting the new idea. This is especially important in oral communication, since listeners will only hear your message once; it is critical that you provide signposts during your speech. You should indicate major transitions between ideas, such as: "We've just seen how the two standard types of data storage operate, now let's look at the advantages and disadvantages of each storage system."

In written form, you can signal transitions by indenting, numbering, or using bullets to highlight information. You can call your reader's attention to key words with italicized or bold print. Take advantage of these devices.

Conclude on a high note.   Two important psychological concepts are at work in communication—primacy and recency. Primacy is the first impression received and recency is the last. People tend to remember the first and last things they read or hear in messages. It's easy to understand why the most important parts of any presentation are the first and last impressions it creates. You establish an initial feeling in your introduction that colors the rest of the presentation, and the impression created during the conclusion influences the audiences' overall evaluation of your message. Since these are the most important segments of your presentation, they warrant the most preparation. You should plan your message with the beginning and end in mind, that is, consider your specific purpose statement as you develop your introduction and conclusion. Some people write the conclusion first because this allows them to organize the rest of their material so it naturally flows into the conclusion.

Reach closure at the end of your speech or written message by summarizing your ideas for a final time. Research shows that this kind of reinforcement helps listeners retain information. Normally people remember less than 20 percent of what they hear or read. If you preview the information in your introduction, reinforce it in internal summaries, and then summarize in the conclusion, you will increase the odds that your audience will remember your ideas.

The last statements you make after your summary should create a sense of closure and add to the memorability of your message. These statements can take a variety of forms. You can call for action, reinforce your audiences' commitment to action, or establish feelings of good will (see Table 3 for further sugges-

tions). For example, you might emphasize legitimacy by highlighting several authoritative quotes, emphasize the "I'm here to help" theme, predict conditions in the future, underscore the utility of your proposal by emphasizing its impact on the bottom line, or use an emotional appeal to increase commitment and loyalty.

Support Your Points

Choose a variety of support.   There are many reasons to use supporting materials, or evidence, as you develop your message. Most research concludes that supporting material makes a great difference in the impact of ideas. This is true even if you are not well known to your receivers or if they find your credibility moderate to low. What kind of support should you choose? Table 4 illustrates some of the many kinds of supporting materials available. Messages are strongest when they are built upon a variety of supporting materials. For example, reinforce statistics on profit sharing with a specific instance, such as how those numbers will affect a person on the assembly line.

When you select an introduction or conclusion, ask yourself if it orients your audience to your purposes and clearly signals the beginning or ending of your speech.
1. Refer to the subject or occasion.
2. Use a personal reference or greeting.
3. Ask a rhetorical question.
4. Make a startling statement.
5. Use a quotation.
6. Tell a humorous story.
7. Use an illustration.
8. Issue a challenge or appeal.
9. Use suspense.
10. Appeal to the listener's self-interest.
11. Employ a visual aid.
12. Refer to a recent incident.
13. Compliment the audience or a member of the audience.
14. Refer to the preceding speaker.
15. Request a specific action.

Table 3   Types of Introductions and Conclusions

Examples	Specific instances that illustrate the point or clarify the idea: for example, "Our plants in Detroit and Sacramento use Quality Circles."
Statistics	Numbers that express relationships of magnitude, segments, or trends: for example, "Currently, a full 32% of our workforce is involved in Quality Circle decision-making, and that is up 17% over the past two years."
Testimony	The opinions or conclusions of others, particularly experts: for example, "After studying our plants, professor Henry Wilson of the Harvard School of Business observed that American workers are not group motivated. He concluded that 'American workers cannot be expected to respond well to Quality Circles for that reason.'"

Table 4 Types of Supporting Materials

Consider your listeners when choosing your support.

The kind of supporting materials you choose partially depends on your audience. If the evidence is new to them, it will have more impact on them. Live videotapes, recordings, or actual photos also have greater impact. People who are highly dogmatic are more affected by evidence than are persons who are not so dogmatic. Of course, people are likely to believe evidence that agrees with their own position more than evidence that does not. So their initial position determines the extent to which they will find evidence believable. If your receivers find the source or types of evidence to be believable or credible, it will be more effective (see Table 5).

Use visual aids as support.

There are as many reasons to use visual aids as there are types of visual aids (see Table 6). Visual aids help people process and retain data (Seiler, 1971). In addition to enhancing comprehension and memory, visual aids can heighten the persuasive impact of your ideas if they engage receivers actively in the communicative exchange. Your credibility and your persuasiveness are enhanced by good visual aids. With these functions in mind, remember that visual aids should be simple, clear, and professional (see Table 7). The purpose of a visual aid is to augment your presentation, not replace it or distract from it. Unfortunately, this last point is lost by many professionals who treat presentations as slide shows in which

There is a great deal of research on the use of supporting materials or evidence in oral presentations. The following patterns seem to emerge:

1. If you have low to moderate credibility, evidence will probably increase your persuasive effectiveness.
2. There seems to be minimal difference between emotional and logical evidence.
3. Using evidence is usually better than not using it.
4. There seems to be little difference between biased sources and objective sources in their final impact on audiences.
5. Good speech delivery may improve the potency of evidence when sources of the evidence are unknown or have low credibility.
6. Evidence can reinforce the long-term effectiveness of persuasion.
7. Evidence is most effective when listeners are not familiar with it.
8. People are more likely to believe evidence that agrees with their own position.
9. Highly dogmatic people are more affected by evidence than are less-dogmatic people.
10. Evidence produces more attitude change when the course and source qualifications are provided.
11. Speakers with low credibility are seen as more credible when they cite evidence.
12. Using irrelevant evidence or poorly qualified sources may produce an effect opposite to what the speaker intends.

Table 5 Using Supporting Materials
Source: Charles U. Larson, *Persuasion,* 6th ed. (Belmont, CA: Wadsworth, 1992), pp. 202–203. Copyright © 1992 by Wadsworth Publishing Company. Reprinted with the permission of the publishers.

According to research, using effective visual aids in an oral presentation:

- makes your presentation up to 50% more memorable.
- significantly clarifies complex or detailed information.
- portrays you as more professional and better prepared.
- speeds up group decision making.
- shortens meeting time by up to 28%.
- makes your message 43% more persuasive.

Table 6   Functions of Visual Aids
Sources: Michael Osborn and Suzanne Osborn, *Public Speaking* (Boston: Houghton Mifflin, 1991), p. 231; Bruce E. Gronbeck et al., *Principles of Speech Communication,* 11th ed. (New York: HarperCollins, 1992), p. 191.

screen displays and even sound effects—not the presenter—become the center of attention.

Computer-aided graphics make it easier than ever to supplement your main ideas with visual materials. They also make it easier to create cluttered, excessive visual and sound images that distract the audience from your strategic message. Select and design visual aids to reinforce your strategy and ideas, and to make them clearer. Keep in mind that each type of visual aid communicates information in a different way. In general, visual aids such as slides, photographs, and posters can help an audience *feel* the way you do. They enhance the emotional dimension of a presentation. On the other hand, descriptive or written materials help an audience *think* the way you do. Numbers and charts reinforce cognitive processes; photographs reinforce

As you prepare your visual aids, ask yourself the following questions:

- Can I avoid making the visual aid the most important aspect of my speech? Will it be more than just an ornament?
- Can I translate complex numbers into bar or line graphs for easier comprehension?
- Am I comfortable with using the visual aid? Have I practiced with it so using it is natural, and it does not break the flow of ideas in my speech?
- Is it large enough to be seen by everyone without straining?
- Is all the printing short and neat?
- Is the visual aid colorful and involving? Studies show color highlights aid recall of information.
- Are my visual aids professional: neat, attractive, and accurate?
- Have I made the necessary arrangements for special visual aids in advance?
- Can I use the visual aid without blocking my audience's view of it? Will I be able to maintain good eye contact with my listeners while using the visual aid?
- Can I avoid reaching across my body or waving the visual aid in front of my face?
- Can I avoid distracting my listeners by keeping the visual aid covered or out of sight before and after I use it?
- What will I do if the visual aid fails to work? Am I prepared for unexpected contingencies such as a burned-out projector bulb or a room that cannot be darkened?
- Have I planned for assistance or volunteers in advance if they are needed?
- Will a pointer be needed?
- Will all charts be secured so I don't have to hunt for them on the floor in the middle of my speech?
- Am I using a variety of visual aids to increase my listeners' interest?
- If I'm using handouts, can I adjust to the distraction caused by passing them around? Can I compete with listeners who will read the handout rather than listen to me?
- Can I speak over the noise of a projector or other machine?

Table 7   Checklist for Using Visual Aids

affective processes. Use tables and graphs to highlight relationships and patterns, not to convey comprehensive data. If necessary, use supplemental handouts of comprehensive tables and charts.

Use an Enhancing Style

Up to this point, the preparation of oral and written messages is very similar. Whether you intend to deliver a speech or write a memo, you need to develop your strategy by identifying your purposes, structuring your message, and supporting your ideas with evidence. The fourth step requires separate treatment of oral and written messages because they are stylistically very different forms of communication. We'll first focus on oral presentations.

Style in Oral Communication

Prepare your notes. The mark of effective presenters is the appearance of effortlessness. Some speakers have such command of their material it appears they are ad libbing. Most of us prefer such a conversational style (see Table 8), but don't be fooled by appearances. Hours of preparation and practice preceded the actual performance. You've already been introduced to the three steps of preparation, but how do you develop the fourth stage of your preparation for oral communication?

After you have carefully considered your strategy, structure, and support, you should prepare your speaking notes. To do this, simply write your key points in a rough outline following the organizational pattern you have chosen. What you do next depends on your method of presentation. Most often, you will speak in a conversational manner that is not memorized or read; this is referred to as extemporaneous speaking. Extemporaneous presentation is desirable because it is natural and flexible; it applies to most situations. To prepare, copy key words on note cards to stimulate your memory; standard pages are often distracting. Write out quotations, statistics, or anything that requires exact wording. Highlight places where you intend to use visual aids, pause for questions, or present an exhibit. To rehearse, go through the speech, phrasing your ideas in language that seems natural. You may find yourself phrasing ideas with different words each time. That is okay. In fact, it will increase the conversational quality of your speech because your words will be typical of oral style and natural expression. It will help you develop flexibility, allowing you to adjust to different wording and flow of ideas.

If the occasion is formal and demands precise wording or exquisite prose, you should prepare a word-for-word manuscript to memorize or read. Then you should rehearse with the manuscript, trying to achieve as much natural flow in the dialogue as possible. This form of presentation is rare, but it may be required for discussing legal and financial issues, making announcements to the press, or conducting special ceremonies. Otherwise, avoid using written scripts and memorization for presentations because they disrupt the natural flow of conversational style and break eye contact with your listeners. Because manuscripts are

---

Folk wisdom holds that giving a speech is just like talking to another person. While it is true that most people prefer a conversational style of public speaking, there are at least three noteworthy differences between giving speeches and holding conversations:

1. Public speaking is more highly structured. It requires more detailed planning and development. Specific time limits may be imposed, and the speaker does not have the advantage of being able to respond individually to listeners.

2. Public speaking requires more formal language. Slang, jargon, and poor grammar all lower speaker credibility, even in informal speech situations. Listeners usually react negatively to poor language choices. In fact, many studies show that some kinds of language, such as obscene language, dramatically lower a speaker's credibility.

3. Public speaking requires a different method of delivery. The speaker's voice must be adjusted in volume and projection, posture is more correct, and distracting mannerisms and verbal habits are avoided.

Table 8 Differences Between Public Speaking and Conversation
Source: Adapted from Stephen Lucas, *The Art of Public Speaking*, 3rd ed. (New York: Random House, 1989).

prepared in written form first, they usually take on the style of written language. Unless you are a practiced speech writer, your manuscript will sound like written rather than oral speech (see Table 9).

Practice your presentation. It is a good idea to rehearse your presentation under simulated conditions—in a similar room, with listeners who can give you suggestions for improvement. Time your presentation so you know if it is necessary to cut or expand your ideas. Research shows that practicing a speech for short periods of time over the course of several days is more successful in reducing anxiety and improving memory than concentrated practice. So give the speech to yourself during breakfast, at your morning coffee break, as you walk to a mid-afternoon meeting, and before bed. Distributed practice is more efficient and yields better results than massed practice.

Practice using your visual aids. This will help you get used to managing them and give you some idea of how long your speech will take with the visual aids. Prepare for the totally unexpected. What if the roar of an overhead plane drowns out your voice? What if the microphone goes dead, a window blows open, or the room becomes extremely hot? Compensate for minor disruptions by slowing your rate, raising your volume a little, and continuing. You will encourage listeners to listen to your message rather than be temporarily distracted. For other disruptions, a good rule of thumb is to respond the same way you would if you were in the audience. Take off your jacket if it is too hot, close the window, raise your voice if listeners can't hear you, or pause to allow a complex idea to sink in.

As you practice, think about how you will channel your anxiety. Most speakers report feeling anxious before they speak; it's normal. To manage your anxiety, channel it into positive energy. Prepare well in advance for the speech—develop your ideas, support them, and practice your delivery. Even if you are anxious, you will have something important to say. It may help to visualize the speaking situation. Close your eyes, relax, and think about how it's going to feel and what your audience will look like as they watch you. Expect to feel a little momentary panic as you get up to speak, it will evaporate as you progress into the speech. Remember to think about your ideas rather than how nervous you feel. Focus on your message. Also remember that anxiety about speaking never really goes away. Most experienced speakers still get podium panic. The advantage of experience is that you learn how to cope by converting your

---

Why do we instantly recognize a memorized speech? Why does a meeting transcript *sound* funny? The answer to both questions is that oral style differs from written style. Memorized speeches from manuscripts reveal their written style, and conversations that are read reveal their oral style. Oral style differs from written style in the following ways:

1. The average sentence length is shorter (about 16 words) in conversations.

2. Vocabulary is more limited in speaking than in writing. "I" and "you" make up almost 8% of the words used in speaking; fewer than 50 words make up almost half of the total vocabulary we use when we speak.

3. Spoken vocabulary consists of more short words.

4. Speakers use more words referring to themselves such as "I," "me," and "we"; listeners rate this as more interesting.

5. More qualifying terms (such as "much," "many," and "a lot") and allness terms (such as "none," "never," and "always") are used in speaking.

6. More phrases and terms indicating hesitation are apparent in speaking, such as "it seems to me," "apparently," "in my opinion," and "maybe."

7. Fewer precise numbers are used in speaking.

8. Speakers use more contractions and colloquial expressions such as "can't," "wouldn't", "wow," and "chill out."

One final note on language: There is some evidence that we use lexical diversity as a cue to a speaker's socioeconomic status, competence, and perceived similarity.

Table 9 Differences Between Oral and Written Styles
Source: Lois Einhorn, "Oral and Written Style: An Examination of Differences," *Southern Speech Communication Journal* (1978): 302–311. Reprinted with the permission of the Southern States Communication Association.

anxiety into energy and enthusiasm. That gives you an extra sparkle as you speak. Above all, don't tell your listeners that you are nervous. This will divert their attention from your ideas to your anxiety. Usually, listeners can't tell that a speaker is nervous—only speakers know, and they should keep that secret.

Convey controlled enthusiasm for your subject. When a survey was given to 1,200 people asking them to identify the characteristics of effective presentations (Peoples, 1988), the results contained adjectives such as flexible, cooperative, audience-oriented, pleasant, and interesting. What was striking about these results is that only the last item on the list of 12 outstanding characteristics was specifically related to the content of the presentations. This suggests that the preceding discussion of effective format, while necessary, is not sufficient to guarantee your success. Put another way, a rambling, poorly organized presentation will surely produce an overall negative evaluation. On the other hand, a well-organized, highly logical, and easy-to-follow presentation that is poorly delivered will also be viewed negatively. This study suggests that style is extremely important in oral communication.

Years of research on student evaluations of classroom teaching performance have consistently shown that enthusiasm is the hallmark of a good teacher. Students will forgive other deficiencies if the teacher obviously loves the subject and is genuinely interested in conveying that appreciation to the students. The same holds true for presenters. Your posture, tone of voice, and facial expressions are all critical indicators of your attitude. Speak standing if you can, move occasionally, and use gestures to convey an attitude of earnestness. Remember, your audience will become infected with your enthusiasm.

Although enthusiasm is important, it must be controlled. Do not confuse enthusiasm with loudness. A good rule is to use vigorous but conversational tones of voice and inflections. Avoid bellowing or preaching at your listeners. Be sure you can be easily heard and that your tone is sufficiently emphatic to convey meaning effectively. In general, your speech should resemble an animated or lively conversation.

Use delivery to enhance your message. Another key to maintaining audience attention is effective delivery. Eye contact is the most important tool for establishing audience involvement. It makes listeners feel as if they are involved in a one-on-one, semiprivate discussion with you. In this culture, we value directness and honesty. One of the expressions of these values is direct eye contact. Effective eye contact means looking directly at members of the audience, one at a time, on a random, rotating basis. Generally, the smaller the group, the longer you can look at each person. Maintaining eye contact is also your primary source of audience feedback as you are presenting. If your audience appears puzzled, you may need to pause and review your key ideas.

It is important to use physical space and body movement to enhance your message. Remember that presentations are like movies, not snapshots. Alternate moving and standing still, speaking and listening, doing and thinking. Intersperse your lecture with chalkboard use, demonstration, audience participation, and audiovisual aids so that no single activity occupies a large portion of the presentation. Add some spice to your presentation by including personal anecdotes, references to members of the group, unusual facts, vital information, and vibrant images. Whenever appropriate, arrange the podium area to accommodate physical movement. Physical movement can be used to punctuate important points, signal transitions, build rapport with a person who asks a question, heighten the interest of particular segments of the audience, and help your listeners stay alert by refocusing their attention.

Other aspects of physical space affect the quality of your presentation. If possible, arrange the podium area and seating in the room to remove distractions. In more intimate settings, group participants so that there is less space between them. Eliminate unnecessary or distracting materials from the podium, such as unused equipment, signs, and displays. Keep your visual aids covered until they are used and keep the chalkboard clean. Focus your listeners' attention on you and your message.

You can use space to convey intimacy or distance. Position yourself roughly in the middle of your audience from left to right and in a spot where you can comfortably maintain eye contact. With this in mind, you can deliberately alter your presentation style to build rapport with members of the audience. Move closer if you intend to build intimacy or tension; move to a comfortable distance when your ideas are neutral.

Gestures can also add to a presentation. They should appear to be spontaneous and natural in order to enhance, rather than distract from, your message. They should be relaxed, not rigid. Use them to accentuate your normal mode of expression. To some extent, when you concentrate on your message, not your movements, the appropriate gestures will come naturally. Remember that your gestures should be smooth, relatively slow, and not too low (below your waist), too high (above your shoulders), or too wide (more than two feet from your body). If you are using a podium, step slightly behind or to the side of the podium so it does not block your listeners' view of your movement. The general rules for gestures change as your audience becomes larger. You must adapt to large groups by making larger, more dramatic gestures.

Avoid any gestures or movement that distracts from your message. Irrelevant movement such as jingling change in a pocket, toying with notes, shifting from foot to foot, twisting hair, or adjusting eyeglasses are annoying. In fact, any movement repeated too often creates a distraction. Practice using a variety of body movements to illustrate or describe, enumerate, add emphasis, or direct attention. For variety, some gestures should involve the entire upper body, not just your dominant hand.

Style in Written Communication

Like oral communication, written communication is a skill; it can be learned. Written communication follows the same three preparation steps as oral communication. The writer determines strategies, structure, and support before actually putting pen to paper. As with effective presentations, good writing draws on careful analysis of the audience and situation. In a business setting, "every document is a response to a problem or opportunity requiring that some consensus be achieved or action taken" (Poor, 1992, p. 38).

There are significant differences between oral and written communication style. Although it lacks the interpersonal dimension of immediacy, written communication offers one tremendous advantage over oral communication—it lasts. Written documents can be retained, studied, duplicated, and filed for the future. This means that they are essentially capable of conveying much more detailed information. While written communication offers these advantages, it also makes different demands on the communicator; written communication demands precision.

Develop mechanical precision in your writing.
Your professional image is judged by the appearance of your written communication. Cross outs, erasures, ty-

pographical errors, or other sloppiness detract from your written message, just as awkward mannerisms can distract from your oral message. Grammatical precision is also required—misspellings, punctuation errors, and poor grammar are marks of uneducated writers. This is certainly not an image you want to convey. You may expect a secretary or clerical worker to catch and correct all these things, and many times that happens. However, when you sign or otherwise endorse the final product, you alone are accountable for any errors it contains. It is essential to develop the habit of proofreading final drafts before you sign them.

Violations of the rules of grammar and punctuation may affect more than just your credibility. They can also disrupt your reader. If the reader is distracted by typos, confusing grammar, or ambiguous pronouns, your ideas may become lost; such errors can cripple the impact of your message. Some recruiters toss out resumes that contain mechanical errors. Their reasoning is that if job applicants can't take the time to proofread a short resume, they may be sloppy on the job, too. Some readers are insulted by poor grammar; others automatically consider themselves superior to the writer. While these may not be logical reactions, they occur, and more important, they block your effectiveness. You may argue that correct grammar and punctuation are not vital. Maybe not, but you take a chance every time you present careless work to another reader. Consider the campaign of Charles Day for a seat on local government. His campaign flyers, delivered house to house, carried the banner, "Vote Charles Day for School Bord." Would you want a man who apparently can't spell making decisions on academic matters for your neighborhood schools? The impression is that if you don't have the time or incentive to check your own writing, you won't pay attention to details in the work of others.

Practice factual precision in your writing.
It's obvious that getting the facts right is important. If you send a memo calling for a meeting but record an incorrect meeting date, you'll suffer the consequences of inconveniencing others. Accuracy is critical but that's just the beginning. It's up to the writer to create sentences so that the meaning is unmistakably clear to the reader. Many times writers know the facts but omit important details in writing. Omission occurs when you have all the facts or circumstances but as you write, you assume the reader knows the facts. Write with your reader in mind. This assumes that you have analyzed

who your readers are and understand what information they need and expect. What basic information is important for readers to know in order to understand your message? Instead of starting with the central part of the message, provide the background first, such as: "In response to your memo of February 2, requesting corrections to our policy on grievances, we have taken three actions. First . . ." If you're not sure what to include, ask someone who doesn't know the details of the situation to read what you have written.

Ambiguity is another barrier to clear writing. Many times we write as we speak, throwing in phrases as we would speak them. Unlike speakers, writers can't use nonverbal cues to convey specific meanings or associations. Since readers may not have the advantage of asking questions or getting immediate feedback, they are left to determine associations for themselves. Consider how ambiguity creates a lack of precise factual meaning in this memo:

> The next meeting of the department is scheduled for next week. Matt Olsen has told Leo Robinson to report on the union elections. His report will follow announcements. We will elect new officers at our upcoming meeting.

This memo doesn't pass the standard test of clear writing. If the memo was sent on Friday and received on Monday, which week contains the meeting? Who is giving the report? The pronoun "his" causes confusion since it could refer to either Matt Olsen or Leo Robinson. Which "upcoming meeting" will result in the election of officers? Will it be the meeting called by the memo or another "upcoming meeting"? Because it can breed confusion, annoyance, and wasted time, such a sloppy memo can have an adverse effect on the relationship between the writer and recipients that can affect their subsequent communication. Seen in this light, the memos a manager routinely writes are an important factor in managing relationships strategically and productively.

Construct written messages with verbal precision.
Achieving verbal precision is different from mechanical or factual precision. Verbal precision is based on the accuracy of the words chosen to express the ideas. In an ideal world, words would provide the exact meaning you intended, but words can't replicate reality. Rather, words are symbols of objects and ideas. Add to this inexact representation the reader's own sub-

tle shadings of meaning, and you can see why it's difficult to achieve verbal precision. Put another way, a word has two levels of meaning: its denotation, or the meaning agreed upon by most people who use the word, and its connotation, or the personal dimension of meaning brought to the word by the receiver.

Communication depends on a blend of both denotative and connotative meanings. Consider the noun "Greenpeace." Its denotative reference is to a specific international environmental organization. The connotative meaning varies widely. For many environmentalists, Greenpeace is leading a worthy crusade. However, for some governments and companies, the organization is, at best, a nuisance. These are the connotative references of a single word. Consider the difficulty in creating the right blend of denotative and connotative meaning in entire documents. You need to be aware of both types of meaning of the words you use. Frequently, you may recognize your own connotative meaning but be unaware of how others may react. While connotation is often a personal matter, you can attempt to judge this meaning by thinking from your receiver's viewpoint. What is their most likely reaction?

The key to verbal precision in writing is clarity. The fundamental questions you must ask yourself are: "Does the word or phrase convey my meaning without confusion?" or "Could anyone reading this memo for the first time understand the ideas directly and simply?" A secondary question is whether the written message conveys unintentional meanings stimulated by connotative meanings of words or phrases. The impact of connotations once more underlines the importance of knowing your audience and of being aware of what is appropriate for one audience or another.

Pay attention to tone.
The tone of your writing is directly related to your diction, or word choices. For example, compare these two statements: "Our company will purchase the product" and "We'll buy it." The second sounds more informal because it uses pronouns and a contraction. In general, longer words and sentences tend to convey a more formal tone.

Using the appropriate level of formality in your writing calls for you to analyze the nature of the writing situation. An invitation to a reception for the company's board of directors calls for formal language. When you are writing to strangers or up the chain of command, it is safer to be formal. When you are communicating across or down the chain, you often may be informal. However, a letter of reprimand to a subordinate should be formal in tone.

Tone in business writing goes beyond its relative formality. It reflects on the nature of the writer as a person and therefore affects how the reader feels about the writer. Its impact can be significant and often unexpected. For example, a terse letter may be interpreted as sarcastic or angry even if the writer did not intend sarcasm or anger. Consider a customer who writes a long letter expressing problems with a product. What would the customer think if this response were mailed back: "Thank you for your letter of January 12. We always enjoy hearing from our customers." Although this response has the trappings of courtesy, it seems insincere and perhaps sarcastic. It hardly seems that the respondent read the customer's letter—there is nothing about its contents—or that the letter was "enjoyed." Although the response shows factual and mechanical precision, the tone is inappropriate and potentially damaging to the relationship with this customer.

In most cases, even disappointing news can be expressed in a positive way. Consider an employer who responds to a job applicant by writing, "In a company as well respected as ours, we rarely have time to consider applications such as yours." Not only is the news bad, the arrogant tone also needlessly humiliates the applicant. A response with a more positive tone might be: "We read your application with interest but currently do not have any openings in your specialties. Best wishes with your continued search." The news is still bad, but the polite tone shows respect for the applicant and promotes a professional image of the company.

Compare the following sentence and its more positive version: "Because of recent heavy demand, we will be unable to ship the items you ordered until July 15," and "Although recent demand has been heavy, we will be able to ship the items you ordered July 15." A slight variation in wording here changes a tone of helplessness to one of helpfulness.

Under most business writing conditions, you should be cordial. You should express tact and friendliness appropriate to your relationship with the reader. This attitude will have a positive effect on your word choices, which in turn will more likely convey an appropriate tone.

One area of modern business writing where failing to pay attention to tone has cost many bad feelings and lost time is electronic mail, or E-mail. By its nature, E-mail encourages rapid-fire exchanges, especially when busy workers face an in box filled with messages, many of which are ill considered and unclear. E-mail is not a phone conversation in which tone of voice and other cues can clarify your meaning and in which you can read the listener's vocal cues. However, many E-mailers seem to forget the difference. They don't state the context of their message; they don't give needed background information; they don't organize their message; they don't make careful word choices that convey a cordial tone. By not taking the time to consider their message in light of the situation and the receiver, E-mailers can convey inappropriately demanding tones or disapproving tones if their requests aren't met promptly. The antagonism created by the poor tone of E-mail messages can delay solving the business problem at hand and affect negatively the work relationships of the E-mailers.

Know the proper format.   Like it or not, first impressions count even in written communication. Sloppiness suggests that the writer doesn't take the message seriously; odd or unconventional formats hint that the writer is ignorant or unprofessional. You should become acquainted with the physical layout of letters, memos, proposals, and other common forms of written business communication. Others expect you to have this basic knowledge; many handbooks and computer software programs are available to guide you in the development of these formats. Some companies have style guides that precisely prescribe the formats for all documents representing the company.

While there are several acceptable formats for written communication such as business letters, the reader should be able to pick up specific information at a glance. In the business letter, this information includes: The intended recipient of the letter, the sender, the sender's address for return correspondence, any enclosures, and recipients of copies of the letter. All of this information is separate from the body of the letter and should be clearly visible.

Because memos are intended to communicate within an organization, their format is different from that of letters. Instead of business letterhead, memo letterhead is used. Basic information can also be obtained at a glance. The top of the memo should include: To, From, Date, and Subject headings. Usually salutations and closings are not considered necessary within an organization.

Proposals are much lengthier and require special attention to supporting information such as tables, graphs, and charts. The best ways to represent such data can be found in readily available resources on business writing.

Whatever the final format, there is one objective in all written business communication: Your message should be simple, direct, and clear. Anything that interrupts your reader's movement through your writing limits its effectiveness. Any imprecision—a mechanical blunder, a factual omission, or a strange word—calls attention to itself and, like an odd gesture in spoken communication, diverts attention away from your ideas. As a writer, you must aim at clear, direct transmission of your message.

Supplement Your Presentation by Responding to Questions and Challenges

Prepare thoroughly to handle questions.
Answering questions and responding to objections is a vital part of the communication process because it allows us to interact directly with our listeners. We can learn about how our listeners are thinking and their responses to our ideas from their questions; it's a two-way street.

The key to formulating effective responses is the same as the key to developing good speeches—careful preparation. Read broadly and talk with experts in your field. Don't read just the material that supports your point of view but also read what the opposition is saying. The best defense can be a good offense, and this is no exception. Ask your colleagues to critique your material, discuss their questions and objections with them, and collect supporting documentation or evidence. You can also practice your responses. Begin by considering what your listeners might ask or find someone opposed to your position who will list questions for you. Then, practice your responses to these questions.

Despite your best efforts, you may get an overwhelmingly hostile response from your listeners. Don't be afraid to take a stand that disagrees with them. People may not agree with you but they will respect your sincerity. If someone throws you a curve, don't apologize or bluff your way through with an inadequate response. Be honest and direct, tell them if you don't have the answer. Invite them to discuss the problem further at a later time and follow up on your invitation. The next time someone asks the same question, you will be prepared.

When challenged, answer in a specific format.
Respond to objections in an orderly manner. In general, answer questions as succinctly as possible. Rambling answers may make it appear as though you are hedging. They also suggest an inability to think concisely. You can answer objections in four steps:

1. **Restate the objection.** This gives you time to think, shows your interest, and makes sure that everyone understands the question. Restatement recognizes the objection and clarifies it for everyone in the audience.

2. **State your position.** Give a concise, direct statement of what you believe to make it clear where you stand.

3. **Offer support for your position.** This is the critical part of the response. Provide evidence that shows your position is the right one.

4. **Indicate the significance of your rebuttal.** Show the impact of adopting your position. Offer reasons for doing so.

Following the four steps we've outlined, a good response to an objection might take this form:

1. "Joe has stated that a management-by-objectives system won't work in our factory because supervisors don't want input from the cutting floor (restatement of the objection).

2. I think that a management-by-objectives system will work and that it will increase worker satisfaction (statement of your position).

3. I'm basing my position on a group of studies done in our Newark plant last year. Output increased 0.5 percent during the first month, and more importantly, workers reported more job satisfaction. They had fewer sick days too (support for the position).

4. If our plant is similar to the Newark plant—and I think it is—then I believe our supervisors will notice the same gains here. Until Joe can provide us with a reason to stick with the current system, I think we ought to give the new one a try—we stand to get more output and better job satisfaction (significance of rebuttal)."

Practice this format until it becomes automatic. It builds up your own case while responding to the objection. Since this format rationally shores up your position, it increases your credibility as well. And, it increases the chances that others will agree with you.

Maintain control of the situation. You need to balance being sensitive to feedback and flexible enough to respond to legitimate concerns with avoiding prolonged, unproductive interchanges. Recognizing everyone's right to ask questions or offer alternative positions is important because it grants audience members respect. On the other hand, you also have every right to decide what is relevant for consideration. You shouldn't allow one or two members of your audience to dictate the pace or direction of your presentation. This places you in a position of weakness that undermines your credibility. If you should alter your position, make certain that the majority of your listeners view it as a responsible shift rather than an effort to placate a minority voice.

Keep exchanges on an intellectual level. Arguments and rebuttals can degenerate into name-calling in which little is settled. Effective communication is more likely to occur when the calm voice of reason dominates than when you squabble with your listeners.

You'll soon learn that people don't always ask questions just because they want information. Some people crave attention; others may sabotage your position if they perceive your ideas as a threat. Planning for these possibilities will give you more options; foresight enables you to respond appropriately. You might answer hostile questions with further questions, drawing out your interrogator and regaining the offensive. Or, you might broaden the discussion. Don't get trapped into an argument with one person. Involve others to determine if this is an isolated concern or a legitimate issue. Finally, you might express your willingness to discuss special or detailed issues but defer extensive discussion until the end of your presentation.

Summary and Behavioral Guidelines

A key aspect of management is communication, and formal presentations are an essential communication tool. Therefore, effective managers must be able to create effective informative and persuasive messages. You can enhance your speaking and writing with thorough preparation and repeated practice. This chapter has outlined a number of guidelines based on the Five Ss model:

1. Formulate a **strategy** for the specific audience and occasion.

2. Develop a clear **structure.**

3. **Support** your points with evidence adapted to your audience.

4. Practice presenting your material in a **style** that will enhance your ideas.

5. **Supplement** your presentation by effectively responding to questions and challenges.

Strategy

1. Identify your general and specific purposes.

2. Tailor your message to your audience.

   ▶ Understand their needs, desires, knowledge level, and attitude toward your topic.

   ▶ Make sure your approach is audience centered.

   ▶ Present both sides of the issue if your audience is hostile or uncommitted.

3. Meet the demands of the situation.

   ▶ More formal situations demand formal language and sentence structure.

   ▶ Informal situations allow slang and less rigid language use.

Structure

4. Begin with a forecast of your main ideas.

   ▶ Catch your audience's attention as you begin.

   ▶ Provide them with a reason for listening or reading.

   ▶ Give them an outline of the message so they can follow along.

5. Choose your organizational pattern carefully.

   ▶ Start with what your listeners already know or think.

   ▶ Use organization to increase your credibility.

   ▶ Move from familiar to unfamiliar, simple to complex, old to new, or use another continua for organizing your thoughts.

- Make no more than three to five main points in oral communication.

6. Use transitions to signal your progress.

7. Conclude on a high note.

   - Take advantage of greater audience attention at the conclusion of your message.

   - Reach closure by reinforcing through a summary of your ideas.

   - Use your last statements to call for action, reinforce the commitment to action, or establish a feeling of goodwill.

Support

8. Choose a variety of support.

   - The most effective support is not well known to your listeners.

   - Support increases your credibility.

   - You may use a wide variety of supporting material.

9. Consider your audience when choosing your support.

   - New evidence and live videotapes have more impact.

   - The audience's initial position determines the extent to which they find evidence believable.

   - Using evidence is better than not using evidence.

10. Use visual aids as support.

    - Visual aids have a dramatic impact on comprehension and retention.

    - Visual aids also enhance persuasion.

    - Keep visual aids simple and effective.

Style in Oral Communication

11. Prepare your notes.

    - Remember, the crucial effect is conversational style.

    - Extemporaneous presentation requires limited notes combined with frequent delivery practice.

    - Formal occasions demand precise wording that requires a manuscript or memorized speech.

12. Practice your presentation.

    - Use distributed practice rather than massed practice.

    - Practice using your visual aids and plan for the unexpected.

    - Plan to channel your speaking anxiety.

13. Convey controlled enthusiasm for your subject.

    - Effective speakers communicate excitement about their topics.

    - Your posture, tone of voice, and facial expressions all indicate your attitude.

    - Your speech should resemble an animated conversation.

14. Engage your audience with effective delivery.

    - Eye contact is the most critical tool.

    - Use physical space and body movement to enliven your message.

    - Use space to convey intimacy or distance.

    - Use gestures to accentuate your normal mode of expression.

    - Avoid any movement that distracts from your message.

Style In Written Communication

15. Develop mechanical precision in your writing.

    - Project a professional image.

    - Errors may distract your readers and disrupt the impact of your message.

16. Practice factual precision in your writing.

    - Accuracy ensures that your meaning will be communicated clearly.

    - Ambiguity prevents factual precision.

17. Construct written messages with verbal precision.

    - Words cannot replicate reality.

    - Consider denotative and connotative meanings of words as you write them.

    - The key to verbal precision is clarity.

18. Pay attention to tone.

   ▶ Tone is directly related to word choice.

   ▶ Adjust the tone of your message to the formality of the situation.

   ▶ Tone affects how readers feel about the writer.

   ▶ Writing should express appropriate cordiality.

   ▶ Positive phrasing is preferable to negativity.

19. Know the proper format.

   ▶ You are responsible for creating an impression of professionalism.

   ▶ Business letters, memos, and proposals all have special formats.

Supplement: Questions and Answers

20. Anticipate questions and thoroughly prepare responses.

   ▶ Rehearse answers to difficult questions.

   ▶ Handle hostile listeners with honesty and directness.

21. Respond to objections in an orderly fashion.

   ▶ Restate the objection.

   ▶ State your position.

   ▶ Offer support for your position.

   ▶ Indicate the significance of your rebuttal.

22. Maintain control of the situation.

   ▶ Balance the demands of specific individuals with the interest of the group.

   ▶ Keep exchanges on an intellectual level.

   ▶ Plan for the questioner who has a personal agenda.

Skill Practice

Exercises in Making Effective Oral and Written Presentations

Speaking as a Leader

As illustrated in the opening case about Taylor Billingsley at Apex Communications, one of the major challenges facing leaders is the requirement to deliver a wide range of presentations. Effective communicators must be skilled at both informing and inspiring. They must be able to hold their own with hostile audiences as well as impress content experts and instill confidence in novices. They must be skilled at building consensus, pointing new directions, and explaining complex topics. This exercise, adapted from Richard Linowes, provides an opportunity to practice speaking on a variety of leadership topics.

Assignment

To practice playing this important leadership role, prepare a talk and a memo on one of the following topics. Your speech should last from three to five minutes, unless you are otherwise instructed. Your memo should not exceed two pages. Create a context for your communication by assuming a management role in a familiar organization. Before beginning, explain the details of the context to your audience (either orally or in a written summary). Briefly explain your organizational position, the makeup of the audience, and their expectations of your presentation. (For the memo, attach a one-page background statement.) The specific content of your communication is less important than how well it is prepared and how persuasively it is delivered. Prepare to respond to questions and challenges.

In preparing your presentation, review the behavioral guidelines at the end of the Skill Learning section. The checklist in this exercise may also be useful. You will receive feedback based on the criteria shown in the Observer's Feedback Form in Appendix I.

Topics for Leadership Talks

1. **Taking Charge of an Established Group.** The speaker is a manager newly assigned to a group that has worked together under other managers for some time.

2. **Announcing a New Project.** The speaker is announcing a new undertaking to members of his or her department and is calling on all to rally behind the effort.

3. **Calling for Better Customer Service.** The speaker is motivating all employees to be as attentive and responsive as possible to customers.

4. **Calling for Excellence and High-Quality Work.** The speaker is motivating all employees to perform their jobs with a commitment to meeting the highest-possible standards.

5. **Announcing the Need for Cost Reductions.** The speaker is requesting that everyone look for ways to cut expenditures and immediately begin to slash spending.

6. **Commending for a Job Well Done.** The speaker is extolling a group of people who have worked very hard for an extended period to produce outstanding results.

7. **Calming a Frightened Group of People.** The speaker is endeavoring to restore calm and confidence to those who feel panic in the face of distressing business developments.

8. **Addressing a Challenging Opposition.** The speaker is presenting a heartfelt belief to a critical, even hostile, audience.

9. **Mediating Between Opposing Parties.** The speaker is serving as judge or arbiter between two groups who are bitterly opposed on a key issue.

10. **Taking Responsibility for Error.** The speaker is a spokesperson for an institution whose actions have produced an unfortunate result that affects the audience.

11. **Reprimanding Unacceptable Behavior.** The speaker is taking to task certain individuals who have failed to perform up to required levels.

12. **Petitioning for Special Allowances.** The speaker is presenting the case for an institution seeking certain rights that must be authorized by some external body.

Checklist for Developing Effective Presentations

1. What are my general and specific objectives?

2. What is the context of my communication? (My audience, the situation, etc.)

3. How will I open and close the communication?

4. How will I organize my information?

5. How will I get and keep the attention of my audience?

6. What supporting materials will I use?

7. What visual aids (graphs, charts, objects, etc.) will I use?

8. How will I tailor the presentation to this audience?

9. What format will I use in my presentation?

10. What questions or responses will likely occur?

Quality Circles at Battle Creek Foods

One of the newest innovations in group decision making, quality circles (QCs), has recently received considerable attention among U.S. manufacturers. Their interest in this technique stems from its having been described by the Japanese as critical to their recent manufacturing success. Ironically, Edward Deming, an American, first brought the notion of "statistical quality control," a management tool, to the Japanese in the early post–World War II years. The Japanese combined these ideas with the assumption that the person who performs a job is the one who best knows how to identify and correct its problems. As a result, the Japanese, with Deming's help, developed the "quality circle." A quality circle is a group of people (usually about 10) who meet periodically to discuss and develop solutions to problems related to quality, productivity, or product cost.

The purpose of this exercise is to give you an opportunity to make a presentation on this important topic.

Assignment

You are the Director of Personnel at Battle Creek Foods, a leading manufacturer of breakfast cereal. Productivity has been sagging industry-wide, and your organization is starting to see its effect on profitability. In response, you have been asked by the corporate executive committee to make a 20-minute oral presentation (or prepare a five-page memo) on quality circles. The committee has heard that QCs have been initiated at several plants by your leading competitor, and it would like your recommendation as to whether Battle Creek Foods should follow suit. The committee's only previous exposure to QCs is what each member has read in the popular press. Using the following reference material, prepare a presentation on quality circles. Explain the QC structure and process, and the advantages and disadvantages of QCs. The final section of the presentation should include a recommendation regarding their adoption at your plants. Prepare to respond to questions and challenges.

In preparing your presentation, refer to the behavioral guidelines for effective presentations at the end of the Skill Learning section and the checklist in the preceding exercise. You will receive feedback based on the Observer's Feedback Form in Appendix I.

A Look at Some of the Evidence

Quality circles, on balance, appear to be making a positive contribution to product quality, profits, morale, and even improved employee attendance (Dubrin, 1985, pp. 174–185). The widespread attention QCs have received in recent years has led logically to their evaluation by both businesspeople and researchers. Here we will rely on several types of evaluation methods, sampling first the positive evidence, and then the negative.

Favorable Outcomes with QCs

Honeywell, a high-technology electronics firm, has become a pioneer in the application of QCs in North America. Honeywell currently operates several hundred QCs in the United States. Typically, about a half-dozen assembly workers are brought together every two weeks by a first-level supervisor or team leader. "We feel that this type of participatory management program not only increases productivity," says Joseph Riordan, director of Honeywell Corporate Productivity Services, "but it also upgrades the quality of work life for employees. Line workers feel that they are more a part of the action. As a result, we find that the quality of work improves and absenteeism is reduced. With this kind of involvement, we have, in many cases, been able to increase the capacity of a line without the addition of tooling or extra shifts."

Honeywell used the quality circle method to manage the problem of winning a renewable bid for a government contract. "Here was a situation," Riordan relates, "where we already had cut our rejects down, where all of the learning had effectively gone out of the process." The problem was assigned to the quality circle representing that particular work area. "They came up with a suggestion for further automating the process that enabled us to improve our competitive position by about 20 percent and win the contract."

In an attempt to determine the appropriateness of QCs to North American firms, a team of researchers set up a one-year field experiment at a metal fabricating facility of an electronics firm.

Eleven quality circles, averaging nine production employees each, were established. Performance was measured by a computerized monitoring system created from the company's existing employee performance reporting system. Both quantity and quality measurements were taken. Employee attitudes were also assessed, using the Motivating Potential Score (MPS) of the Hackman-Oldham Job Diagnostic Survey.

The major result of the circle program was its positive impact on reject rate, as shown in the top half of Figure 3. Reject rates per capita for quality-circle participants dropped by one-third to one-half of the former rates by the time the program had run three months. Surprisingly, the reject rates for the control group increased during the same period.

An explanation offered by the researchers for these results is that circle members tackled the issues of internal communication as a top priority item. For example, one of the initial projects implemented by the QCs was improving training manuals and procedures, including translating materials into a worker's native language if the worker desired. Careful attention to better training in fundamentals prevented many errors.

Circle members also made fewer errors. In addition, the defective parts the circle members did make tended to be less expensive to scrap or rework into usable parts. The explanation given for these results is that circle training instructs employees how to prioritize problems on the basis of dollar impact on the company. The cost savings generated by the lower reject rate represented a 300-percent return on the cost of investment in the program.

The impact of QCs on participants' level of work satisfaction was equally impressive. Results shown in Figure 3 indicate that the Motivating Potential Score (MPS) for the circle participants increased, while the control group showed a decrease. No other changes were present in the work environment that would impact the experimental group differently than the control group. The researchers therefore concluded that the improvement in employee job attitudes could be attributed to the circle training program and the problem-solving activity. The job characteristic most influenced by the quality activity was skill variety: the extent to which a job requires a variety of skills.

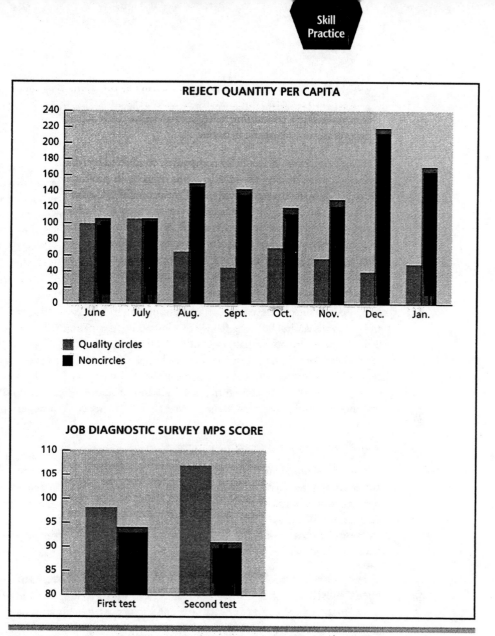

Figure 3 Impact of Quality Circles on Employee Performance and Attitudes

Negative Outcomes with Quality Circles

Despite the favorable outcomes reported, many negative results have also been reported. A review of the results of the first surge of QC activity in the United States revealed that as many as 75 percent of initially successful programs were no longer in operation after a few years. Even Lockheed, one of the American pioneers in this method, had decreased its involvement with quality circles. Robert Cole, a recognized authority on the Japanese workforce, made these pessimistic remarks:

> [The] fact is that the circles do not work very well in many Japanese companies. Even in those plants recognized as having the best operating programs, management knows that perhaps only one-third of the circles are working well, with another third borderline, and

one-third simply making no contribution at all. For all of the rhetoric of voluntarism, in a number of companies the workers clearly perceive circle activity as coercive. Japanese companies face a continuing struggle to revitalize circle activity to ensure that it does not degenerate into ritualistic behavior.

A study of quality circles in 29 companies, conducted by Matthew Goodfellow, found only eight of them to be cost-effective in terms of gains in productivity. Management consultant Woodruff Imberman investigated the 21 unsuccessful QC efforts and found four major causes of failure. First, in many firms, the employees intensely disliked management. Their antagonism carried over into the quality circles, which some employees perceived to be a management ploy to reduce overtime and trim the workforce by increasing productivity. Second, most organizations did a poor job of selling the QCs. Instead of conducting individual discussions with employees, they relied on flip-charts, booklets, and formal management presentations. The workers were left wondering, "What's in it for me?"

Third, the supervisors chosen to lead the circles received some training in human relations and group dynamics, but they felt that little of this information satisfied the specific needs of their own departments. Fourth, most of the 21 firms regarded the QC programs merely as a way of improving the efficiency of production techniques. They did not realize that QCs cannot succeed unless top management is willing to shift its philosophy toward emphasizing good relations among employees and between management and workforce. This last point hints at the importance of establishing the conditions that allow a quality circle program to succeed.

Key Elements of a Successful Program

Quality circle programs show some variation from company to company, whether these companies are engaged in manufacturing or service. They may differ in how frequently they meet, how much authority is granted to the team leader or supervisor, whether they use a group facilitator in addition to a supervisor, and how much coordination there is with the existing quality-control department. Based on the judgments of several observers, the successful programs have certain elements in common.

Quality circles work best in firms where good employee-management relations already exist. QCs are not likely to succeed in organizations suffering from acrimonious union-management conflict or high levels of distrust between employees and management.

Top management is committed to the program. Without commitment from top management, the initiation of a QC program is inadvisable. Instead, the director of a circle project should first prepare reports on other companies where QCs have been successful and present them to top management.

Circle leaders use a participative leadership style. Laurie Fitzgerald, a QC consultant, advocates the "leader as a worker for the members" concept. When the circle leader takes on a highly authoritarian role, the members are usually unresponsive.

The right people and the right area are selected. For quality circles to be effective, the program manager has to be enthusiastic, persistent, and hard-working. The facilitator or team leader must be energetic and cooperative. Also, another important step in getting the program off the ground is to select an area of the company where one can expect cooperation and enthusiasm from participants.

Program goals are stated explicitly. Objectives should be made clear in order to avoid confusion or unreasonable expectations from the circle program. Among the goals of QC programs are improving product quality, increasing productivity, improving communications between workers and supervisors, decreasing product costs, improving the quality of work life, and preparing people for future supervisory assignments.

The program is well publicized throughout the firm.   Once the program is started, information about it should be disseminated widely throughout the company. Better communication results in less resistance and fewer negative rumors about the program. The content of the communication should be open and positive.

The program starts slowly and grows slowly.   A gradual introduction of the program helps expose people to new concepts and helps reduce doubts about its intention and potential merit.

The QC program is customized to meet the needs of the firm.   A subtle source of failure in some QC programs is the use of a canned set of procedures that don't fit local circumstances. A QC participant whose work is data processing may have difficulty with the translation of a case from the aerospace industry. A workable compromise is to use standard training as a framework and build on it with the unique problems of the firm in question.

Quality circles are used as a method of employee development.   A key purpose of these circles is to foster personal development of the participating workers. If managers intend to install a QC as a tool for their own selfish gain, they would do better not to begin.

Management is willing to grant recognition for ideas originating in the circles.   If management attempts to manipulate the circle volunteers or take away from them the credit for improvements, the program most likely will backfire. More will be lost than gained.

Membership is voluntary.   As with job enrichment and all forms of participative management, employee preference is an influential factor. Employees who desire to contribute their ideas will generally perform better than employees who are arbitrarily assigned to a QC.

Achievements of quality circles are recognized as results of group, not individual, effort.   Recognizing them as such decreases showboating and competitiveness and increases cooperation and interdependence within the group or department. Quality circles, not individual employees, receive credit for innovations and suggestions for improvement.

Ample training is provided.   Program volunteers generally need some training in conference techniques or group dynamics. At a minimum, the circle leader will need skills in group-participation methods. Otherwise, he or she will wind up lecturing about topics such as quality improvement and productivity improvement. Leaders and participants will also need training in the use of whatever statistical and problem-solving methods are to be used. Following are eight major problem-solving techniques and their purposes.

1. Brainstorming is used to identify all problems, even those beyond the control of circle members.

2. A check-sheet is used to log problems within the circle's sphere of influence within a certain time frame.

3. A Pareto chart graphically illustrates check-sheet data to identify the most serious problems, that is, the 20 percent of the problems that cause 80 percent of the major mistakes.

4. A cause-and-effect diagram graphically illustrates the cause of a particular problem.

5. Histograms or bar charts are graphed to show the frequency and magnitude of specific problems.

6. Scatter diagrams or "measles charts" identify major defect locations, which show up as dense dot clusters on the pictures of products.

7. Graph-and-control charts monitor a production process and are compared with production samples.

8. Stratification, generally accomplished by inspecting the same products from different production areas, randomizes the sampling process.

Creativity is encouraged.   As illustrated above, brainstorming or variations thereof fit naturally into the quality-circle method and philosophy. Maintaining an attitude of "anything goes" is particularly important, even if rough ideas must be refined later. If half-processed ideas are shot down by the leader or other members, idea generation will extinguish quickly.

Projects are related to members' actual job responsibilities.   Quality circles are not arenas for amateur speculation about other people's work. People make suggestions about improving the quality of work for which they are already responsible. They should, however, be willing to incorporate information from suppliers and customers.

The Arguments For and Against Quality Circles

A major argument for quality circles is that they represent a low-cost, efficient vehicle for unleashing the creative potential of employees. In the process, highly desirable ends are achieved, such as improvements in the quality of both products and work life. Quality circles, in fact, are considered part of the quality of work life movement.

Another favorable feature of these circles is that they are perceived positively by all—management, workers, the union, and stockholders. A firm contemplating implementing such a program thus runs no risk of either internal or external opposition. (It is conceivable, however, that opposition will be forthcoming if management fails to act on quality-circle suggestions.)

Quality circles contribute to organizational effectiveness in another important way. They have emerged as a useful method of developing present and future managers. Recently, a major computing manufacturing firm established a quality circle program. After the program had been operating for two years, the director of training observed that the supervisors who were quality circle leaders were significantly more self-confident, knowledgeable, and poised than other supervisors who were attending the regular training program. The director believed that the supervisors' involvement in the QC training programs and activities had been the major contributor to this difference.

One major criticism of quality circles is that many of them are not cost effective. Furthermore, even more pessimistic is the criticism that the reported successes of QCs may be attributable to factors other than the actual quality circle program. One explanation is that the attention paid to employees by management may be the force behind the gains in productivity and morale (the well-known Hawthorne effect). Another possible explanation of the successes of quality circle programs is that the gains are due to improved group dynamics and problem-solving techniques. Therefore, an entire QC program need not be conducted just to achieve these gains.

A discouraging argument has been advanced that quality circles may not be suited to North American workers. Matsushita Electric, a leading user of the quality circle method in Japan, does not use circles in its U.S. plant (located in Chicago) because it does not consider the American worker suited to circle activities. Perhaps Matsushita management believes that Americans are too self-oriented to be group-oriented.

Quality circles may prove to be breeding grounds for friction and role confusion between the quality-control department and the groups themselves. Unless management carefully defines the relationship of quality circles vis-à-vis the quality-control department, much duplication of effort (and therefore waste of resources) will inevitably result.

Exclusive reliance upon volunteers for the circles may result in the loss of potentially valuable ideas. Many nonassertive people may shy away from participation in the circles despite their having valid ideas for product improvement.

Some employees who volunteer to join quality circles may do so for the wrong reasons. The circle may develop the reputation of being "a good way to get away from the line for a while and enjoy a coffee break and a good bull session." (To counter such an abuse of the quality circle program, QC group members might monitor the quality of input from their own group members.)

Guidelines for Action

An early strategic step in implementing a quality circle is to clarify relationships between the circle and the formal quality-control department. Otherwise, the quality-control department may perceive the circle as a redundancy or threat. One effective arrangement is for the quality circle to complement the quality-control department; the QC department thus does not become subject to the loss of authority.

Membership in the circle should be voluntary and on a rotating basis. In many instances, a team member will soon run out of fresh ideas for quality improvement. Rotating membership will result in a wider sampling of ideas being generated. Experience suggests that group size should be limited to nine.

Quality circles should be implemented on a pilot basis. As the circle produces results and wins the acceptance of managers and employees alike, it can be expanded as the demand for its output increases.

Do not emphasize quick financial returns or productivity increases from the output of the quality circles. The program should be seen as a long-range project that will raise the quality consciousness of the organization. (Nevertheless, as noted in the report from Honeywell, immediate positive results are often forthcoming.)

Management must make good use of many of the suggestions coming from the quality circle yet still define the limits of the power and authority of the circle. On the one hand, if none of the circle's suggestions is adopted, the circle will lose its effectiveness as an agent for change. Circle members will become discouraged because of their lack of clout. On the other hand, if the circle has too much power and authority, it will be seen as a governing body for technical change. Under the latter circumstances, people may use the circle for political purposes. An individual who wants to get a technical modification authorized may try to influence a member of the quality circle to suggest that modification during a circle meeting.

Training in group dynamics and methods of participative management will be particularly helpful. It may also prove helpful at the outset to appoint a group facilitator (an internal or external consultant) who can help the group run more smoothly.

<u>Appendix I</u>

Scoring Keys and
Supplemental Materials

Self-Awareness (page 36)

Scoring Key

Skill Area	Items	Assessment Pre-	Post-
Self-disclosure and openness to feedback from others	1, 2, 3, 9, 11	_20_	_____
Awareness of own values, cognitive style, change orientation, and interpersonal orientation	4, 5, 6, 7, 8, 10	_____	_____
Total Score		☐	☐

Comparison Data

Compare your scores to three comparison standards: (1) Compare your scores with the maximum possible (66). (2) Compare your scores with the scores of other students in your class. (3) Compare your scores to a norm group consisting of 500 business school students. In comparison to the norm group, if you scored

55 or above	you are in the top quartile.
52–54	you are in the second quartile.
48–51	you are in the third quartile.
47 or below	you are in the bottom quartile.

Interpreting the Defining Issues Test (page 37)

The possibility of misusing and misinterpreting this instrument is high enough that its author, James Rest, maintains control over the scoring procedure associated with its use. Some people may interpret the results of this instrument to be an indication of inherent morality, honesty, or personal worth, none of which the instrument is intended to assess. A scoring manual may be obtained from James Rest, Minnesota Moral Research Center, Burton Hall, University of Minnesota, Minneapolis, MN 55455.

Our purpose is to help you become aware of the stage of moral development you rely on most when facing moral dilemmas. To help determine that, the following lists present the stage of moral development each statement associated with each story reflects. By looking at the four statements you selected as most important in deciding what action to take in each situation, you can determine which stage of development you use most often.

After you have done this, you should discuss which action you would take in each situation and why, and why you selected the statements you did as the most important ones to consider.

The Escaped Prisoner (page 37)

1. Hasn't Mr. Thompson been good enough for such a long time to prove he isn't a bad person? (Stage 3)

2. Every time someone escapes punishment for a crime, doesn't that just encourage more crime? (Stage 4)

3. Wouldn't we be better off without prisons and the oppression of our legal system? (Indicates antiauthoritarian attitudes.)

4. Has Mr. Thompson really paid his debt to society? (Stage 4)

5. Would society be failing what Mr. Thompson should fairly expect? (Stage 6)

6. What benefits would prison be apart from society, especially for a charitable man? (Nonsense alternative, designed to identify people picking high-sounding alternatives.)

7. How could anyone be so cruel and heartless as to send Mr. Thompson to prison? (Stage 3)

8. Would it be fair to all the prisoners who had to serve out their full sentences if Mr. Thompson was let off? (Stage 4)

9. Was Ms. Jones a good friend of Mr. Thompson? (Stage 3)

10. Wouldn't it be a citizen's duty to report an escaped criminal, regardless of circumstances? (Stage 4)

11. How would the will of the people and the public good best be served? (Stage 5)

12. Would going to prison do any good for Mr. Thompson or protect anybody? (Stage 5)

The Doctor's Dilemma (page 38)

1. Whether the woman's family is in favor of giving her an overdose or not. (Stage 3)

2. Is the doctor obligated by the same laws as everybody else if giving her an overdose would be the same as killing her? (Stage 4)

3. Whether people would be much better off without society regimenting their lives and even their deaths. (Indicates antiauthoritarian attitudes.)

4. Whether the doctor could make it appear like an accident. (Stage 2)

5. Does the state have the right to force continued existence on those who don't want to live? (Stage 5)

6. What is the value of death prior to society's perspective on personal values? (Nonsense alternative, designed to identify people picking high-sounding alternatives.)

7. Whether the doctor has sympathy for the woman's suffering or cares more about what society might think. (Stage 3)

8. Is helping to end another's life ever a responsible act of cooperation? (Stage 6)

9. Whether only God should decide when a person's life should end. (Stage 4)

10. What values the doctor has set for himself in his own personal code of behavior. (Stage 5)

11. Can society afford to let everybody end their lives when they want to? (Stage 4)

12. Can society allow suicides or mercy killing and still protect the lives of individuals who want to live? (Stage 5)

The Newspaper (page 39)

1. Is the principal more responsible to students or to the parents? (Stage 4)

2. Did the principal give his word that the newspaper could be published for a long time, or did he promise to approve the newspaper one issue at a time? (Stage 4)

3. Would the students start protesting even more if the principal stopped the newspaper? (Stage 2)

4. When the welfare of the school is threatened, does the principal have the right to give orders to students? (Stage 4)

5. Does the principal have the freedom of speech to say "no" in this case? (Nonsense alternative, designed to identify people picking high-sounding alternatives.)

6. If the principal stopped the newspaper, would he be preventing full discussion of important matters? (Stage 5)

7. Whether the principal's order would make Fred lose faith in the principal. (Stage 3)

8. Whether Fred was loyal to his school and patriotic to his country. (Stage 3)

9. What effect would stopping the paper have on the students' education in critical thinking and judgments? (Stage 5)

10. Whether Fred was in any way violating the rights of others in publishing his own opinions. (Stage 5)

11. Whether the principal should be influenced by some angry parents when it is the principal who knows best what is going on in the school. (Stage 4)

12. Whether Fred was using the newspaper to stir up hatred and discontent. (Stage 3)

The Cognitive Style Instrument (page 41)

Scoring Key

To determine your score on the two dimensions of cognitive style, circle the items on the next page that you checked on this instrument. Then count up the number of circled items and put your scores in the spaces below.

	Gathering Information		*Evaluating Information*	
1a	1b	13a	13b
2a	2b	14b	14a
3b	3a	15a	15b
4b	4a	16b	16a
5a	5b	17b	17a
6b	6a	18a	18b
7b	7a	19a	19b
8a	8b	20a	20b
9a	9b	21b	21a
10b	10a	22a	22b
11a	11b	23b	23a
12a	12b	24a	24b

2	10	1	3
Intuitive Score	**Sensing Score**	**Thinking Score**	**Feeling Score**

Comparison Data

	Intuitive	*Sensing*	*Thinking*	*Feeling*
Males	5.98	6.02	6.08	5.20
Females	6.04	5.96	6.94	5.06

Note: The *Instructor's Manual* contains more comparison data from other respondent groups. These will help you compare your own scores with those of others.

The Locus of Control Scale (page 43)

Scoring Key

Count up the number of items you selected of those listed below:

2a	5b	9a	12b	16a	20a	23a	28b
3b	6a	10a	13b	17a	21a	25a	29a
4b	7a	11b	15b	18a	22b	26b	

Total Score [ ]

Comparison Data

Corporate business executives	Ave: 8.29	Sd: 3.57
Elite career military officers	Ave: 8.29	Sd: 3.86

Note: See the *Instructor's Manual* for more comparison data.

Tolerance of Ambiguity Scale (page 45)

Scoring Key

Having intolerance of ambiguity means that an individual tends to perceive situations as threatening rather than promising. Lack of information or uncertainty, for example, would make such a person uncomfortable. Ambiguity arises from three main sources: novelty, complexity, and insolubility. These three subscales exist within the instrument.

High scores indicate a greater *intolerance* for ambiguity. To score the instrument, the *even-numbered* items must be reverse-scored. That is, the 7s become 1s, 6s become 2s, 5s become 3s, and 4s remain the same. After reversing the even-numbered items, sum the scores for all 16 items to get your total score.

The three subscales also can be computed to reveal the major source of intolerance of ambiguity: novelty (N), complexity (C), or insolubility (I). Here are the items associated with each subscale.

Item	Subscale	Item	Subscale	Item	Subscale	Item	Subscale
1	I	5	C	9	N	13	N
2	N	6	C	10	C	14	C
3	I	7	C	11	N	15	C
4	C	8	C	12	I	16	C

(N) Novelty score (2, 9, 11, 13)   _____

(C) Complexity score (4, 5, 6, 7, 8, 10, 14, 15, 16)   _____

(I) Insolubility score (1, 3, 12)   _____

Total Score [   ]

Comparison Data

Average range: 44–48

FIRO-B (page 46)

Scoring Key

To derive your interpersonal orientation scores, refer to the table on the next page. Note that there are six columns, each with *items* and *keys*. Each column refers to an interpersonal need listed in the chart at the bottom of the page. *Items* in the column refer to question numbers on the questionnaire; *keys* refer to answers on each of those items. If you answered an item using any of the alternatives in the corresponding key column, circle the item number on this sheet.

When you have checked all of the items for a single column, count up the number of circled items and place that number in the corresponding box in the chart. These numbers will give you your strength of interpersonal need in each of the six areas. The highest possible score is 9. The lowest score is 0. Refer to the explanations in the chapter in order to interpret your scores and for some comparison data.

Expressed Inclusion		Wanted Inclusion		Expressed Control		Wanted Control		Expressed Affection		Wanted Affection	
Item	Key	Item	Key	Item	Key	Item	Key	Item	Key	Item	Key
1	1-2-3	28	1-2	30	1-2-3	2	1-2-3-4	4	1-2	29	1-2
3	1-2-3-4	31	1-2	33	1-2-3	6	1-2-3-4	8	1-2	32	1-2
5	1-2-3-4	34	1-2	36	1-2	10	1-2-3	12	1	35	5-6
7	1-2-3	37	1	41	1-2-3-4	14	1-2-3	17	1-2	38	1-2
9	1-2	39	1	44	1-2-3	18	1-2-3	19	4-5-6	40	5-6
11	1-2	42	1-2	47	1-2-3	20	1-2-3	21	1-2	43	1
13	1-2	45	1-2	50	1-2	22	1-2-3-4	23	1-2	46	5-6
15	1	48	1-2	53	1-2	24	1-2-3	25	4-5-6	49	1-2
16	1	51	1-2	54	1-2	26	1-2-3	27	1-2	52	5-6
___		___		___		___		___		___	
Score		Score		Score		Score		Score		Score	

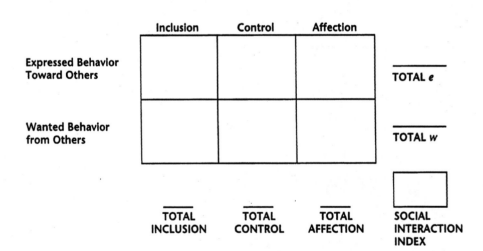

Comparison Data

Averages:		
	TOTAL *e:*	13.4
	TOTAL *w:*	15.9
	TOTAL INCLUSION:	11.9
	TOTAL CONTROL:	8.5
	TOTAL AFFECTION:	8.9
	SOCIAL INTERACTION INDEX:	29.3

Stress Management (page 82)

Scoring Key

Skill Area	Items	Assessment Pre-	Assessment Post-
Eliminating stressors	1, 5, 8, 9	_____	_____
Developing resiliency	2, 3, 6, 7	_____	_____
Short-term coping	4, 10	_____	_____
		Total Score	☐

Comparison Data

Compare your scores to three comparison standards: (1) Compare your score against the maximum possible (60). (2) Compare your scores with the scores of other students in your class. (3) Compare your scores to a norm group consisting of 500 business school students. In comparison to the norm group, if you scored

50 or above	you are in the top quartile.
45–49	you are in the second quartile.
40–44	you are in the third quartile.
39 or below	you are in the bottom quartile.

Time Management (page 83)

Scoring Key

To determine how effective you are as a manager of your time, give yourself the following number of points for the boxes you checked:

Points	Frequency
0	Never
1	Seldom
2	Sometimes
3	Usually
4	Always

If you completed only Section I of the instrument, double the scores for each category.

Add up your total points for the 40 items. If you scored 120 or above, you are an excellent manager of your time both personally and at work. If you scored between 100 and 120, you are doing a good job of managing your time, and making a few refinements or implementing a few hints will help you achieve excellence. If you scored between 80 and 100, you should consider improving your time management skills. If you scored below 80, training in time management will considerably enhance your efficiency. (See note at top of the next page.)

Note: Sometimes people have markedly different scores in the two sections of this instrument. That is, they are better time managers at the office than in their personal lives, or vice versa. You may want to compute your scores for each section of the instrument and compare them.

Type A Personality Inventory (page 84)

Scoring Key

The Type A personality consists of four behavioral tendencies: extreme competitiveness, significant life imbalance (typically coupled with high work involvement), strong feelings of hostility and anger, and an extreme sense of urgency and impatience.

Scores above 12 in each area suggest this is a pronounced tendency.

Research suggests that the hostility aspect of the Type A personality is the most damaging to personal health.

Competitiveness		Life Imbalance (Work Involvement)		Hostility/Anger		Impatience/Urgency	
Item	Score	Item	Score	Item	Score	Item	Score
1	_____	2	_____	3	_____	4	_____
5	_____	6	_____	7	_____	8	_____
9	_____	10	_____	11	_____	12	_____
13	_____	14	_____	15	_____	16	_____
17	_____	18	_____	19	_____	20	_____
21	_____	22	_____	23	_____	24	_____
Total	[ ]	Total	[ ]	Total	[ ]	Total	[ ]

Total Score [   ]

Creative Problem Solving (page 138)

Scoring Key

Skill Area	Items	Assessment Pre-	Post-
Rational Problem Solving	1, 2, 3, 4, 5	_____	_____
Creative Problem Solving	6, 7, 8, 9, 10, 11, 12, 13, 14, 15	_____	_____
Fostering Innovation	16, 17, 18, 19, 20, 21, 22	_____	_____

Total Score [   ]

Comparison Data

Compare your scores to three comparison standards: (1) Compare your score against the maximum possible (132). (2) Compare your scores with the scores of other students in your class. (3) Compare your scores to a norm group consisting of 500 business school students. In comparison to the norm group, if you scored

105 or above	you are in the top quartile.
94–104	you are in the second quartile.
83–93	you are in the third quartile.
82 or below	you are in the bottom quartile.

How Creative Are You? (page 140)

Scoring Key

Circle and add up the values assigned to each item. The values are as follows:

	A Agree	B Undecided or Don't Know	C Disagree		A Agree	B Undecided or Don't Know	C Disagree
1.	0	1	2	10.	1	0	3
2.	0	1	2	11.	4	1	0
3.	4	1	0	12.	3	0	−1
4.	−2	0	3	13.	2	1	0
5.	2	1	0	14.	4	0	−2
6.	−1	0	3	15.	−1	0	2
7.	3	0	−1	16.	2	1	0
8.	0	1	2	17.	0	1	2
9.	3	0	−1	18.	3	0	−1

	A Agree	B Undecided or Don't Know	C Disagree		A Agree	B Undecided or Don't Know	C Disagree
19.	0	1	2	30.	−2	0	3
20.	0	1	2	31.	0	1	2
21.	0	1	2	32.	0	1	2
22.	3	0	−1	33.	3	0	−1
23.	0	1	2	34.	−1	0	2
24.	−1	0	2	35.	0	1	2
25.	0	1	3	36.	1	2	3
26.	−1	0	2	37.	2	1	0
27.	2	1	0	38.	0	1	2
28.	2	0	−1	39.	−1	0	2
29.	0	1	2				

40. The following have values of 2:

energetic	dynamic	perceptive	dedicated
resourceful	flexible	innovative	courageous
original	observant	self-demanding	curious
enthusiastic	independent	persevering	involved

The following have values of 1:

self-confident	determined	informal	forward-looking
thorough	restless	alert	open-minded

The rest have values of 0.

Total Score [ ]

Comparison Data

95–116	Exceptionally creative
65–94	Very creative
40–64	Above average
20–39	Average
10–19	Below average
Below 10	Noncreative

Innovative Attitude Scale (page 142)

Scoring Key

Add up the numbers associated with your responses to the 20 items. When you have done so, compare that score to the following norm group (consisting of graduate and undergraduate business school students, all of whom were employed full time). Percentile indicates the percent of the people who are expected to score below you.

Score	Percentile
39	5
53	16
62	33
71	50
80	68
89	86
97	95

Applying Conceptual Blockbusting

The Bleak Future of Knowledge (page 179), Keith Dunn and McGuffey's Restaurant (page 180)

Observer's Feedback Form

After the group has completed its problem-solving task, take the time to give the group feedback on its performance. Also provide feedback to each individual group member, either by means of written notes or verbal comments.

Group Observation

1. Was the problem defined explicitly?
   a. To what extent was information sought from all group members?
   b. Did the group avoid defining the problem as a disguised solution?
   c. What techniques were used to expand or alter the definitions of the problem?

2. Were alternatives proposed before any solution was evaluated?
   a. Did all group members help generate alternative solutions without judging them one at a time?
   b. Did people build on the alternatives proposed by others?
   c. What techniques were used to generate more creative alternatives for solving the problem?

3. Was the optimal solution selected?
   a. Were alternatives evaluated systematically?
   b. Was consideration given to the realistic long-term effects of each alternative?

4. Was consideration given to how and when the solution could be implemented?
   a. Were obstacles to implementation discussed?
   b. Was the solution accepted because it solved the problem under consideration, or for some other reason?

5. How creative was the group in defining and solving the problem?

6. What techniques of conceptual blockbusting did the group use?

Individual Observation

1. What violations of the rational problem-solving process did you observe in this person?

2. What conceptual blocks were evident in this person?

3. What conceptual blockbusting efforts did this person make?

4. What was especially effective about the problem-solving attempts of this person?

5. What could this individual do to improve problem-solving skills?

Answers and Solutions to the Creativity Problems

Solution to the Roman numeral problem (page 152).

"S"IX or "6" or VI

Solution to the matchstick problem in Figure 1 (page 153).

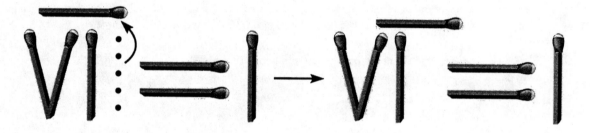

Placing the match at the top turns the figure into a square root sign. The square root of 1 equals 1 ($\sqrt{1} = 1$).

Answer to the Shakespeare problem in Figure 2 (page 154).
5 inches. (Be careful to note where page 1 of Volume 1 is and where the last page of Volume 4 is.)

Common terms applying to both water and finance (page 155):

banks	deposits	capital drain
currency	frozen assets	sinking fund
cash flow	float a loan	liquid assets
washed up	underwater pricing	slush fund

Answer to the Descartes story (page 155).
At the foundation of Descartes' philosophy was the statement, "I think, therefore I am."

Solution to the block of wood problem in Figure 3 (page 155).

Source: McKim, 1972.

By turning the block with the bottom facing us, we see that it becomes a circle and fills the circle hole completely. By turning the block with the dark side toward us, we see that it becomes a square and fills the square hole completely. By turning the block to the side with the light side facing us, we see that it becomes a triangle and fills the triangle hole completely.

Solutions to the nine-dot problem in Figure 4 (page 156).

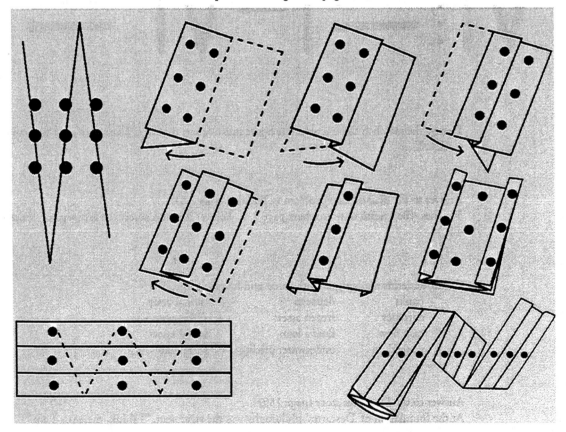

Solutions to embedded-patterns problem in Figure 5 (page 157).

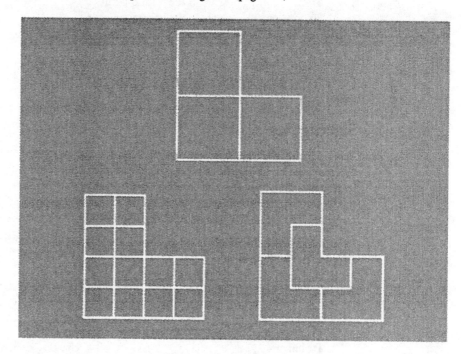

Solution to the fractionation problem in Figure 7 (page 166).

Communicating Supportively (page 190)

Scoring Key

Skill Area	Items	Assessment	
		Pre-	Post-
Knowledge of Coaching and Counseling	1, 2, 20	_____	_____
Providing Effective Negative Feedback	3, 4, 5, 6, 7, 8	_____	_____
Communicating Supportively	9, 10, 11, 12, 13, 14, 15, 16, 17, 18, 19	_____	_____
Total Score		[ ]	[ ]

Comparison Data

Compare your scores to three comparison standards: (1) Compare your score against the maximum possible (120). (2) Compare your own scores with the scores of other students in your class. (3) Compare your scores to a norm group consisting of 500 business school students. In comparison to the norm group, if you scored

99 or above	you are in the top quartile.
93–98	you are in the second quartile.
87–92	you are in the third quartile.
86 or below	you are in the bottom quartile.

Communication Styles (page 191)

Scoring Key

Part I: Identify the type of response pattern that you rely on most when required to be a coach or a counselor by adding the numbers you gave to the response alternatives in Part I. The chapter discusses the advantages and disadvantages of each of these response types. The most skilled supportive communicators score 9 or above on Reflecting responses and 6 or more on Probing responses. They score 2 or less on Advising responses and 4 or less on Deflecting responses.

Part II: Circle the alternative that you chose. The most skilled communicators select alternatives 1a, 2b, 3a, 4b, and 5a.

Part I

1. a. Deflecting response _____   3. a. Probing response _____

   b. Probing response _____   b. Deflecting response _____

   c. Advising response _____   c. Advising response _____

d. Reflecting response	_____	d. Reflecting response	_____
e. Deflecting response	_____	e. Probing response	_____
2. a. Reflecting response	_____	4. a. Reflecting response	_____
b. Deflecting response	_____	b. Probing response	_____
c. Advising response	_____	c. Deflecting response	_____
d. Reflecting response	_____	d. Deflecting response	_____
e. Probing response	_____	e. Advising response	_____

Part II

1. a. Problem-oriented statement
   b. Person-oriented statement
2. a. Incongruent/minimizing statement
   b. Congruent statement
3. a. Descriptive statement
   b. Evaluative statement

4. a. Invalidating statement
   b. Validating statement
5. a. Owned statement
   b. Disowned statement

Diagnosing Problems and Fostering Understanding

United Chemical Company (page 219), Byron vs. Thomas (page 221)

Observer's Feedback Form

As the observer, rate the extent to which the role-players performed the following behaviors effectively. Place the initials of each individual beside the number on the scale that best represents performance. Identify specific things that each person can do to improve his or her performance.

Rating
1 = Low
5 = High

Action

MAX *Role 1*	Sue *Role 2*	Jack *Role 3*	
_____	_____	_____	1. Used problem-oriented communication.
_____	_____	_____	2. Communicated congruently.
_____	_____	_____	3. Used descriptive communication.
_____	_____	_____	4. Used validating communication.
_____	_____	_____	5. Used specific and qualified communication.
_____	_____	_____	6. Used conjunctive communication.

_____	_____	_____	7. Owned statements and used personal words.
_____	_____	_____	8. Listened attentively.
_____	_____	_____	9. Used a variety of response alternatives.

Comments:

Gaining Power and Influence (page 226)

Scoring Key

Skill Area	Item	Assessment	
		Pre-	Post-
Gaining power			
(Personal characteristics)			
Expertise	1	_____	_____
	10	_____	_____
Personal attractions	2	_____	_____
	11	_____	_____
Effort	3	_____	_____
	12	_____	_____
Legitimacy	4	_____	_____
	13	_____	_____
(Position characteristics)			
Centrality	5	_____	_____
	14	_____	_____
Criticality	6	_____	_____
	15	_____	_____

Total Scores

Organization 1 _____   Organization 5 _____

Organization 2 _____   Organization 6 _____

Organization 3 _____   Organization 7 _____

Organization 4 _____

Team Development Behaviors (page 418)

Scoring Key

Skill Area	Items	Pre-	Post-
		Assessment	
Diagnosing team development	1, 16	8	_____
Managing the forming stage	2–4	12	_____
Managing the conforming stage	6–9, 13	_____	_____
Managing the storming stage	10–12, 14, 15	_____	_____
Managing the performing stage	5, 17, 18, 19	_____	_____
Total Score		76	

Comparison Data

Compare your scores to three comparison standards: (1) Compare your score against the maximum possible (144). (2) Compare your scores with the scores of other students in your class. (3) Compare your scores to a norm group consisting of 500 business school students. In comparison to the norm group, if you scored

90 or above	you are in the top quartile.
77 to 89	you are in the second quartile.
63 to 76	you are in the third quartile.
Below 63	you are in the bottom quartile.

Jimmy Lincoln (page 463)

Role-Analysis Worksheet

1. If you are observing a team meeting being conducted, put check marks by the roles performed by the team members you are observing each time they make a comment or display behavior that matches one of the roles listed below. If you are analyzing your own team after it has completed its meeting, put names of team members next to the roles they played. (See pages 433–435 in the text for definitions of these roles.)

Task-Facilitating Roles

Direction-giving   _____

Information-seeking   _____

Information-giving   _____

Elaborating   _____

Coordinating   _____

Monitoring   _____

Process-analyzing   _____

Reality-testing   _____

Enforcing   _____

Summarizing   _____

Relationship-Building Roles

Supporting   _____

Harmonizing   _____

Tension-relieving   _____

Energizing   _____

Developing   _____

Facilitating   _____

Processing   _____

Blocking Roles

Overanalyzing   _____

Overgeneralizing   _____

Fault finding   _____

Premature decision making _____

Presenting opinions as facts _____

Rejecting _____

Pulling rank _____

Dominating _____

Stalling _____

What suggestions do you have for improvement in the team members' performance?

Making Oral and Written Presentations

Speaking as a Leader (page 489), Battle Creek Foods (page 491)

Observer's Feedback Form

Rating   *Action*
1 = Low
5 = High

Strategy

_____ 1. Identified the general and specific purposes.

_____ 2. Tailored the message to the audience's needs, attitudes, knowledge level, and so forth.

_____ 3. Met the expectations of the audience by using appropriate language and style.

Structure

_____ 4. Began with a forecast of the main ideas and captivated the audience's interest by giving them an important reason to listen.

_____ 5. Chose an appropriate organizational structure, for example, moved from familiar to unfamiliar and simple to complex.

_____ 6. Used transitions, including internal summaries, to signal progress.

_____ 7. Concluded on a high note; reinforced major points; summarized key actions.

Support

_____ 8. Used a variety of supporting information, examples, and so forth, to increase the credibility and understanding of major points.

_____ 9. Used supporting material (both the content and format of evidence and illustrations) appropriate for the audience.

_____ 10. Used effective, simple visual aids to enhance comprehension and retention of the message.

Style in Oral Communications

_____ 11. Used notes to create a conversational style.

_____ 12. Presentation had obviously been well-rehearsed, including the use of visual aids, and so forth.

_____ 13. Conveyed controlled enthusiasm for the subject through the tone of voice, posture, and facial expressions.

_____ 14. Engaged the audience through effective eye contact, physical arrangement of the room, and appropriate gestures.

Style in Written Communication

_____ 15. Document was mechanically precise, that is, it contained no errors that detracted from the message.

_____ 16. Document was factually precise, that is, the content was accurate.

_____ 17. The choice of words communicated the message clearly and unambiguously.

_____ 18. The tone matched the topic and the audience (e.g., formality, emotion, directness).

_____ 19. Used the appropriate format for the type of correspondence.

Supplement: Questions and Answers

_____ 20. Handled questions and challenges thoughtfully, candidly, and assertively.

_____ 21. Responded to objections in an orderly manner, for example, restated the objection, restated your position, offered further support for your position, and explained the significance of your rebuttal.

_____ 22. Maintained control of the meeting by balancing the demands of specific individuals with the interests of the group and keeping the discussion focused on the issues.